STUDIES IN COMMONWEALTH LITERATURE

Edited by
Mohit K. Ray

ATLANTIC
PUBLISHERS & DISTRIBUTORS (P) LTD

Published by

ATLANTIC

PUBLISHERS & DISTRIBUTORS (P) LTD

7/22, Ansari Road, Darya Ganj,
New Delhi-110002
Phones : +91-11-40775252, 23273880, 23275880, 23280451
Fax : +91-11-23285873
Web : www.atlanticbooks.com
E-mail : orders@atlanticbooks.com

Branch Office
5, Nallathambi Street, Wallajah Road,
Chennai-600002
Phones : +91-44-64611085, 32413319
E-mail : chennai@atlanticbooks.com

Printed in India at Glorious Printers, A-13, D.S.I.D.C., Jhilmil Industrial Area, Delhi-110095

Preface

Commonwealth Literature was officially born or at least named as such in a Conference at Leeds University in 1964 and its official confirmation came with the floating of a new journal, *The Journal of Commonwealth Literature*, also founded at Leeds in 1964, and the formation of the International Association of Commonwealth Literatures, ACLALS in 1965. However, the term Commonwealth Literature, though loosely used, was in vogue since the 1950s to refer to the literatures in English produced in the commonwealth countries.

According to literary historians there are some epistemological problems with a term like "colonial literature" because one was not sure whether a work like *Oroonoko* (1688) by Aphra Behn, dealing with the situation of the black in colonial Surinam, could be considered a part of colonial literature. Many critics think that the term Commonwealth Literature was invented to keep American literature out of fray. Thus, Commonwealth Literature today stands for literature[s] in English written only in the commonwealth countries outside the Anglo-American tradition. What is common between the diverse members of the commonwealth, in spite of their different calendars of independence, is that all these countries shared the common colonial experience. In the widely different and distant countries like India and Nigeria, Canada and Kenya, Australia and Pakistan, we can discern the varying patterns of common human experience and emergence of cultural nationalism leading to an emphasis on their distinctiveness in literary heritage and assertion of cultural identity. Commonwealth Literature thus presents a rich variety of aesthetic and cultural experience.

The essays collected in this volume spanning different countries and periods try to offer a taste of this interesting variety.

Basavaraj Naikar examines the nature of the conflict between cultural nationalism of Africa and the British colonialism as reflected in Chinua Achebe's archetypal novel, *Things Fall Apart.*

Mallikarjun Patil examines how Gabriel Okara's novel *The Voice* registers the radical social changes that come about in the wake of the opposition to the feudal social system.

Rajendra Chetty examines *Other Secrets* of the South African writer, Farida Karodia, who spent many years in Canada, as expression of diaspora.

Rajendra Chetty makes a perceptive analysis of the writings of Ahmed Essop, a South African writer of Indian extraction, and develops the thesis that for a proper evaluation of the marginalized life of the minorities the South-African writing must be seen as a multilingual, multicultural product.

Elsa Linguanti examines writings of Salman Rushdie, David Malouf, and Wilson Harris to argue that multiculturalism must be complemented by crossculturalism or interaction between the East and the West for a proper assessment of a literary work. Linguanti picks up three texts, one each, of Rushdie, Malouf and Harris to suggest that faithful expression of originality calls for assiduous crossculturalism and interanimation of cultures.

Kalpana Purohit in her brief but incisive study of Patrick White's *Tree of Man* explores the symbolic structure of the novel and how it contributes to, and reinforces, the final vision of harmony and fulfilment.

C.C. Mishra in his article brings under sharp focus the distinctive features of Rohinton Mistry in his criticism of the ecological imbalance brought about by industrialization and argues that ecological balance can be preserved as long as man's cultural values are in harmony with the forces of nature.

Rashmi Gaur makes an incisive study of Michael Ondaatje's Booker winning novel, *The English Patient,* in terms of socio-cultural shifts brought out by colonialism.

B. Indira analyses Beatrice Culletin's *In Search of April Raintree* to show how history is sometimes rewritten to rob a people of its identity.

Dipankar Chakrabarti examines Aurobindo's *Savitri* from a postcolonial perspective and contends that this celebrated work is intended to elevate the mortals to the level of divinity.

P.N. Sinha offers a fresh look at the Indian Mutiny through his masterly analysis of Malgonkar's novel *The Devil's Wind* which uses the raw materials of history, interprets them from the Indian point of view, and yet remains a powerful novel; a fine specimen of the literature of power rather than the power of literature while it also reveals Malgonkar's vision of life.

K.M. Pandey analyses the different levels of journey used in Gur Charan Das's *A Fine Family* and shows how the journey as metaphor lends pivotal support to the theme of the novel and sustains it.

Stella tries to see the contrastive technique used by Jhumpa Lahiri as a function of her expatriate position as an insider-outsider.

In a fine critical exegesis Rama Kundu interprets Kamala Das's "Introduction" in the dialogic imagination of Bakhtin, analyses the polyphonic nature of the text and sheds light on the energy dynamics of the poem.

Suka Joshua studies some of the South Asian poets and shows with many illustrative references how these poets develop images which are indigenous in nature as products of their own imagination, experience and environment.

Uday Shankar Ojha argues that K.S. Venkataramani's *Murugan, the Tiller* as an authentic reproduction of the contemporary society constitutes a slice of valid history and maps out the Gandhian dream of rural India.

Gajendra Kumar and Kuldeep Kumar point out the lacunae of the contemporary postcolonial theory and carry conviction when they plead that a new meaningful postcolonial theory has to be evolved from the postcolonial ethos.

Kh. Kunjo Singh argues that *Voss* is essentially concerned with Australia's search for identity.

In "Cultural Contention in Australian Aborigine Women Autobiographies" Jyotirmay Tripathy questions the image of the fixed indigenous identity of the aborigines and argues that the formation of identity is an on-going process which is formed discursively with culturally and temporally located meanings.

C.C. Mishra examines *Lajja* as a faithful transcript of the social reality of the ethnic crisis of the minority community of Bangladesh.

Kh. Kunjo Singh tries to identify the theme of landscape and national identity as the common feature of commonwealth poetry.

Alka Gopal holds that Indian English literature, and particularly Indian English fiction has outgrown the stage of servility to imperialism and has begun to assert its own distinct identity since 1980s.

Mohit K. Ray explores an aspect of the Canadian literary scene—its awareness of the binary oppositionalities of the Canadian Society—with particular references to Margaret Craven's novel *I Heard the Owl Call My Name* which projects the native Canadian life in a remote island in British Columbia and an outsider's eventual merging into it, and thus suggests the possibility of a unique harmonious solution.

I take this opportunity to thank all the contributors to this volume for their well-researched papers. I also thank my colleague Professor Rama Kundu for her valuable assistance.

It is my pleasurable obligation to offer my sincerest thanks to Dr K.R. Gupta, Managing Director of the Atlantic Publishers and Distributors, for inviting me to edit this volume and rendering all possible help to make it successful.

MOHIT K. RAY
Editor

CONTENTS

1

Colonial Conflict in *Things Fall Apart*

BASAVARAJ NAIKAR

Chinua Achebe is one of the major writers from Africa who has depicted the colonial encounter between the Africans and the British in all his novels. *Things Fall Apart* happens to be his earliest novel, which captures the spirit of the African society during the transitional period. It delineates the encounter between the tribal *i.e.* Igbo culture and the British culture necessitated by the historical force of colonialism. Okonkwo, the protagonist of the novel, is a representative of native African culture. The values and ideals of African culture are presented elaborately and contrasted with the British and Christian culture.

Okonkwo is a popular man in his society and known for his heroism throughout the nine villages. Even as a young man of eighteen, he has brought honour to his village by throwing Amalinze the Cat. He is an embodiment of courage and success, which happens to be the highest ideal of Igbo culture. "He has no patience with unsuccessful men. He had had no patience with his father" (6). Okonkwo's father Unoka provides a sharp contrast to him. Unoka is lazy, improvident, a debtor and a drunkard. He is poor, a loafer and a miserable failure. "Unoka was never happy when it came to wars. He was in fact a coward and could not bear the sight of blood" (6). Unoka's weaknesses contrastively highlight the heroic qualities of Okonkwo. "When Unoka died he had taken no title at all and he was heavily in debt. Any wonder then that his son Okonkwo was ashamed of him? Fortunately, among these people a man was judged according to his worth and not according to the worth of his father. Okonkwo was clearly cut out for great things. He was still young but he had won fame as the greatest wrestler in the nine villages. He was a wealthy farmer and had two barns full of yams, and had just married his third wife. To crown it all he had taken two titles and had shown incredible prowess in two tribal wars. And so although Okonkwo was still young, he was already one of the greatest men of his time. Age was respected among his people, but achievement was revered" (7-8). Okonkwo is an embodiment of heroism, the highest ideal of his culture. "He was a man of action, a man of war. Unlike his father he could stand the look of blood. In Umuofia's latest war he was the first to bring home a human head. That was his fifth head; and he was not an old man yet. On great occasions such as the funerals of a village celebrity he drank his palm wine from his first human head" (10). Although a warrior, he is not a cruel man. "But his whole life was dominated by fear, the fear of failure and of weakness" (12). There is a conspicuous contrast between Okonkwo and his father. "Okonkwo was ruled by one passion—to hate everything that his father Unoka loved. One of those things was gentleness and another was idleness" (13). A similar contrast may be seen between him and his son Nwoye. Nwoye is lazy and cowardly. Okonkwo is deeply worried about his son's delicate nature. Thus both father and son of Okonkwo provide a good contrast to and highlight his heroism.

The heroism of Okonkwo is pressed into service when there is a war between Umuofia and Mbaino. When the daughter of Umuofia is killed in Mbaino, Okonkwo is sent there as the proud and imperious emissary of war, he treated with great honour and respect. Two days later he returns with Ikemefuna, a lad of fifteen and a young virgin. According to the decision of elders, the young virgin has to replace Ogbuefi Udo's murdered wife and Ikemefuna has to live in Okonkwo's household as he belongs to the whole clan. Initially Ikemefuna is afraid to stay in Okonkwo's household, but later he overcomes his sense of fear and shyness. Okonkwo is a short-tempered man who beats his wives for slightest reasons. He is not demonstrative in his expression of love and affection for his kinsmen or friends, as he believes in the view that demonstration of delicate feelings is a sign of weakness. "Okonkwo never showed any emotion openly, unless it be the emotion of anger. To show affection was a sign of weakness; the only thing worth demonstrating was strength" (26).

In spite of his heroism, Okonkwo is unlucky to lead a poor life because of his father's irresponsibility. For example, he has no yams to sow in his farm. He, therefore, approaches Nwakibie and requests him to lend him four hundred yams. "I have cleared a farm but have no yams to sow [...]. I am not afraid of work [...]. I began to fend for myself at an age when most people still suck at their mothers' breasts. If you give me yam seeds I shall not fail you" (20). Nwakibie who appreciates Okonkwo's hardworking nature agrees to lend him four hundred yams. Okonkwo eagerly plants the seed yams, but unfortunately the crop is scorched by the hot sun and lack of rains at the right time and by too much of rain at the wrong time. But, in spite of the failure of crops, Okonkwo faces the dire situation very boldly.

Because of his angry nature, Okonkwo beats his wife Ojiugo in the Sacred Week of Peace. Ezeani, priest of the earth goddess Ani, views his violation of the tribal rules very seriously. Ezeani visits Okonkwo's house and points out his sin and warns him, "Your wife was at fault, but even if you came into your *obi* and found her lover on top of her, you would still have committed a great evil to beat her" (28). He warns Okonkwo that the earth goddess who is insulted by the latter may refuse to give her increase. His tone changes from anger to command, "You will bring to the shrine of Ani tomorrow one she-goat, one hen, a length of cloth and a hundred cowries" (28). Although Okonkwo is an angry man by nature, he obliges the priest of the earth goddess because of his respect to the tribal gods, goddesses and cultural rules.

On some other occasion, Okonkwo grows angry and beats his second wife for plucking a few leaves from the banana tree in the compound. When he is taking out his locally made rusty gun for hunting, his second wife murmurs about guns that never shot. Okonkwo is so impulsive that when he overhears her words, he aims his loaded gun at her and presses the trigger. There is a loud report. The frightened wife clambers over the dwarf wall of the barn. Then Okonkwo examines her and heaves a sigh of relief to know that she is not hurt.

Okonkwo, who is a hero by the tribal standard, enjoys

watching the wrestling matches arranged in his village. That, obviously, gives him a vicarious pleasure. He is happy to note his son's development, which he attributes to Ikemefuna's company. "He wanted Nwoye to grow into a tough young man capable of ruling his father's household when he was dead and gone to join the ancestors. He wanted him to be a prosperous man, having enough in his barn to feed the ancestors with regular sacrifices" (47).

Although Ikemefuna has developed a filial attachment to Okonkwo, he has to be killed according to the rules of the clan. He is, therefore, caught in a dilemma between affection and cruel duty. Ezeudu, the oldest man in Umuofia tells Okonkwo, "Yes, Umuofia has decided to kill him. The Oracle of the Hills and the Caves has pronounced it. They will take him outside Umuofia, as is the custom, and kill him there. But I want you to have nothing to do with it. He calls you his father" (51). As per the arrangement, Ikemefuna is taken out of the village. He carries a pot of wine on his head. A few men and Okonkwo follow him. After covering sufficient distance, one of the men is supposed to kill Ikemefuna from behind. But when the plan is unexpectedly upset, Okonkwo is forced by the circumstances to kill Ikemefuna much against his wish but only to overcome his fear of failure and cowardice. "As the man who had cleared his throat drew up and raised his matchet, Okonkwo looked away. He heard the blow. The pot fell and broke in the sand. He heard Ikemefuna cry, 'My father, they have killed me!' as he ran towards him. Dazed with fear, Okonkwo drew his matchet and cut him down. He was afraid of being thought weak" (55). Okonkwo remains morose and refuses to have any food for two days.

Okonkwo who is an advocate of success and heroism worries about Nwoye's cowardice and Ezinma's courage. He tells Obierika that "I am worried about Nwoye. A bowl of pounded yams can throw him in a wrestling match. His two younger brothers are more promising. But I can tell you, Obierika, that my children do not resemble me" (58). About Ezinma he feels that "She should have been a boy" (58).

Although Okonkwo is courageous by nature, he respects the rules of his clan and accepts the punishment for the crime that he inadvertently commits. When Ezeudu's funeral is being conducted in the darkness, Ezeudu's sons are dancing the traditional farewell to their father, Okonkwo's gun explodes and kills Ezeudu's son. "The drums and the dancing began again and reached fever heat. Darkness was around the corner, and the burial was near. Guns fired the last salute and the cannon rent the sky. And from the centre of the delirious fury came a cry of agony and shouts of horror. It was as if a spell had been cast. All was silent. In the centre of the crowd a boy lay in a pool of blood. It was the dead man's sixteen-year-old son, who with his brothers and half brothers had been dancing the traditional farewell to their father. Okonkwo's gun had exploded and a piece of iron had pierced the boy's heart" (112). The crime committed by Okonkwo happens to be the female one and he has to undergo the punishment according to the rules of the clan. "The only course open to Okonkwo was to flee from the clan. It was a crime against the earth goddess to kill a clansman, and a man who committed it must flee from the land. The crime was of two kinds, male and female. Okonkwo had committed the female, because it had been inadvertent. He could return to the clan after seven years" (113). Okonkwo has to undergo a period of exile for seven years. He, therefore, flees along with his family to his motherland Mbanta, a little village, before the break of dawn. The wrathful natives of his village destroy his property. "As soon as the day broke, a large crowd of men from Ezeudu's quarter stormed Okonkwo's compound, dressed in garbs of war. They set fire to his houses, demolished his red walls, killed his animals and destroyed his barn. It was the justice of the earth goddess, and they were merely her messengers" (113). Okonkwo has no choice but to accept the punishment as part of expiation of his sin.

Okonkwo takes the help of his maternal uncle Uchendu, builds his compound and three huts for his habitation and cultivates a piece of land. By nature, he ambitious and has a great passion to become one of the lords of the clan. But circumstances beyond his control have made him utterly desperate and helpless. Uchendu, therefore, tries to cheer him up by advising him to take the emergency in his stride and face it boldly. "A man belongs to his fatherland when things are good and life is sweet. But when there is sorrow and bitterness he finds refuse in his motherland. Your mother is there to protect you. She is buried there. And that is why we say that mother is supreme [...]. Your duty is to comfort your wives and children and take them back to your fatherland after seven years. But if you allow sorrow to weigh you down and kill you, they will die in exile [...]. You think you are the greatest sufferer in the world. Do you know that men are sometimes banished for life? Do you know that men sometimes lose all their yams and even children? I had six wives once. I have none now except that young girl who knows not her right from her left. Do you know how many children I have buried—children I begot in my youth and strength? Twenty-two. I did not hang myself, and I am still alive. If you think you are the greatest sufferer in the world ask my daughter, Akueni, how many twins she has borne and thrown away" (122). Uchendu's words of encouragement and consolation seem to have given Okonkwo some courage to face the challenges of life. He leads the exilic life in his motherland, Mbanta with a sense of resignation.

By the time Okonkwo's exile comes to an end, he learns about many changes taking place in African life due to colonial forces. The white men have entered the country. The Africans initially resent their presence. The Christian missionaries start converting the Africans who are not very strong in their cultural moorings. "Chielo, the priestess of Agbala, called the converts the excrement of the clan, and the new faith was a mad dog that had come to eat it up" (130). The colonial encounter between the white and the black involves religious conflict. The defenders of Christianity *i.e.* missionaries try to denigrate the native religion and wean the natives towards their own religion. "We have been sent by this great God to leave your wicked ways and false gods and turn to Him so that you may be saved when you die" (132). Although some of the spirited Africans argue against Christianity, the weak ones like Nwoye, Okonkwo's son is attracted to it. "[...] there was a young lad who had been captivated. His name was Nwoye, Okonkwo's first son. It was not the mad logic of the Trinity that captivated him. He did not understand it. It was the poetry of the new religion, something felt in the marrow" (134). Conversion to Christianity continues amidst all odds and obstacles. Okonkwo who is popularly known as the 'Roaring Flame' is infuriated to learn about his son's conversion to

Christianity. He ruminates over the matter very deeply, "How then could he have begotten a son like Nwoye, degenerate and effeminate? Perhaps, he was not his son. No! he could not be. His wife had played him false. He would teacher her! But Nwoye resembled his grandfather Unoka, who was Okonkwo's father. He pushed the thought out of his mind [...]. He sighed heavily [...]. And immediately Okonkwo's eyes were opened and he saw the whole matter clearly. Living fire begets cold impotent ash. He sighed again, deeply" (140).

The colonial situation in Africa has brought not only a new religion, but also a new government both trying to attract and control the natives. Under the influence of Christianity, one of the native converts kills the sacred python thereby triggering off a serious conflict between the missionaries and the natives. Okonkwo does not like to tolerate such womanish acts of abomination. He gnashes his teeth in disgust. He believes that such things may never happen in his fatherland.

After the completion of seven years exile in his motherland Mbanta, Okonkwo returns to his fatherland *i.e.*, Umuofia. But he is surprised to see the effect of colonialism there also. "But apart from the church, the white men had also brought a government. They had built a court where the District Commissioner judged cases in ignorance. He had court messengers who brought men to him for trial" (158). The spread of Christian religion, government and law is strongly resented by Okonkwo. He asks his close friend Obierika, "But I cannot understand these things you tell me. What is it that has happened to our people? Why have they lost the power to fight?" (159). In spite of native resistance to the white man's religion, Christianity continues to attract the weak-minded people. It is a great humiliation to Okonkwo to learn that his son Nwoye has now become Isaac and been sent to the new training college for teachers in Umuru. Okonkwo's helplessness is complete. He is very sad to notice the change that has come over in Umuofia during his exile in Mbanta. "The clan had undergone such profound change during his exile that it was barely recognizable. The new religion and government and the trading stores were very much in the people's eyes and minds [...]. Okonkwo was deeply grieved. And it was not just a personal grief. He mourned for the clan, which he saw breaking up and falling apart and he mourned for the warlike men of Umuofia, who had so unaccountably become soft like women" (165).

When Mr Brown, the moderate missionary is replaced by Mr Smith, the liberal one, the conflict between native religion and the Christian church grows conspicuous. When Enoch, an over-zealous convert, son of the snake-priest, kills and eats the sacred python, it creates a great disturbance in the clan. The natives attribute this abomination to the influence of the church. They, therefore, rush to the spot and destroy the church, thereby having a sense of satisfaction.

The natives do not know that Christianity is protected by the Christian law system represented by the local District Commissioner. The District Commissioner calls a meeting of six native men at his headquarters. When Okonkwo and other five men go to attend the meeting, they are arrested rather unexpectedly. They are insulted by the court officers. Their heads are shaved by the official barber. Okonkwo and his five companions feel an unprecedented humiliation in their life. Okonkwo is so furious with the white men that he tells his companions in prison, "We should have killed the white man if you had listened to me" (176). All the six prisoners are released only after some fine is given to the court by the public.

The experience of imprisonment has exasperated Okonkwo beyond measure. He sleeps with little that night and swears vengeance. "If Umuofia decided on war, all would be well. But if they choose to be cowards he would go out and avenge himself" (179). Okonkwo and other elders of his village conduct a meeting and deliberate about the course of action that they have to follow in the interest of solidarity of their clan. They know that their clan is divided and that they have to do the painful duty of rooting out the Christians as well as Christianized natives. They know that they have to face a new problem, which was not faced by their fathers. Okika expresses it very comprehensively, "They have broken the clan and gone their several ways. We who are here this morning have remained true to our fathers, but our brothers have deserted us and joined a stranger to soil their fatherland. If we fight the stranger, we still hit our brother and perhaps shed the blood of a clansman. But we must do it. Our fathers never dreamt of such a things, they never killed their brothers. But a white man never came to them. So we must do what our father would never have done [...]. We must root out this evil. And we must do it *now*. We must bale this water now that it is only ankle deep [...]" (183). When they are deliberating about the integrity and solidarity of their clan, a messenger comes there and tells them, "The white man whose power you know too well has ordered this meeting to stop (184). Such an order from the white man is too much for Okonkwo to bear. Impulsive as he is, Okonkwo cannot differentiate between the white man and his messenger. "In a flash Okonkwo drew his matchet. The messenger crouched to avoid the blow. It was useless. Okonkwo's matchet descended twice and the man's head lay beside his uniformed body" (184). The meeting of natives meant for consolidation of views and positive action ends up in tumult. The murder of the messenger committed by patriotic Okonkwo is considered as a crime by the Christian law. The District Commissioner arrives at Okonkwo's compound along with an armed band of soldiers and court messengers in order to arrest him. Okonkwo perhaps knows that he would be arrested once again by the British officers and thinks that it is better to die with a sense of dignity than to suffer indignity at the hands of the alien people. He, therefore, hangs himself to death by a tree behind his compound. Obierika takes the District Commissioner and his soldiers to the spot. "Then they came to the tree from which Okonkwo's body was dangling, and they stopped dead" (186). Although it is a sin according to the clan to commit suicide, Okonkwo is driven to do so by way of protest against the predatory culture. Obierika rightly and ferociously tells the District Commissioner, "That man was one of the greatest men in Umuofia. You drove him to kill himself; and now he will be buried like a dog [...]" (187). The Commissioner orders the dead body of Okonkwo to be lowered and asks the messenger to bring all the people concerned to the court. One may easily see that there is no alignment between the African tribal culture and the Western civilization. The Commissioner who believes in the white man's civilizing mission learns many a lesson from his administrative experience in Africa. The superstitions, beliefs, strange customs, mythological thinking etc. of the African tribes do not agree with the rational modes of Western life. The Western man is compelled by the contingencies of his stay in Africa to educate himself rather slowly and educate other white men in course of time. The Commissioner, therefore, wants to write a book about his experiences in Africa which will make interesting reading: "In the many years in which he had toiled to bring civilization to different parts of Africa he had learn a number of things. One of them was that a District Commissioner must never attend to such undignified details as cutting down a hanged man from the tree. Such attention would give the natives a poor opinion of him. In the book, which he planned to write, he would stress that point. As he walked back to the court he thought about the book. Everyday brought him some new material. The story of this man who had killed a messenger and hanged himself would make interesting reading. One could almost write a chapter on him [...]. He had already chosen the title of the book, after much thought: *The Pacification of the Primitive Tribes of the Lower Niger*" (187).

Things Fall Apart is, thus, the story of Okonkwo's resistance to the colonial power of the British. Whereas he has taken his exilic punishment by the clan in his stride, he cannot tolerate the disintegrating presence of the British in his land. A staunch believer in personal heroism and honour, he cannot stand any humiliation by the strangers *i.e.* white men. For him death is preferable to dishonour. The British Government in Africa may break him, but can never bend him. Okonkwo, thus, becomes a spokesman of his cultural values and becomes a martyr. But one may also note a tragic element in his martyrdom. While resistance to the foreign power is not wrong, as it is part of his patriotic agenda, the manner in which he expresses it is rather disconcerting. Far from thinking of the pros and cons of his action, he plunges into misdirected action rather rashly and impulsively like Macbeth thereby wasting his precious life. But his posture of resistance is very admirable. However, it is part of the irony of life that his resistance and sacrifice do not help retain the unity and solidarity of his society and culture in the context of colonial conflict between two cultures. His society and culture disintegrate in spite of his opposition because of the British religious, administrative, legal and economic forces, which are more powerful than the native ones.

Chinua Achebe has delineated the colonial conflict between the two cultures very convincingly and beautifully from an insider's perspective through the employment of African brand of English, which is impregnated with African idioms, proverbs and cultural semiotics thereby giving a poetic dimension to the prose narrative. *Things Fall Apart* achieves the quality of a parable and the stature of a classic by projecting an almost archetypal picture of the Calibanesque resistance to the presence of Prospero in his cultural island. Okonkwo is especially dear to the Indian reader as he easily invites comparison with Indian freedom fighters like Rani Chennamma of Kittur, Rani Laxmibai of Jhansi, Raja Bhaskararao Bhave of Naragund and Nana Saheb Peshwa in different details and degrees. *Things Fall Apart* may easily be compared and contrasted with Tom Gibson's *A Soldier of India,* Malgonkar's *The Devil's Wind* and Basavaraj Naikar's *The Sun Behind the Cloud.*

WORKS CITED

Chinua Achebe. *Things Fall Apart* (First Indian Edition). New Delhi: Arnold Heinemann, 1975. All the page references are to this edition.

2

Gabriel Okara's *The Voice* : A Novel about Awakening

MALLIKARJUN PATIL

Nothing is more pleasure than reading of a racio-cultural novel like Gabriel Okara's *The Voice*, which has become a classic today. Like the Indian 'Big Three' R.K. Narayan, Mulk Raj Anand and Raja Rao, or like his own contemporaries Chinua Achebe and Wole Soyinka, the great Nigerian novelist Mr Gabriel Okara has written his only one novel *The Voice* way back in 1950's. As in the case of Raja Rao's *Kanthapura*, Okara's novel deals with a radical social change *The Voice* celebrates the educated and awakened hero Okolo's interrogation of the feudal socio-political system. This way the hero bears a resemblance to Okonkwo of Achebe's *Things Fall Apart* or Murty of Raja Rao's *Kanthapura.* Okolo also reminds us of Kafka and Sarte's rebellious characters. The work is a classic. In his Introduction to this novel the critic Arthur Ravenscroft says, "One of the unexpected, and certainly one of the happiest, byproducts of former British Imperialism is that some of the most interesting writing in English today comes from former British colonies that are now independent nations."[1] The novel is certainly an interesting and imaginative piece of writing possessing the simplicity of a parable and the poignancy of an epitaph. Margaret Laurence writes, 'The novel is certainly one of the most memorable novels to have come out of Nigeria."[2] This view is shared by all.

God, believe or not, created man and world. Great weaknesses made man's life meaningless. Then there came a saviour either in the form of a human or a superhuman, but humankind rejected him. Even the sense-awakener is insulted. This can be the gist of Okara's novel *The Voice*. The novel beautifully begins:

> Some of the townsmen said Okolo's eyes were not right, his head was not correct. This they said was the result of his knowing too much book, walking too much in the bush, and others said it was due to his staying too long alone by the river.[3] (23)

Man is not yet prepared to face a hero and human society does not want to face a rebellion. Alternatively, does it wish to undergo any revolution for its good? When Okolo comes to Amatu to live a life of goodness, the feudal town views him as an enemy. Autocracy is the rule of the Old World. So is the case of Amatu where the tale of the novel is set.

Izongo, the Chief of Amatu does not like the scientific-tempered men like Okolo live in Amatu as they will threaten his power and position. So are the Elders of his Council, just his yes-men. The harassment makes the awakened hero flee. The native situation of this kind and its sensibilities are best depicted by the author:

> They moved nearer. Okolo stood. They moved and suddenly pounced on Okolo. Okolo and the men fell to the ground. Hands clawed at him, a thousand hands, the hands of the world. Okolo twisted, struggled and kicked with his shadow, with all his life and, to his astonishment, he saw himself standing free. He ran. Running feet followed. He ran. A million pursuing feet thundered after him. He ran fast his house without knowing and ran into another. A woman-giving suck to her baby screamed. Out Okolo sprang and ran. The running feet came nearer the caring nothing feet of the world. They did not look at him. He turned to a corner. A dog barked at him. Okolo ran. (28)

The sorriest situation at the beginning of his stay stuns Okolo. Therefore, afraid of his life, he hides in Tuere's house, who then bargains for him. The woman who is now classed with him supports Okolo. No sooner this happens than, Izongo with a big crowd turns up and takes away the protagonist for a drilling enquiry where Okolo is brought already beaten:

> 'Hear him,' Izongo said with his lips on the edge of the jug. He took a sip of the palmwine. 'Hear him,' he repeated after swallowing the palmwine. 'Always asking questions. Questions will take you nowhere. I keep telling you these teaching words. He looked at the Elders and they nodded their heads vigorously on agreement.
>
> 'Untie my hands. This is no question [...]. All I ask from you is let me be free.' At this Izongo laughed and the Elders this time taking the cue also laughed.
>
> '[...] Indeed, you have been dreaming since you came and I have been trying to wake you since yesterday,' Izongo said with a wise voice and looked at the Elders. They nodded their heads and mumbled their agreement. (41-42)

Abadi, though a highly educated member of Amatu, turns insensitive to the current problem. Praising Izongo and praising the traditional way of life, he starts quipping Okolo of his secondary school education. He observes "Okolo's mouth is foul and the citizens of Amatu should not listen to him." Stressing the importance of collective responsibility, Izongo looks at Okolo to death. He asks the victim to fall in the line:

> 'Keeping your thoughts in your inside alone will not do,' Chief Izongo said grinning. 'Your hands will only be untied if you agree to be one of us.'
>
> 'No!' Okolo said. 'No, never!' (57)

Gabriel Okara says, by this wonder held the Chief Izongo, the learned Abadi and the whole crowd. The petulance of Izongo and the loyalty of all those to him caused a decree that Okolo who has caused so much of embarrassment to Amatu must leave the town forever.

Be it as it may, that Okolo is a man of different mettle. Having been orphaned in his childhood, with whatever education he has, due to bitter experiences, Okolo has become a revolutionary. He wants to face the world and decides to improve it whatever his way. He tells this to Tebeowei when the latter advises him to avoid his search for *it* (reformation).

> 'How can I change my inside?' he said. 'The chair you are sitting on now is made of Abaru, a cheap softwood. Not so?'

> 'Yes.' 'Well, what will you call a person who says it is made of Iroko?'
>
> 'Perhaps he does not know.'
>
> 'I mean a person who knows Abura and Iroko. What will you call him?'
>
> 'A person who speaks not the straight thing.' (49)

A man of so much of social concern, learned and human, Mr Okolo has the boldest chest to declare the universal truth: 'The world is no longer straight.' The following displays his cry of the universe:

> 'If you put a black paint over a white paint does it mean there is no white paint? Under the black paint, the white paint is still there and it will show when the black paint is rubbed off. That's the thing I am doing—trying to rub off the black paint. Our fathers' insides always contained things straight. They did straight things. Our insides were also clean and we did the straight things until the new time came. We can still sweep the dust out of our houses every morning.'
>
> 'But the heap of dirt is more than one man's strength, Okolo. It may bury you,' Tebeowsi said.
>
> 'But we must start clearing, even if it is only by basketfuls. Chief Izongo does not want me to do even that.'
>
> 'I know, Okolo, but you must see the fact of the new time. Everybody's inside is now filled with money, cars, and concrete houses and money is being scattered all around. If any falls at my feet, I stoop and pick it up. If I don't and kick it away, I will be called a know-nothing man and I will be kicked away.'
>
> 'But I cannot stoop to pick up such things. Let my hands remain tied. Let me have no money, no friends, no house, no clothes. I like it so,' said Okolo. (50-51)

Okolo's ouster means Okolo's going to the town of Sologo. Even a cross section of people in the cone target Okolo. His giving shelter to a girl while rain came leads him to a serious trouble. The mother-in-law of the girl threatens him. The time Okolo lands at Sologo, he is dragged by a couple of miscreants to a big man's house where he is tortured. His reporting of it to a constable amounts but to no avail. Amidst the world, which is in earning and spending, Okolo hurries to a hotel. His right conduct evokes laughter. Since he is frightened and has a high morality, the hotelier asks him simply to laugh at the world's ills. He says as if logs in river man have to float in the direction of winds' command. Besides, the following three wall sayings shock Okolo:

1. 'Even the white man's Jesus failed to make the world fine. So let the spoilt world spoil.'
2. 'Eat and drink O, die one day we go.'
3. 'If we die tomorrow Mammy later go bury we.' (82-83)

The world considers Okolo a madness-afflicted fellow. Suddenly someone on the pretext of taking him to the big man's house pulls him to a white man who, though a sensible fellow, rates Okolo an insane. The dialogue between Okolo and the white man is quite arresting:

> The white man raised his eyes and looked at Okolo from head to foot. Then he rested his elbows on the table and clasped his hands in front of him.
>
> 'You speak English, of course?'
>
> 'Yes,' answered Okolo.
>
> 'You want to see the Big One?'
>
> 'Yes.'
>
> 'What about?'
>
> 'I want to ask him if he has got it.'
>
> 'Have you ever heard of the word psychiatrist?'
>
> 'Yes.'
>
> 'Do you know what a psychiatrist does?'
>
> 'Yes.'
>
> 'Have you consulted of one?'
>
> 'No.'
>
> 'Why not?'
>
> 'Because I do not need his services.'
>
> 'I think you need his services badly.' (86)

Thus, an upright person in a morally desolate world looks useless. What else can Okolo do now after having seen the beset human phenomena? He wishes to return to Amatu, his native.

What a wonder! The time Okolo turns up to Amatu, under the order of Izongo, all Amatu people have started merry-making. Eating, drinking and drumming resound there. In spite of Tuere's strongest binding, Okolo rushes to have a look at Izongo's celebration of the seventh day of his departure. Ironically on the very celebration of it. Okolo returns. Lying between the deep and devil, Izongo stops the revelry and summons the Elders. The Council of Elders decides to dispatch Okolo except Abadi who does not favour the decision. This indicates Okolo created awakening. However, Izongo with his trusted men conspires and the next day he dispatches Okolo in a boat. The boat as preplanned takes him to a whirlpool and Okolo and Tuere who followed him, meet their tragic end.

Shakespeare says man is kind but men are cruel. What is this collective 'men' but society. Nothing is more tragic than the fact that society is never prepared to have an individual like Okolo who can cleans it morally, socially, or in any field for that matter. The fate of a Socrates or a Gandhi is always the same 'assassination.'

However, this does not mean a great man does not achieve anything. Usually the impact of such man is felt after his death. As for Okolo, he greatly awakens people. At the outset only, the witch Tuere also succumbs to his straightforwardness. She defends him right until the end even dying with him, while Ukule, a cripple lives only to tell their unprecedented tale. Abadi being gradually awakened towards Okolo changes his mind. Still there are Tebeowei, Tiri and many mute Amatu people who get awareness due to Okolo's prophecy. Even the hotelier of Sologo and the white man calmly support Okolo's cause against the feudal system.

The novel is an allegory depicting the decline of sanctity everywhere—in the Ijaw tribe, in Nigeria and in the entire world. L.S.R. Krishna Sastry observes:

> Although the novel apparently deals with the situation in a Nigerian village, its allegorical implications are clear. Amatu is Nigeria or Africa itself in miniature and what happens there is more or less a paradigm of the general human condition in the modern world, which devoid of abiding values is receding farther and farther away from

> peace, happiness and truth. Material values hold the sway and people have no use for love and trust and honesty. Civilization is thus but an external façade.
>
> Okolo, which means the voice, is the inner voice, the voice of Truth and Goodness. He is the 'rebel' who is the prophet, who is in advance of his fellow human beings. He sees through the malady of modern life and realises that it is only that can redeem humanity. The author chooses to leave *it* nameless, probably to suggest that while we know that something is missing, there is no way identifying it. Chief Izongo is a reactionary and tries to perpetuate his sway. The convenient mechanism, which helps to impose his will on the people, is the Elders' Council! The voice of Reason, Truth and Goodness, although pure, is weak and cannot hold, whereas evil is backed by numbers. The novel thus represents the confrontation between Good and Evil.[4]

This interesting piece of fiction, like Raja Rao's *Kanthapura* consists of several touches linguistic features. The language and style employed by Okara are appealing. The author local-colours the novel just to transliterate the native Nigerian socio-cultural sensibilities. Stylistic devices like syntactic inversions, repetitions, odd sentences, transliterations and the like render a kind of poetic appeal to his prose. Besides heralding a heroic message to humanity about the beauty and truth of life, the novel as an experiment, freshening our linguistic taste. Indeed, it is a classic ever written by an African.

REFERENCES

1. Arthur Ravenscroft. *Introduction*, Gabriel Okara's *The Voice*, 1.
2. Margaret Laurence, qt. by Arthur Ravenscroft, *Ibid.*
3. All references to the text are from Gabriel Okara's novel *The Voice.*
4. L.S.R. Krishna Sastry. "Novel as Prophesy: Gabriel Okara's *The Voice*" *Commonwealth fiction*, ed. R.K. Dhawan, New Delhi, 199.

3

FARIDA KARODIA'S *OTHER SECRETS*

RAJENDRA CHETTY

Farida Karodia was born and raised in the Eastern Cape in South Africa. She has taught in South Africa and Zambia and spent twenty-six years in Canada where she wrote radio dramas for the Canadian Broadcasting Corporation. Karodia returned to South Africa from exile in Canada in 1994 during the time of the first democratic elections in the country. She reworked her first novel, *Daughters of the Twilight,* published by The Women's Press in 1986, but was not available in South Africa at that time because of the apartheid regime's proscription of alternate black writings. She has turned it into an epic three-part novel, *Other Secrets,* newly published by Penguin. It explores the mother-daughter relationship in the running crisis of the apartheid situation, updating it to include new family alignments in the post-apartheid South Africa.

Karodia's oeuvre includes *Coming Home and Other Stories* (1988), *A Shattering of Silence* (1991) and *Against an African Sky* (1994). Two of her short stories of note are "The Red Velvet Dress" in *Opening Spaces: An anthology of Contemporary African Women's Writing* (1999) edited by Yvonne Vera and "Friends" in *Her Mother's Ashes 2: More Stories by South Asian Women in Canada and the United States* (1998) edited by Nurjehan Aziz.

A pertinent question in the analysis of *Other Secrets* is how did the exile from South Africa for over three decades influence Karodia's writing? Her response is that if she had not gone into exile, she might never have written. It was a whole chain of circumstances that got her started. One of these was writing radio plays for the Canadian Broadcasting Corporation. She wanted to write, but did not know how to get started. A producer suggested that she do a script. The theme of those radio plays was what was happening in South Africa during the years of the struggle. The radio plays served as a springboard to writing short stories and then novels.

Other Secrets is written into three distinct parts, *Daughters, Mothers* and *Other Secrets*. Karodia's first novel, *Daughters of the Twilight* (1986) was reworked to form the first part, *Daughters*. Why and how did she rework the text to form the opening section of *Other Secrets*? Karodia explains that *Mothers* and *Other Secrets*, the new parts, are a continuation of the opening *Daughters*. Basically *Daughters* has remained the same; just some of the details like names have changed—the writer fictionalised the name of the town from Sterkstroom to Soetstroom. But, in fact, all three parts can be considered as distinct books within the one new book. She adds that she wrote them initially as a trilogy. Thereafter, she had to go back and change it to read as one novel. In the old *Daughters of the Twilight*, there was always the promise of a later book. Karodia outlines that she always knew that she had to come back to Yasmin, the chief protagonist, and tell the rest of her story. She was motivated to write the text by a few things that happened in her life.

Other Secrets covers four generations of women's lives spanning two continents. When Karodia was asked to share her feelings on writing this work, she replied:

> It took a long time. I started parts two and three in 1994. I have been working on it since then. The way I write is that I don't sit down and work on just one project. I work simultaneously on different projects to maintain my interest.[1]

When writers work simultaneously with more than one text, one is inclined to question the occurrence of overlaps in the themes or cross-pollination among the different works in progress. Karodia insists that no such overlaps are evident in the texts and her illustration is interesting:

> I have just finished an early draft of a new manuscript that I have been working on together with *Other Secrets* and it is a totally different story. It is a story of an old woman

and is set in Canada. It is her last day; she dies at the end of that day. She does not know it and reflects on her life.

One of the most remarkable characteristic of the writings of Karodia's text and those of other African exiles like Ezekiel Mphahlele, Can Themba, Breyten Breytenbach, Lauretta Ngcobo, etc., is the fine South African nuance that feeds into their writing during exile. Karodia succinctly outlines the influence of exile on the psyche of the writer:

> I was so homesick. It is reflected in *Other Secrets*. It took me about 10 years to get over my despair with living abroad and being away from South Africa. You need strong feelings for writing. If I hadn't been homesick, I am sure that I would not have been able to write. I find solace and comfort in my writing. You never lose those images of the landscape; they are always there with you. If I shut my eyes I can see the landscape of the Eastern Cape where I grew up. I have not been back there, yet I still conjure images of the area.

Several of the post-1994 South African stories are autobiographical or semi-autobiographical, where the childhood self is treated as other, and challenged by changes taking place in the present. Memory effects the passage into the future and enables moral re-alignment. Texts like J.M. Coetzee's *Disgrace* (1999), Gillian Slovo's *Red Dust* (2000) and Farida Karodia's *Other Secrets* are examples of the evocative, and unmistakably new South African writings that exemplify the seeping, cumulative signs of change. How are Karodia's personal feelings reflected in *Other Secrets*?

> They are not all personal experiences at all. I really got into the head of Meena, the main character and narrator. I don't think Meena is really like me. She is a character that I created and that I felt very sympathetic towards. I also admire her sister Yasmin, a very gutsy woman. I did use some of my personal experiences in Meena's and Yasmin's characters, although I never had a sister myself. They are two totally different characters. But, I could link some of my experiences. Maybe, they were the emotions that I felt at particular times of my life, which I linked to the two. It is almost like a schizophrenic kind of thing with the two girls.

> I grew up in Sterkstroom, a very lonely life. I did not have many friends and we were the only Indian family in the town. So the setting is quite authentic. However, while I gave the town the name of Sterkstroom, I became bogged down psychologically, emotionally and intellectually in that setting, but then as soon as I changed the name to Soetstroom it released me. One can't really pin down autobiographical experiences in *Other Secrets.* There are things like exile, my passport was revoked—but those were just little things by comparison.

Karodia notes in her text that it was relatively common in the days before mass relocation (the Group Areas Act decreed that the different races shall live apart) to find solitary Asian traders living and conducting business in the heart of the white rural communities. Isolated because of their racial and cultural differences, the Indian families, who were mostly traders in the white areas, built walls around themselves—"surviving like bits of flotsam in a hostile sea, practising their religion and conducting their daily routine as inconspicuously as possible." Sisters Yasmin and Meena, their parents and grandmother are among those who live behind the walls, helpless to control their destinies in the arid years of apartheid, but not entirely without hope [...]. Yasmin's strivings bring her some of what she wants in life, but not without the tragedy of rape and exile compounded by long-concealed secrets that seem to be passed from mother to daughter.

The leitmotif in *Other Secrets,* like in Jung Cheng's *Wild Swan's* (1991), is the complex relationship between mothers and daughters. Karodia acknowledges that the motif existed right from the inception of her writings. She wanted to write about really strong women. However, she emphasises that she didn't want to sideline the father, but she saw him as absolutely helpless. Karodia articulates very strongly from a gender perspective that:

> Women, I feel, always had the power to change and create. For me, they are the most important elements in the story. I come from a family with very strong women. That was the influence on me. It was a natural progression to write about strong women.

With such a strong gender standpoint, one would be inclined to easily categorise Karodia's writings as feminist. Interestingly enough, she strongly refuses to be categorised as a feminist. She thinks that every writer uses some of the influences that she had on her life. One has to delve into one's own history, and Karodia's evolves from such strong women. She does not see it as a feminist tendency. She was very protective of Papa, not in a feminist way, perhaps in an endearing way. This is what he was, an old man, and she loved the character of Papa, but she could not give him power that non-feminist writers would have liked to see because that was not his character.

A recurring theme in the text is "fatherhood." It is significant that both in Yasmin's and Soraya's lives, the issue of fatherhood is questioned and the theme is juxtaposed within the dominant female discourse of the text. Karodia takes delight in explaining the use of the theme since it correlates with the title of the text:

> The secret is in the lives of both sisters. This is the other secret, the irony of the story; the father was so attached to Yasmin, yet he was not really her father. Who is her father? This is where the other secret comes in. It is not your ordinary run of the mill secret. It is the final secret. I loved that secret.

Another reason to put Karodia's writings in the feminist box is the absence of the male voice in this text. She is quick to point out that it is just not a male story, because you could not be a strong male in the apartheid society. As a male you never had the power, no political power, no economic power, so where would your strength be? The ordinary non-white men ended up as alcoholics. A lot of them became derelicts.

> Even if I had given Papa the strength, even if I had made him a younger person he would never have been able to do anything to alter their circumstances, not in that particular era.
>
> Women, on the other hand, held the family together at home. The kitchen was a site of comfort, it created a feeling of being at ease and it was a familiar site. Their power was in the house. You find this everywhere. Wherever you have a group of women, they open up to each other. There is a bonding that goes on—female bonding.

> I speak from personal experience. I feel very comfortable in the kitchen. Maybe it is a historical thing too. This is where we have always been. This comment is going to get me into a lot of trouble, especially with women in the workforce, women in positions of power, etc.

Central to the South African texts is the question of race and identity. Most South African writers have a morbid fascination for politics, and opposition to apartheid motivated much of their writings. Examples that come to mind are Bloke Modisane, Ellen Kuzwayo, Alan Paton, Nadine Gordimer, Ashwin Desai, and Athol Fugard. The invasion of the private realm by politics meant that even writers who might usually have ignored politics were forced to deal with it. The personal relationships that might otherwise have been their focus were moved into the political realm. Karodia also addresses race and identity questions in her text. However, she insists that, unlike *A Shattering of Silence* (1991), she did not want to write from a political context.

> But, I couldn't do it without referring to the political situation of the day because it affected your life in many ways. Reclassification of race did take place and people were forced out of their homes, so how could I avoid those issues?

Karodia outlines the difficulty of growing up under apartheid, the repression and oppression that prevented the young girls from experiencing life to the fullest: "It was like having your legs cut off just as you were learning to walk. You saw others—whites—living differently, having what you could never have simply because you were not the right colour. It made you bitter. Yasmin was beautiful and vivacious and thought she had the world at her feet, but she was stopped dead by the system which controlled our lives" (Karodia 431).

The tragedy of growing up under apartheid is that despite the fact that Yasmin had "more in her little finger" than all the white girls in Soetstroom put together, she was always on the outside looking in. They were envious of her because she was beautiful and confident, but at the same time they disdained her, knowing that she would never be their equal because she was a coolie meid. The terms "coolie" and "meid" were derogatory labels used against Indians and black women respectively. It is interesting to note that as part of the Black Consciousness Movement, the vulgar labels used against the oppressed were juxtaposed in their life narratives, but this time within an affirmative context, as part of black pride. Examples of "coolie" texts that come to mind include Kesaveloo Goonum's *Coolie Doctor* (1990), Jay Naidoo's *Coolie Location* (1989), and Reshard Gool's *Cape Town Coolie* (1990).

Issues of sexuality were markedly absent from black South African writings pre-1994. Writers like Breyten Breytenbach, Andre Brink and Stephen Gray did not hesitate to include sexual issues in their poetry and novels. When one compares *Other Secrets* with Karodia's earlier writings, one has to acknowledge that the directions on sexuality in this text are unexpected, and one is keen to know what the catalyst was?

> You couldn't really be honest about Meena and Yasmin without touching on it. The sexual issues are part of their characters, of who they are: Meena being a virgin at twenty-two and Yasmin obviously not. I deliberately set out to do this. Nothing influenced me. I just wanted to be honest about their characters.

Farida Karodia is considered one of the important writers within the sub-genre of South African Indian writings in English, alongside Ahmed Essop, Ronnie Govender, Jayaprega Reddy, Achmat Dangor, Essop Patel and Shabbir Banoobhai. South African Indian writers have their own authentic identity—they have their own necessity, they seek their own forms and often, through a combination of simplicity and daring, by directness and an unembarrassed handling of feeling, achieve artistic effects of insight and profound disturbance. The black writers (African, coloured and Indian) had to carve their own literary path through a myriad of obstacles: state harassment, academic hegemony over literature, resource constraints, western literary codes, prejudice of critics, racism, etc. The academe (largely white) also arrogantly posited a distorted conception of what literature is, how value should be appropriated and, more specifically, what constitutes South African cultural capital.

The marginalisation of indigenous knowledges and African writers is currently being addressed by the academe, which is transforming from an elite, exclusive institution to embrace all the writings of the land. Pertinent questions that one needs to ask black writers would concern the dynamics and process of writing. Karodia outlined that when she embarked on *Other Secrets*, she did have a plan, however, her writing style defies description:

> I knew the end of the story. I work backwards. However, I don't always stick to the end of the story—it changes. In *Other Secrets* I did change the end. The story ended much earlier. But then, I had to go back; I wanted to add more to the story. The original ending is still in the book, but I went beyond that, further.

Do other writers influence an author's writing style, and what is the nature of this influence? Ahmed Essop notes that he was influenced by V.S. Naipaul, R.K. Narayan, Ruth Jhabvala and Anita Desai while Ronnie Govender's repertoire of influence is wide and they include Arthur Miller, Philip Roth, Paulo Freire, Augusto Boal, Wole Soyinka, Bertolt Brecht, Rabindranath Tagore, Dambudzo Marechera, R.K. Narayan, Rohinton Mistry and J.M. Coetzee. Karodia's response to the greatest influence on her as a writer was a stark contrast to Essop and Govender:

> There has been no other writer that has had a great influence on my work or me. I am fairly solitary. It can't be a person. I read a lot of diverse stuff. I read everything. I like the more obscure writers. I don't focus on one particular writer. I rather not read South African writers. Not because of any reason—I don't want to be influenced. I am moving away from South African settings. I want to branch out and write things that are also set elsewhere. Hence my new book is set in Canada. I went to India and wrote a collection of short stories during the monsoon.

However, she does acknowledge that the influence could be other than a writer. Coming back to South Africa has been one.

> It was the experience of coming back just before the first democratic elections of 1994. It was then that *Other Secrets* took off the ground in terms of the writing.

Karodia is a hot publishing property, like many black female writers in South Africa due to the marginalisation and exclusion of women's writings by the academe and the androcentric publishing houses. She has just completed a novel set in Canada. The working title, *A Long Journey Home*, has to be changed since it sounds like Rohinton Mistry's *Such a Long Journey* (1999). She confesses that she has used some interesting concepts and techniques. The structure is also quite different from her other novels, she claims:

> I wrote in the first person narrative and the rest of the story is told in the third person. Some of the story is told in the immediate presence, while the rest is in the past. They are not flashbacks. It is the way the story develops. There is this old woman trying to figure out what went wrong in her past, what has brought her to this point in time. Once again, an extremely strong woman. But, I do have some interesting men in this novel.
>
> My other work is set in a small town in the Karoo (in South Africa); it is more of a young person's story. A film crew arrives in a small town that has not been part of the South African change after democracy. My other concurrent project is the collection of short stories that reflect my experiences in India.

Who does a South African Indian writer envisages as her audience in the new democratic South Africa? Karodia maintains that she would like to write for everyone. It is interesting to note that although she refutes the categorisation of her text as feminist, she thinks *Other Secrets* is especially written for women. She states succinctly that her text mirrors particularly the experiences of South African Indian women, however, it is a story that everybody can get something out of.

NOTE

1. This article is based on an interview that Rajendra Chetty conducted with Farida Karodia on the o ccasion of the release of *Other Secrets* in July 2000 at her home in Gauteng, South Africa.

WORK CITED

Karodia, F. *Other Secrets*. Johannesburg: Penguin, 2000.

4

ON THE FRINGE OF AFRICA: AHMED ESSOP

RAJENDRA CHETTY

Introduction

Ahmed Essop is a South African writer of Indian descent. His oeuvre includes three collections of short stories, *The Hajji and Other Stories*, 1978, (which received the Olive Schreiner Award in 1979), *Noorjehan and Other Stories* (1990) and *The King of Hearts and Other Stories* (1997). His two novels are *The Visitation* (1980) and *The Emperor* (1984). Essop s stories have been translated into German, Dutch and French. In the foreword to *The Hajji and Other Stories* Nadine Gordimer commented that Essop is simply so true to his insights and observations that nothing appears to be, or is, contrived. Lionel Abrahams (1978: i) observed that Essop's style is simple and direct, his subtlety is born out of nothing more or less than his fascination with the endlessly varied ways of the human heart. Thence the power to amuse, delight, move and challenge us. Thence an achievement of a timeless sort. In an endeavour to shift South African Indian writings in English to the centre of South Africa's reception, appreciation and teaching of English literature, I find it appropriate to research a community bard who takes up the responsibility of recording individual histories of the "other," and in the process provides a unique dimension of South African life.

From the Margins to the Centre

The colonial history of South Africa and its legacy of cultural and linguistic domination have resulted in a situation where the literatures of the majority of South Africans were relegated to the margins of institutional, social and cultural life. The exclusion of writings by black writers like Ezekiel Mphahlele, Peter Abrahams, Ngugi wa Thiongo, Wole Soyinka, Can Temba, Ahmed Essop, Ellen Kuzwayo, and Farida Karodia was the principal mode by which power was exercised by the white academe. Literary discourse was also trapped within the colonial and apartheid paradigm since it largely reflected rather than challenged thinking in which people were categorised and separated. With the advent of democracy in 1994 in South Africa, there has been a paradigm shift from the margin to the centre—there is now an intense focus on the hidden texts of the "other" (African, Indian and coloured). One of the current approaches to literature reception is transdisciplinarity. Through its self-reflexivity it attempts not simply to accumulate knowledge, but to ask what constitutes knowledge, why and how, and by whose authority, certain modes of understanding are certified as knowledge and others as non-knowledge (Zavarzadeh and Morton 1994: 66). It is also a transgressive form of redrawing the map of South African literature in a fashion that opens up new space for emergent radical and revolutionary subjectives. It was not only texts that were marginalised, but also African literary theories. Students were exposed to Aristotle, Leavis, Richards and Derrida, but they did not hear of Jane Watts, Ursula Barnett, Leopold Senghor, Cesaire, Homi Bhabha or Edward Said. Feminism too was restricted to the Anglo-American theories with little regard for the African, Asian and South African writings which are more relevant to the context of racial oppression.

Michel Foucault examines a number of concepts that express the theme of continuity in *The Archaeology of Knowledge* (1972): *tradition, influence, development (period), spirit, genre, book, oeuvre* and *author*. These concepts were integral in the process of exclusion of black writings. The concept *author* would be used to illustrate the argument. The traditional notion of the *author* and the author's intention is polemic when one considers the development of new codes in black autobiography within the social, literary and political situation in South Africa. Autobiographical texts like Ezekiel Mphahlele's *Down Second Avenue* (1959), Bloke Modisane's *Blame Me on History* (1963), Ellen Kuzwayo's *Call Me Woman* (1985) and Kesaveloo Goonum's *Coolie Doctor* (1990) focus on the communal experiences of the community. The autobiographer becomes a spokesperson and representative of the people. A central focus is the people's demand for liberation and there is little emphasis on the cult of the author or the author as source and origin. The autobiographical genre was adapted to the needs of the writers'—where the urge to protest was interwoven with the urge towards self-discovery. There was a reconstruction of the people's identity (black consciousness) rather than an individualistic consciousness.

Indian Location and Politics

Ahmed Essop's fiction is firmly rooted in the Indian community of Johannesburg. Like Ronnie Govender, a prolific South African playwright, Essop also explores the lives, tragedies and pathos of the Indian community and his stories are set in the 1960s, the time of forced removals and open repression by the white Afrikaner regime. According to the Group Areas Act of 1953 which forced the different races to live separately, Essop had to move to an Indian area called Lenasia. He comments succinctly on the milieu of his stories in an interview:

> I lived in a place called Fordsburg for about 15 years. It was essentially an Indian suburb, but there were people from other groups who also lived there. Nearby was the suburb called, Pageview, also known as Vrededorp. We lived very closely with each other, many houses had shared walls and it was a sort of Casbah—a communal existence. People visit you, you talk to your neighbours, and there was this joy in Fordsburg and Pageview. In Lenasia we live as the whites live, with high walls and edges and so on, but in Fordsburg and Pageview doors were always open, you could walk into anybody's home at any time. There was no need to phone them and make appointments. People walked in the streets and sat on the porches and verandas and there was a kind of friendship, a close-knit community (Chetty 1999: 273).

It is, therefore, not surprising that most South African writers have a morbid fascination for politics, and opposition to apartheid motivated much of their writings. Much South African writing over the years gave attention to documenting the atrocities perpetrated by the government *e.g.*, the dispossession and relocation of Indian communities is central to the writings of Ronnie Govender (1996) and Ahmed Essop while the detention and struggle of political prisoners is covered widely in the poetry of Achmat Dangor, Essop Patel, Farouk Asvat and Shabbir Banoobhai. Political activists like Indres Naidoo, Mewa Ramgobin, Kesavaloo Goonum and Dinesh Narandas wrote of their incarceration, frequently with accompanying torture and the unwarranted death of comrades. Peck (1997: 9) notes that the invasion of the private realm by politics meant that even writers who might usually have ignored politics were forced to deal with it. The personal relationships that might otherwise have been their focus were moved into the political realm.

Totalitarian politicisation meant that virtually no realm of personal relationships was left free of politics. The state also issued a long list of censorship laws resulting in writers fearing censorship and imprisonment with the concomitant turning to allegory or poetry as a means of expression. Unfortunately, not all South African critics have made an attempt to understand literary works in their social contexts. The tension between the social commitment to the freedom struggle and the aesthetics of arts has been the cardinal debate of the academe. Albie Sachs in his controversial commentary *Preparing Ourselves for Freedom* (1990), complained that the "solidarity criticism" had ill served South African literature over the years of apartheid. Sachs' seems to deny that it was the liberation forces that wanted writers to line up with the appropriate ideology and to voice appropriate sentiments, a pressure that many resented deeply. Stephen Watson was most vociferous in his rejection of the demand to turn poetry into a weapon in the struggle. Ahmed Essop, when asked to comment on the debate between political activism and those that wrote about themes other than protest, outlined:

> There are also the human relationships and the personal relationships and so on. I see no reason why that should be excluded from literature. The realities of apartheid intrude into many of my stories, but the people of Fordsburg achieve a distinctive identity through their personal dilemmas and concerns. South African life involves a complexity of issues, not only apartheid (Chetty 1999: 273).

The human element was predominant in Essop's writings. He was exposed to the different aspects of life in the community. There were humour, joy, marriages, funerals and so on. His writings present a comprehensive whole, rather than selecting one aspect, the apartheid aspect, the aspect of oppression—that (apartheid) was one aspect of our lives, it should not constitute our entire life.

South African critics have often distinguished between those writers who linked their work with political activism and those that wrote about themes other than protest. The concepts *literature* and *value* in South Africa was politicised—it was governed by crude and monolithic views of what literature and value should be. The political discourse cannot be separated from the concept value. Literature is a cultural artefact produced and consumed within a cultural hegemony and it can also be considered a bearer of a particular ideology that will either legitimate or undermine the *status quo* (Lockett 1993: 2). Lockett contends that what is considered good literature or literature of value, like all other cultural artefacts in South Africa, had been defined within the apartheid paradigm and specifically created by white men making the race/gender question inevitable. One therefore rightly speaks of norms and values: the dominant and the other.

The literature acceptable to the dominant hegemonic discourse of the establishment conformed to the great English tradition. The marginalised black writers, like Essop, on the other hand, challenged this value system with their own distinctive political agenda of Africanism, Communism, Black Consciousness, etc., their own social and economic forces (alternative publishing houses, magazines like *Staffrider*, poetry recitals at mass meetings, funerals and protests) and their own codes of writing made famous by the Black Consciousness artists. Oliphant (1992: 17) explained further this dichotomy in values in South Africa when he argued that the articulation of private, personal and subjective themes were complacently equated with excellence by the dominant conservatives and the exploration of historical and social themes by the radical writers was viewed as aesthetic impoverishment. The attack from the aesthetic domain is often the formlessness, excessive particularisation and public character of black writing—

characteristic symptoms of the Eurocentric versus Afrocentric debate.

Marxist criticism has recognised the close relationship between literary works and the social milieu. Eagleton (1983) and Apple (1990) maintain that no culture is neutral, all literature is political and serves somebody's interest. Art for art's sake simply underlines the capitalist trend of separating art from society. The black writers' aims of social and political liberation would not be hampered by the centralised literary conventions or traditional views of writing. The process of conferring value in literature must be interrogated to reveal how the dominant paradigm of racism, sexism and class consciousness influences value.

Essop was able to carefully tread the fine line between politics and aesthetics in his stories. He notes:

> I think that one can combine aesthetics with reality, the apartheid situation is an aspect of reality, and art, I think, has to write about reality. So aesthetics and reality, the human experience, have to be combined. The socio-political reality is just one part of my life that I wish to present. I refuse to limit the scope of my art and I also resist the attempt to pigeonhole my writings (Chetty 1999: 274).

The onslaught against the black writers during the apartheid era was intense and the draconian censorship laws ensured that much of the writings were banned or proscribed. Essop's comments on the negative aspects of writing during apartheid are interesting and he maintains that his survival lay with the alternate publishing avenues. He was very fortunate in that he appeared at a time when there were a number of literary journals such as *Contrast, Seseme* and *Staffrider* which published his writings and there were publishing houses like Ravan Press which were not afraid of including protest works.

The South African Indian writers have their own authentic identity—they have their own necessity, they seek their own forms and often with writers like Essop and Ronnie Govender, through a combination of simplicity and daring, by direction and an unembarrassed handling of feeling, they achieve artistic effects of insight and profound disturbance. It is interesting to note that the South African critic Lionel Abrahams (1978) draws parallels between Essop's writings and that of V.S. Naipaul and Herman Charles Bosman. Essop grew up on Dickens and Conrad. South African literature never appeared in the prescribed lists of readings at school right up to the 1990s. The first South African book that Essop read was the Olive Schreiner classic *A Story of an African Farm* (1883). He acknowledges the profound influence that V.S. Naipaul, R.K. Narayan, Ruth Prawer Jhabvalla and Anita Desai had on his formation as a writer:

> It was these Indian writers who were my favourite. One gets influenced by writers, but it is essential to keep one's own perception, style, and the aesthetic part is one's own. The question is: How are you going to present that work? That you will have to work out on your own (Chetty 1999: 274).

Essop's oeuvre consists of both short stories and novels. Although his distinct style permeates both the genres, one is tempted to know how they differ in the actual writing:

> There are segments of experience that can be put into a short story form and other segments that require a larger canvas so I found that I could write a short story in three pages and another in ten. And then, of course, for the novels, *The Visitation* and *The Emperor,* I realised that what I had to say had to take a novel form. The short story is very demanding because you want to exclude everything that does not focus on what you want to convey in terms of the message; It can be a segment of experience, or it may be a character that I wish to create, or some meaning I wish to convey. But, I have to do that artistically. What I like of the short story form is that I can spend a lot of time on the sentences, syntax, choice of words and the diction. I enjoy the fine workmanship and also I write with a pen and then I type it, so I am still very primitive in that I do not use the wordprocessor (Chetty 1999: 275).

When Essop works on short stories, it is the locality, the milieu, that links them to make a collection. However, one must confess that his stories follow quite naturally. Many of his stories are set in Fordsburg and Pageview, and they are linked geographically. Some stories are set in Lenasia and few are set in Eldorado Park,

Durban and overseas. Essop, like Govender in *At the Edge and Other Cato Manor Stories* (1996), links his stories with their particular locality. Both the writers use the actual names of the streets, buildings and townships, unlike Narayan who invents place names like *Malgudi.* Critics often see such writings as (semi)autobiographical. However, Essop rejects the notion that his writings are autobiographical.

The autobiography has been one of the most common sub-genres both during South Africa's struggle for freedom and the post-apartheid period. It is not only the politicians like Nelson Mandela (*Long Walk to Freedom*), Helen Suzman (*Memoirs*), Desmond Tutu (*Hope and Suffering*), or Kesaveloo Goonum (*Coolie Doctor*), but also writers and artists who took readily to autobiographical writings. In fact, several South African stories are autobiographical or semi-autobiographical, where the childhood self is treated as other, and challenged by changes taking place in the present. Memory effects the passage into the future and enables moral re-alignment. Autobiographies that come to mind are Mark Behr's *The Smell of Apples* (1994), Stephen Gray's *An Accident of Birth* (1993), and Jay Naidoo's *Coolie Location* (1990). Many of the stories in *Noorjehan and Other Stories* are characteristic of autobiographical writings. Essop outlines that there are experiences in life which he uses. There are people that he knows. He recreates that imaginatively so that they are not quite the people that he knows:

> No one has come to me and said, look, that's me. There was no Mr Moonreddy. The writer uses his experience. Sometimes the story may be close to a character in the community but it is not the same character. For example, the character Gool, the gangster; There was a man in Fordsburg who had that sort of power and reputation. When I wrote the story, I wanted a man who is very intelligent, and also a man who reads. Apparently, our local gangsters could not read, although they had this great power. Gool also had great admiration for beauty. So he is quite a different man to the local gangster. And then of course in "The Novel," a story in *The King of Hearts and Other Stories,* a renowned Fordsburg gangster comes to visit me and claims that he is the character in the novel *The Visitation.* He tries to re-enact some of the

> incidents in the novel. And that was one of my funnier stories. Many people identify my stories with our gangsters. A local gangster who passed away a few years ago in Fordsburg was told of this book in which he appeared. He was very pleased, of course he did not read (Chetty 1999: 275).

Many of the issues in *The Emperor* were Essop's ideas on education—he was a high school teacher of English for over two decades. Some of the incidents are actual events, for instance, there was a teacher who had been charged in the Chief Magistrate's court for not doing his daily forecast. It was a male teacher, not the character Zenobia in the novel, so in the whole process he had to recreate the events in his stories. Essop acknowledges that the demands of fiction are quite different from writing history or autobiography.

Another unique perspective to Essop's writings is the major feminist issues on different levels in *Noorjehan and Other Stories* that he explores. What made him one of the few male and black writers that tackled the question of women's rights? It is the character Zenobia Hansa in *The Emperor* who is the epitome of a feminist activist. Essop explains that as far as Islamic religion goes, the woman has complete rights, even the right to divorce her husband. Further, like Farida Karodia (*Other Secrets*, 2000) he needed women characters who are strong. It was also the women in the political movement that influenced him. He was part of the Unity Movement as well as the Black Consciousness Movement for a period and he came to know political stalwarts like Amina Cachalia and Ruth First. Essop drew from his experiences of strong women. However, he insists that none of the women characters are real—I am not writing sociology or biography. I have to re-create and give them qualities.

Many South African writers of Indian descent refused to be categorised as Indian writers. Ronnie Govender correctly maintains that he is a South African writer, not an Indian writer. Essop's stance on the issue differs:

> [The] category relates to a particular group of people and their experiences in their own localities created by apartheid. But, I think even if there was no Group Areas Act, Indians would live together, in that we share certain

> cultural values and there is also a joy in community living (Chetty 1999: 277).

Essop's stories manifest themselves most immediately as mirrors on the life of the Indian community, and in a larger sense, South Africa as a whole. A tale like "Jericho Again" bemoans the apartheid demolition of Fordsburg and the exile of the inhabitants to Lenasia.

He finds the categorisation unproblematic and notes that there is enough South African Indian literature already, and the more that we have the better especially within the current context of the *African Renaissance* in South Africa.

> Indians are moving away from their group areas, but areas like Lenasia will lie intact for many years, I think, because of shared values. I think all of our writers are not writing parochially, they are also dealing with human nature, and human nature is essentially the same all over the world, although values are shifting. Whatever I wrote was not confined to Indians only. I always tried to present a larger human dimension. Not only here but also outside (Chetty 1999: 278).

Conclusion

Re-reading Ahmed Essop's writings has led to a re-think of local writings within postcolonial situations. One of the findings is the urgent need to expose students to the multi-cultural South African context and to give significance and value to marginalised knowledge like local Indian writings in English. A reason cited for the exclusion of "other" writings (*e.g.* popular writings, women's writings, black writings, etc.) by the academe is the subjective aesthetic evaluation of its quality—it was viewed as inferior to both the "little" canon of South African writings (Gray 1982) and the canon of traditional English literature. A reflection on the ideological position of Essop, a key South African Indian writer in English along with Farida Karodia, Jayapraga Reddy, Ronnie Govender and Agnes Sam, was an attempt to understand the discursive situations that characterise the South African Indian discourse. The discourses of colonialism and apartheid have made it possible for the construction of the dominant ethnic discourses of Anglo-colonial liberalism and Afrikaans nationalism with the consequent exclusion of "other writings."

A valid approach to the various branches of South African writings seems more and more to require a view of them not so much as parts of generalised international traditions but as forming a multi-lingual product arising primarily out of the needs and compulsions of this country and its many people. It was not only persistent state interference or the lack of resources for the promotion of local literature that had a negative effect on writers like Essop, it was also academics who insisted on a particular Western perspective of what literature is, how value should be appropriated and, more specifically, what constitutes South African writing.

WORKS CITED

Abrahams, L. "Introduction." *The Hajji and Other Stories,* by A. Essop. Johannesburg: Ravan.

Apple, M.W. *Ideology and Curriculum.* New York: Routledge, 1990.

Chetty, R.P. A Community Bard: Interview with Ahmed Essop. *Alternation.* 6.1 (1999) 272-78.

Eagleton, T. *Literary Theory: An Introduction.* Minneapolis: U of Minnesota P, 1983.

Essop, A. *The Hajji and Other Stories.* Johannesburg: Ravan, 1978.

——. *The Visitation.* Johannesburg: Ravan, 1980.

——. *The Emperor.* Johannesburg: Ravan, 1984.

——. *Noorjehan and Other Stories.* Johannesburg: Ravan, 1990.

——. *The King of Hearts and Other Stories.* Randburg: Ravan, 1997.

Foucault, M. *The Archaeology of Knowledge and the Discourse of Language.* New York: Pantheon Books, 1972.

Govender, R. *At the Edge and Other Cato Manor Stories.* Pretoria: Manx, 1996.

Gray, S. *English South African Literature in the Last Ten Years: A Survey of Research Developments.* Inaugural Address. Johannesburg: Rand Afrikaans University, 1982.

Lockett, C. "Strangers in your Midst: A Study of South African Women's Poetry in English." MA diss. University of Natal, 1993.

Oliphant, A.W., ed. *Essential Things.* Johannesburg: COSAW, 1992.

Peck, R. *A Morbid Fascination. White Prose and Politics in Apartheid South Africa.* London: Greenwood Press, 1997.

Sachs, A. Preparing Ourselves for Freedom. African National Congress Discussion paper. *Weekly Mail* (February 1990).

Zavarzadeh, M. and D. Morton. Theory as Resistance: Politics and Culture after (Post) Structuralism. London: Guilford Press, 1994.

5

ORIGIN, ORIGINS, ORIGINALITY: SALMAN RUSHDIE'S *EAST, WEST*, DAVID MALOUF'S *ANTIPODES* AND WILSON HARRIS'S *THE WOMB OF SPACE*

ELSA LINGUANTI

A Bridge between here and there, and now and then

In 1998 we gathered in Turin for a seminar whose title was: "From one Ocean to the Other: the Expressions of Originality." The group included academics studying Anglophone, Francophone and iberophone literary cultures. It was the twenty-fifth anniversary of our meetings.

The first thing that came to my mind when I saw the title/subject of that meeting, was (a typical case of idiolectic association) the moment, almost twenty years ago, when I had opened what was then the latest novel by the West-Coast Canadian Jack Hodgins, entitled *The Resurrection of Joseph Bourne, or A Word or two about Those Port Annie Miracles,* published in 1979, and found, among the epigraphs, a quotation from *An Imaginary Life,* by the Australian David Malouf, which in the previous year, 1978, had been a real revelation for me.

> What else should our lives be but a continual series of beginnings, of painful settings out into the unknown, pushing off from the edges of consciousness into the mystery of what we have not yet become, except in dreams [...].[1]

At the time, it seemed to me that, across the oceans, from one hemisphere to the other, the voices of the two writers were rising in unison to remove limits, borders, thresholds, signs of division and separation ("the edges"), and to draw closer, starting again from scratch every time, to a potential idea of man: "what we have not yet become," or "what we might have been," to quote a more recent verse of Fay Zwicky, the Australian poetess.[2]

Twenty years after the publication of those books, among the various possibilities suggested by the title/subject of the seminar, I decided to follow a route which linked together two specific works: the first, a collection of stories, *East, West* by Salman Rushdie, published in 1994, which forms a link across the oceans because it visits India, and the West of Christopher Columbus and Hamlet, Prince of Denmark, narrating also of encounters between the two worlds; the second, David Malouf's collection of stories published in 1985, *Antipodes*, because the stories connect Australia with Italy, Belgium and Austria. Worth mentioning seemed also the volume *12 Edmonstone Street* in which Malouf describes, with his meditations and comments, the two most important addresses where he has lived for the longest periods: 12, Edmonstone Street, Brisbane, Australia and Campagnatico, in the province of Grosseto, Italy, and tells of a trip of his to India.[3]

The third book I refer to, a collection of essays by Wilson Harris, *The Womb of Space*, moves the subject ("From One Ocean to the Other") onto a totally metaphorical level.[4]

As regards "the expressions of originality," we know that the word "expression" indicates language, and in our case, literary language. What is not so easy to define is the meaning of "originality." It is true that the word is used in our professional, critical-academic jargon to mean an innovation (something is born *orior* and is therefore new), *in contrast to* an imitative respect for tradition, and thus the word has to do with a semantic field that Western histories of literature discuss freely, displaying a fair degree of certainty. However, then what kind of tradition(s)? All the writers using English in our times are fully acquainted with the tradition of Western culture, even if they were born in countries bordering on other oceans, but at the same time other traditions have either partially influenced them (the Aborigines in Australia, the Maoris in New Zealand, the

Indians in Canada) or wholly permeated them (that of the Indian subcontinent in the specific case of Rushdie, of Africa with its different nations, of the West Indies, etc., in other cases) with their different stories, legends, myths and interpretations of the world, and their different techniques of narrating and of composing poetry. Thus originality is a term that invites reflection.

Etymologically speaking (*orior, origo*), the word is connected with birth and origins, as we consider them in a spatial synchronic sense (origination). In this sense, the writers that we study are natives of, and were born on, the shores of other oceans, and come to us from far away: Rushdie, for example, from India to London, as an expatriate, Malouf from Australia, but with Lebanese and British connections, to Campagnatico, but not on a stable basis.

But origins may also exist in a diachronic sense, as Wilson Harris does not fail to observe; he comes originally from Guyana (but what a mixture of ethnic, biological and cultural components in the person of Harris!). Reflecting upon origins, upon the Origin, is a cultural imperative for Harris. In order to find the "gateway" that makes it possible to go beyond limits, edges, borders, thresholds, and all kinds of signs of division and separation that keep man imprisoned in the monolith of the dominant culture, Harris searches for the resources of the imagination "that may alter perception through and away from fixed habit, greed and monoliths of terror" (*WS* XVI), trying to detect the possible alternatives to the 'mainstream' which has become the foundation of the life of man on our planet, and returning to the potential that has been removed, and discarded, but which can and must coexist.

When the origin—seen as a synchronic provenance from other oceans—and the memory of the Origin—seen as a diachronic, fossilized, largely forgotten but potentially coexisting alternative—are combined, the linguistic-literary expression that is created is likewise "original" in the above sense. Not just an originality of literary forms, to which modernism and post-modernism have accustomed us (to saturation point, I might add, arousing the suspicion of a conformity to anti-conformity), but an originality of metaphors which appear to me to be capable of gathering into new *topoi*, in contrast with worn-out fields of metaphor and exhausted, over-worked topics.

On the basis of these premises

1. The contrasting relationship between "the Old Country" and "the New World" is frequently presented in the collection *Antipodes*: on the one hand, philosophy and the music of Beethoven and Mahler, and on the other, "the desolate shore" (*A* 7) which is the Australian continent; on the one hand, Bruges, "our dear sad Bruges," "this old and impressively dead city" (*A* 88), and on the other, the antipodes, where one of the protagonists is "deep in his dream of sunlight and youth" (*A* 90).

But it is not the binary separations that interest Malouf. In the first story, "Southern Skies," an English teacher at Brisbane is the link, "a last link" (*A* 9), between the two worlds, but also the anonymous boy who forms a relationship with him in the story, always riding his bicycle, is "a kind of centaur" (*A* 12) and consequently a creature that belongs to two worlds, both human and non-human, both realist and mythic. The story moves towards a climax, when the boy is presented with a revelation: the beauty, grandeur, and mathematical order of the spectacle of the stars, revealed by the telescope that the English teacher always keeps trained on the "southern sky."

> The sky, which looks so still, is always in motion, full of drama if you understand how to read it. Like looking into a pond. Hundreds of events happening right under your eyes, except that most of what we see is already finished by the time we see it—ages ago—but important all the same. Such large events. Huge! Bigger even than we can imagine. And beautiful, since they unfold, you know, to numbers of infinite dimensions like the ones you deal with in equations at school, but more complex and entirely visible (*A* 18).

The clumsy boy, who is hampered by an excess of adolescent hormones, is overwhelmed by the vision of

> blossoming abstractions, equations luminously exploding out of their own depths, brilliantly solving themselves and playing the results in my head as a real and visible music (*A* 24),

which recalls the passage at the beginning of the third chapter of Joyce's *A Portrait of the Artist as a Young Man*, with the difference that Stephen Dedalus is obsessed with himself, whereas the anonymous boy of "Southern Skies," who is sexually manipulated by the English teacher—with all the ambiguities and the irony of the coincidence—when he perceives the relationship between the stars and mathematics and music, feels as if he is "bursting into the life of things" (*A* 25), and the experience thrusts him beyond his modest individual dimensions.

Roughly at the centre of the collection, in the story "The Only Speaker of his Tongue," a linguist-anthropologist reflects upon the ancient mystery of language:

> O holiest of all things! We touch here on beginnings, go deep under Now to the remotest dark, far back in each ordinary moment of our speaking, even in gossip and the rigmarole of love words and children's games, into the lives of our fathers, to *share* with them the single instant of all our seeing and making, all our long history of doing and being, [...] back before syntax (*A* 69, my italics).

In the language of the aborigine,

> a whole alternative universe, since the world as we know it is in the last resort the words through which we imagine and name it (*A* 69).

In that language, the aborigine

> holds [...] the whole circle of shabby-looking trees, the bushes with their hidden life, the infinitesimal coming and going among grass-roots or on ant-trails between stones, the minds of small native creatures that come creeping to the edge of the scene and look in at us from their other lives (*A* 71).

And in the same way, in the context of a story set in Italy, the non-human world is present in the sound of cicadas, that can be heard in the silence of the siesta,

> whose generations beyond counting might go back here to beginnings. They were dug in under stones, or they clung with shrill tenacity to the bark of pines. It was another language. Immemorial. Indecipherable (*A* 110).

In the last story, "A Medium," there is once again "a link" between two worlds—those of the living and of the dead—and once again an anonymous boy, "standing at an angle to the half-open door" (*A* 158), his attention divided between the music that is being played in one room, and a *séance* that is taking place in the other one. As he answers the music teacher's questions ("she played intervals and I named them, or struck chords and I named them. It wasn't difficult. It was simple mathematics" *A* 159), the boy feels that at a moment of excitement he has gained "a glimpse through a half-open door" (*A* 160) of a reality that is bigger than him, but of which his voice is a part.

Also in *12 Edmonstone Street,* there is on the one hand "the ghost of England" (*ES* 25), and on the other, Australia, like "another planet" (*ES* 35) where the "are invisible," but here too, the adolescent boy's curiosity is aroused by "the magic that glows along a threshold" (*ES* 9), and by verandas, which are "no man's lands, border zones" (*ES* 20), ambiguous places in contact with the house, but also opening on to the street, the night, the world of mystery, and the area below the houses, where clocks and language have not yet been invented, and "the freedom and mystery of a time before houses" dominates (*ES* 47). "The world is full of odd, undisclosed connections" (*ES* 51), he observes, and some photos of creatures that are half-human and half-animal give him "a marvellous sense of possibilities, of how the world of animals and men might be connected" (*ES* 60).

What strikes Malouf on his travels in India is the plural density, the "invigorating, indestructible" inclusiveness (*ES* 110) of a life "closer to primitive beginnings" and perhaps, as a consequence, "further off from the distant, inconceivable end" (*ES* 111):

> India seems never to have heard of this absolute distinction (between the human world and the animal world) on which our superiority and power is based (*ES* 119).

Thus, questions arise, from the antipodes, about "undisclosed connections" and "alternative possibilities," and eyes are turned to "beginnings," in an all-inclusive gaze.

2. In *East, West,* Rushdie explores what Naipaul has so appropriately defined "the enigma of arrival." Stories of cultural distance succeed one another in a truly brilliant programmatic order. In the "East" section, two stories set in India narrate, in a sober, realistic style, single human cases against the background of multitudes. A third story follows, "The Prophet's Hair," which

introduces a note of magic realism: just because they have spent a few minutes in the same environment as the prophet's hair, four lame beggars are healed (and the narrator ironically comments: "They were, the four of them, very properly furious, because the miracle had reduced their earning power by 75 per cent, at the most conservative estimate: so they were ruined men," *EW* 58), and their mother regains her sight.

In the "West" section, Rushdie carries out the far more refined experiment, with a devastatingly parodic effect on present-day stylemes of Western literature, of constructing two post-modern *caprices*, with all the ingredients—including the rewriting of a historical figure (Columbus) and of a canonic literary text (Hamlet), a desecrating intertextuality, a mixture of genres, some Sternian lines ("..../...../...../...../.....," in order to represent "by each dot [...] the conjunction of one toe-tip with the floor," in the stride of young Hamlet, *EW* 74)—amid which he interpolates another typically Western text, the dystopic fanta-sociological tale, "At the Auction of the Ruby Slippers." Nothing is saved here, of the future which hangs inevitably over Western society: in a not-too-distant future, the real world is completely dominated by the fictitious world, and this is "a symbol of the moral decay of our post-millennium culture," says the anonymous narrator (*EW* 94). Individuals who rarely venture out, and live their lives closed inside bunkers, throng to the auction selling "memorabilia junkies" (*EW* 88). "Imaginary beings" are also present here:

> a large majority of us opposes the free, unrestricted migration of imaginary beings into an already damaged reality, whose resources diminish by the day. After all, few of us would choose to travel in the opposite direction (though there are pervasive reports of an increase of such migrations latterly) (*EW* 94-95).

The ruby slippers are highly desirable

> because we believe they can make us invulnerable to witches (and there are so many sorcerers pursuing us nowadays); because of their powers of reverse metamorphosis, their affirmation of a lost state of normalcy in which we have almost ceased to believe and to which the slippers promise us we can return (*EW* 92).

They also promise to take the wearer home, but

> 'Home' has become such a scattered, damaged, various concept in our present travails. There is so much to yearn for. There are so few rainbows anymore. How hard can we expect even a pair of magic shoes to work? They promised to take us home, but are metaphors of loneliness comprehensible to them, are abstractions permissible? Are they literalists, or will they permit us to redefine the blessed word? (*EW* 93)

It is the auctioneers who establish the value of things, of the past, the future and life, and, after this one of the ruby slippers, the following week's auction is to be dedicated to family trees and pedigrees:

> Family trees, coats of arms, royal lineages will be up for sale, and into any of these one may insert any name one chooses, one's own, or one's beloved [...]. Thanks to the infinte bounty of the Auctioneers, any of us, cat, dog, man, woman, child, can be a blue-blood; can be—as we long to be; and as, cowering in our shelters, we fear we are not—*somebody* (*EW* 102-103).

The third section is "East, West," and unlike the verse "Oh the East is the East/ and the West is the West/ and never the twain shall meet," it contains two stories which describe meetings between young people from different backgrounds. In the first one, there is a search for harmony which subsequently proves to be ephemeral, or even dangerous. In the words of one of the two friends, it is a question of trying to find "a [...] way of making a bridge between here-and-there, between my two othernesses, my double unbelonging" (*EW* 141). In the second story, a friendship is compromised by history and politics. In the third story, a young Pakistani in London observes the two worlds pulling the old nurse Certainly-Mary, in opposite directions:

> It was England that was breaking her heart, breaking it by not being India. London was breaking her heart by not being Bombay [...] was it that her heart, roped by two different loves, was being pulled East and West, whinnying and rearing, like those movie horses being yanked this way by Clark Gable and that way by Montgomery Clift [...]? (*EW* 209)

and in spite of the fact that he has acquired British citizenship, he is, in turn, torn in two directions. In his case, however, the verse "home is best" does not work.

> I, too, have ropes around my neck [...] pulling me this way and that, East, West, the nooses tightening, commanding, *choose, choose.*
>
> I buck, I snort, I whinny, I rear, I kick. Ropes, I do not choose between you. Lassoes, lariats, I choose neither of you, and both. Do you hear? I refuse to choose (*EW* 211).

We find here the "double unbelonging," and the need for a "bridge," the refusal to choose between alternatives *as if* they were mutually exclusive, and the much-desired redefinition of "home."

3. It is the relationships on the synchronic level that interest Rushdie in these stories: he deals with current affairs, history and politics.

It is the relationships on the diachronic level that interest Malouf: "beginnings," and alternative possibilities, as well as relationships between the infinitely large and the infinitely small (the stars and insects in the pond), between so-called highly-developed languages and primitive languages, between human and animal languages, between worlds.

Both Malouf and Rushdie, however, work on edges, borders, thresholds, and boundaries, looking for "links," "bridges," something that will allow them/us to share, instead of dividing, what is on either side. In the last few lines of *The Moor's Last Sigh,* the final words of dying Moraes confirm

> our need for flowing together, for putting an end to frontiers, for the dropping of the boundaries of the self.[5]

It is "gateways" that are of interest for Harris: "the elaboration of gateways into the largely submerged territory of the imagination" (*WS* XIX). In order to go beyond "thresholds," "break polarisations," and make a connection, 'melting pots' or 'mosaics' are not sufficient; what is needed is "a body of harlequin features rooted in many cultures" (*WS* 3), from one ocean to the other.

Once all signs of fragmentation, division, separation, opposition and drifting have been excluded, the continuity-contiguity between men, and between men and the created world, favours metaphors that are not based on scraps of reality, but on a fabric without "seams," not on drifting fragments, but on the totality: "the seamless whole."

To begin with, Harris's imagination is always at work amid "the living museum of creation" and "aeons of matter and space" (*WS* XVII), observing "the live tapestry of the universe" (*WS* XVI), in search of "secrets of potentiality" which may reveal "a universe composed of fabrics of mobility akin to thought" (*WS* XVI). His is a "pilgrimage toward forgotten origins."

The *Womb of Space* is a text made up of critical readings which Harris defines as "explorations": the writers that he "explores" are Faulkner, Poe, Jean Toomer, Juan Rulfo, Jean Rhys, Patrick White, etc., and what interests him is the "thread [...] woven into potential heterogeneity, and arching through European, African and pre-Columbian hidden antecedents" (*WS* 6).

With Harris, a completely 'original' language is born: his critical and his creative languages share in an identical, systematic disruption of binary polarisations and are based on metaphors that all tend towards "disrupting symmetries" (*WS* 18), and thus on paradoxes that unite apparently incompatible elements, in search of a "dialogue" (*WS* XVII), "a doorway *into* a break*through* from tragedy"—the tragedy of twentieth century nihilism—(*WS* 45, my italics)—and the prepositions 'into' and 'through' are frequently, almost obsessively, found on every single page.

Harris follows an "irrational coherence" [...] that breaches "conventional logic," moving "against the narrowness of simple logical patterns" (*WS* 4): this is a defence of what Harris calls "asymmetrical" discourse, not because symmetries are false, but because they claim to be universally valid, when instead they are only useful, and at times brilliant, extensions of a superimposed order that reduces the most contradictory phenomena "within patterns of elegant tautology" (*WS* 17). In practice, it is the "symmetrical thinking" which Matte Blanco studies for the unconscious, and whose laws he identifies in *The Unconscious as Infinite Sets, an essay in bi-logic,* that is presented as a language capable of expressing the coexistence of and interaction between two "modes of being" of man: the asymmetrical and the symmetrical, what we use in order to put an order into the organisation of knowledge, but at the same time, more or less unwittingly, to divide and construct rigid boundaries—"obdurate frontiers [...] we must learn to cross," says Harris (*WS* 150)—and the mode of being—"before syntax," as Malouf says—through which we are in contact with the *continuum* of our psychic life.[6] While Matte Blanco claims that symmetrical language is enclitic, in the sense that it needs the support of logical language in order to express itself, in order to express contents that are foreign to rational logic (but in so doing, it uses generalisations, condensations, and all the paradoxes that spring from an absence of the principles of contradiction and of negation), Harris suggests that language should make use of paradoxes (typical of Matte Blanco's 'symmetrical' thought) in order to overcome the resistance of so-called logical language.

> Imaginative sensibility is uniquely equipped by [...] paradox to mirror the inimitable activity of subordinated psyche; inimitable in that no art of total capture or subordination of originality within formula exists despite appearances. Thus the unity or density of *original* expression, in a work of profound imagination, is paradox (*WS* XVII, my italics).

While "the post-modern temperament [...] is committed to dead myth and tamed metaphor" (*WS* 47), it is necessary

> to release profound metaphors [...] to uncover a bridge of forgotten associations between diversity and mutuality, mutual heights/depths, mutual skies/earth, mutual cultures that civilisation has grossly married or eclipsed (*WS* 48).

Clearly, we are in need of "untamable metaphor and myth" (*WS* 47). The metaphor that appears most frequently "to bridge a divide" (*WS* 51) is that of the "rainbow bridge between cultures" (*WS* 29), "rainbow arcs or bridges between cultures" (*WS* 31, 33, 49), which is also "a rainbow arc or bridge of psyche" (*WS* 46), and takes the name of an "alchemical *coniunctio* or true and productive union between man and woman, between one and the other, between culture and culture" (*WS* 37), "between sky and earth" (*WS* 50).

With Harris, we arrive at the re-semanticisation of old metaphors by means of paradox: the river has four banks, and it is not the flow of time that is associated with the flow of its water, but space. In *The Four Banks of the River of Space*, there is one river of the living and one of the dead, and space is a womb.

It is not a question of reconciling opposites:

> not simply a reconciliation of opposites. Such a formula was too uncreative or mechanical. Not just a mechanics of psyche. But a *gathering* up of all that had been experienced in every condition of existence (my italics).[7]

What we are required to do is not to be "blind to originality," "to re-imagine the past, to enter changed spatialities in the past," to enter into "moral twinships with all species and things." There is the metaphor or "overlapping," of "gathering," and above all, of "salvaging," as the "capacity to convert rather than to succumb to, deprivations."[8]

4. In modernism, the dominant metaphor was the fragment, indicating discontinuity and separation. Fragments, ruins, the single occasions, the intermittent moments: pieces that are foreign to one another, and no force exists that can hold them together, except, perhaps, the Form of Art. Henry James distils them, Robert Browning lets them roll down a grassy slope ("Two in the Campagna"), or tries to melt them with gold into a ring, which is, however, the product of art (*The Ring and the Book*). T.S. Eliot piles them up on the shore, James Joyce inserts them into the nostalgia of an ancient form, and, later on, Malcolm Lowry attaches them to the big wheel of a fairground, which moves without making any progress (*Under the Volcano*), and heterogeneous fragments go "slipping past one another" in his story "Through the Panama," which is already a great post-modern experiment.

After the fragment, the drifting, of which *Waterland*, by Graham Swift, may be taken as a representative text: "the fens" are "a low-lying region [...] formed by silt [...], a slow, sly, insinuating agency [...] which shapes and undermines [...], simultaneously accretion and erosion; neither progress nor decay."[9] The protagonist does not expect, or require, a future, and all meaning is absent.

But, while we thought we were in the post-modern era, something new was happening: from the shores of other oceans, we were offered the surprise of "overlapping" connections,[10] of osmosis and metamorphosis, and the thought of the Origin, the origins, of possible, potential alternatives, abandoned but still coexistent.

For the new *topoi* to take shape, a sense of contiguity with the created world and with the Other needed to be revived; observation needed to go beyond the solipsistic boundaries that have made it so arid, settling again with a sense of wonder on the external world; the Other's gaze needed to turn to the Other. East and West, and the antipodes were being connected. The contribution came from far away oceans.

In my opinion, the expressions of originality are to be found in the new dominant metaphors of "links," "bridges," "gateways" ("pushing off the edges," "crossing borders"), which become *topoi* forming the basis for the many stories of relationships between what is on either side of the borders (for example, the only man that Morag can love, in Margaret Laurence's unforgettable novel *The Diviners,* is a métis, while the only man that Ammu can love in Arundathi Roy's novel *The God of Small Things* is an untouchable); other metaphors are those of "overlapping" and sharing, "salvaging" and "gathering," which are at the basis of the many stories about communities (for example, the new community that is reconstructed after the landslide, at the end of Jack Hodgins' *The Resurrection of Joseph Bourne,* etc).

Contiguity with the non-human is presented in various ways: in Robert Kroetsch's *What the Crow Said,* the young Vera is made pregnant by bees, by means of a literalised metaphor; in *The Carpathians,* by Janet Frame, the old Maori woman explains to the protagonist that it is impossible to work with flax if you don't know it, if you don't know how to talk with it; in Malouf's *An Imaginary Life,* Ovid gets lost and finds himself in the countryside:

> We are continuous with earth in all the particles of our physical being, as in our breathing we are continuous with sky. Between our bodies and the world there is unity and commerce.[11]

Continuity with origins it to be found in the revival of contact with ancient myths, no longer exclusively Biblical or Greek, in search of truths of the imagination which have been lost: "Myth [...], like all the past, real or imaginary, must be acknowledged," as Strabo Becker said in Jack Hodgins' *The Invention of the World*, "even if not believed."[12]

"Untamed potential for rebirth in the womb of space" is the formula used by Wilson Harris, to be activated by means of synchronic and diachronic contact, in a constant crossing over and back, through and into.

"Cross-culturalism" goes beyond mere multiculturalism, once again in the metaphor of "crossing": "cross-pollination," according to Rushdie. This is a crossing which takes place in both directions: it is not only Shakespeare familiarised (and parodied) in the tale of Rushdie, or Greek tragedy revisited in a play of the Nigerian Soyinka, or the Dantesque journey of the protagonist of *The Four Banks of the River of Space* by the writer from Guyana, Wilson Harris. It is also the need for Westerners to read the Koran and its commentaries in order to appreciate a book by Nuruddin Farah, or Rushdie's *Satanic Verses*, the ability to read the Mahabharata and classical Indian literature that is being acquired by my colleagues who are experts in English literature produced in India, the usefulness of translating into English the legends of the Canadian Indians, as the poet Robert Bringhurst is doing, before the last elderly Indian who knows them dies.[13] We need to move "through" these oceans, to "open doors" and share cultures.

NOTES AND REFERENCES

1. David Malouf. *An Imaginary Life* (London: Chatto and Windus, 1978) 135; Jack Hodgins, *The Resurrection of Joseph Bourne, or A Word or Two about those Port Annie Miracles* (Toronto: MacMillan, 1979).
2. Fay Zwicky. "Talking Mermaid," *Poems 1970-1992* (St Lucia: U of Queensland P, 1993) 232.
3. Salman Rushdie. *East, West* (London: Jonathan Cape, 1994), henceforth *EW*; David Malouf, *Antipodes* (London: Chatto and Windus, 1985), henceforth *A*; *12 Edmonstone Street* (1985; London: Penguin Books, 1986), henceforth *ES*. This essay was first published in *Africa, America, Asia, Australia* 22 (1998) 7-18.
4. Wilson Harris. *The Womb of Space: The Cross-Cultural Imagination* (Westport, USA: Greenwood Press, 1983), henceforth *WS*.

5. Salman Rushdie. *The Moor's Last Sigh* (London: Jonathan Cape, 1995) 435. In the best paintings of the Moor's mother, "the vision [...] in fact was a vision of *weaving* or more accurately interweaving (227); "a land-sea-scape in which the land could be fluid and the sea stone-dry was her metaphor [...] of the present, and the future she hoped would evolve" (227), and on the water's edge "strange composite creatures slithered to and fro across the frontiers of the elements" (226).
6. Ignacio Matte Blanco. *The Unconscious as Infinite Sets, an Essay in Bi-logic* (London: Duckworth, 1975).
7. Wilson Harris. *The Four Banks of the River of Space* in *The Carnival Trilogy* (London: Faber and Faber, 1993) 317.
8. Wilson Harris. *Jonestown* (London: Faber and Faber, 1996) 133, 137, 166, 168, 189, 194, 214, 223.
9. Graham Swift. *Waterland* (1983; London: Picador, 1992) 8-9.
10. I noticed this metaphor for the first time in a short story by Jack Hodgins in the collection *Spit Delaney's Island* (Toronto: MacMilland, 1976) 15.
11. Malouf 147.
12. Jack Hodgins. *The Invention of the World* (1977; Toronto: Macmillan of Canada, 1978) 316.
13. Robert Bringhurst. *A Story as Sharp as a Knife: The Classical Haida Mythtellers and their World* (Vancouver/Toronto: Douglas & McIntyre, 1999).

6

Tree of Man: Symphonic Structure

KALPANA PUROHIT

Seven years passed between what Patrick White felt to be the disappointing reception of *The Aunt's Story* and the publication of *The Tree of Man (1955)*. During this period, there were times, white confesses, when he considered ceasing to write altogether. But as he explains in his 1958 essay 'The Prodigal Son,' what he saw as the vacuity and mediocrity of modern Australian life suddenly overwhelmed him and he began to plan another novel. He says of it,

> "Because the void I had to fill was so immense, I wanted to suggest in this book every possible aspect of life, through the lives of an ordinary man and woman. But at the same time, I wanted to discover the extraordinary behind the ordinary" indicating that *The Tree of Man* reflects the restored faith of White.

The Tree of Man, which first brought Patrick White to general attention, remains in some ways his most impressive achievement. White's novel prior to this one, *The Aunt's Story* is almost a religious novel celebrating the nature of the human spirit of the soul. There is none of this tentativeness about *The Tree of Man*. This book is about a 'Mystery' and is also more strenuously, a wrestling throughout the life of its protagonist, Stan Parker, with the contradiction of complexities of the spiritual relationship. This trend towards religiosity provides the novelist with a wide framework within which he traces the 'poetry' behind the lives of ordinary people and for this he employs a neat symphonic structure.

The novel is a positive, poetic, affirmative work in which the writer dares to suggest that the lives of even the most ordinary people have some significant shape, structure and value. What is appealing is that White attempts to do this in the large old fashioned, conventional manner by telling us the life story of his characters. Patrick White's successful handling of a traditional form. The family saga, has invited critics to make comparisons with Lowrence and Tolstoy.

There is no doubt that White's intention is to give comprehensive picture of common people and the whole book is pervaded by a sense of the larger rhythms of life, the endless cycles of birth, growth, reproduction, decay and death.

As Vincent Berckley has demonstrated in his essay on *The Tree of Man*, its magnified and beautifully organised structure is one of its most impressive features. It not only enables the novelist to change his angle of observation and perspective but also lends credence to the theme of transcendental experience. In four movements, the pioneer couple are accompanied in their life and development through the stages of innocence, experience, death and reconciliation. The fourness of the seasons and of the elements make up the foundation, in every movement a natural disaster creates a kind of mystic crisis which changes their search for that is constant and firm.

Like the earlier novel, *The Aunt's Story*, this novel too can be said to illustrate a journey of discovery though the general movement is reversed, starting on an optimistic note quite in contrast to the note of apprehension emphasized in Theodora Goodman's journey. In the first *Spring section* of *The Tree of Man* the Parkers feel 'they were limitless' (98) and they feel convinced that they have each other and that harmony will last. "They were close. Their lives had grown together. They would continue in that way, because it was not possible to divide their common trunk." Words to them are too hard to handle, but "it was not necessary, perhaps, to speak, he began to feel in the skin of her hand." The stage of innocence of the young couple is symbolized by spring, morning, the honeymoon; all of which ends with a natural disaster—the flood, which introduce the protagonists to the stage of experience.

In *Part Two, Summer*, the tone is somewhat different,

however, The "moments of true knowledge [...] animating his mind and limbs with conviction, telling him of the presence of God" (186), can obviously not be shared verbally or by other means. "Stan had remained slow with men. It was a kind of unrealized ambition to communicate with them. But so far he had not done this."

There they experience personal failure, Stan when he cannot rescue a victim, Amy when she cannot make part of her life; a boy she has rescued from danger but has to accept his disappearance as suddenly as he appeared. The symbolic language is based on parenthood, maturity and summer, "a time of white dust, and yellow grit," and the natural disaster is a fire which destroys the property called Glastonbury. This fire also destroys Amy's romantic opinion of Madeline Armstrong, the beautiful daughter-in-law to be from a new rich butchering family, and also destroys Stan's escapist love for Madeline as he is rescuing her from the burning building. Towards the end of this summer of experience come "the years of mud and metal" of war.

Stan's spiritual isolation continues, in fact deepens in *Part Three, Autumn*. Now Amy resents the knowledge he cannot communicate, and they both apprehend that their growing apart is incurable. He realizes that she longed for 'permanence' which is illusionary and aware of the fact that vital, deep, experiences cannot be shared or expressed. In a dream, 'he could not lift the lid of that box to show her what he had inside' (308). Nor can be communicate with his son and "give shape to his knowledge" though he tries sincerely and hopefully. So we learn that in the Parker family "each was his own globe, or world of thought."

From this war Stan returns to the stage of spiritual death, to autumn and "a Chalky world of long perspectives." The climatic experience of illumination, attained only in the last moments of life's winter, follows this period of dreary, autumnal, spiritual decay, that what is reiterated once again is the novelist's belief (which constantly surfaces in Patrick White's writings) that suffering alone sweetens the fruit of illumination and spiritual reproachment with the unity.

Finally in *Part Four, Winter* there is a total disintegration of their lives. Their initial paradise is gradually being swallowed by Sydney, the growing metropolis equalling Hell in the symbolic structure, their children are destroyed—Ray is murdered after having lost all honour and dignity in life, and Thelma renounces her identity and personality to the extent that she changes her name to christine (an ironic touch) and joins the ranks of the spiritual dead. "The moments of illumination would not have been for her anyway," her "nonentity was complete" (471-72). Thus the general atmosphere of the last section can be summarized by Madeline's statement: "Lives [...] can only touch, they do not join." Stan dies with a final vision of the harmony and unity whose existence he has glimpsed in a few precious moments earlier in life, convinced at last of his own divinity and his relationship with the universal one, but doubtless alone, all the same.

WORKS CITED

John Barnes. *A Note on Patrick White's Novels.*

White Patrick. "The Prodigal Son," *Australian letters,* Vol. 3.

7

Ecology and Identity Crisis in Rohinton Mistry's Fiction

C.C. MISHRA

> "These temple destroyers, these devotees of ravaging commercialism seem to have a perfect control for nature, and instead of lifting their eyes to God of the Mountains, lift them to almighty dollar."
>
> John Muir
>
> Founder of Sierra Club, California (1892)

Ecological concerns have been the subject of literature since time immemorial. However, the ecological movement in the last few decades has gained considerable momentum and vigorously drawn the attention of the intellectuals, academics, writers and scientists to the grave issue of Man-Land (Nature) relationship. We have but one earth to live in. Naturally, therefore, any threat perception to its flora and fauna, to its biological and physical Nature, has become the central concern in the ecological writings ensuing therefrom. Such environmental crisis that challenges the Mother Earth and makes the Man-Nature relationship too fragile and endangered has acquired an existential dimension. As 'conscious' and 'sensitive' artists, the writers of this world have, time and again, raised their formidable voices of protest against the unmindful destruction of natural resources and the "Civilization's intrusion upon the pristine wilderness." They have written quite vividly and elaborately about the Man's relationship with Nature and the factors which are responsible to disrupt it and create existential problem.

Both the English and Canadian writers have responded to

the ecological relationship between the Man and the Nature around them differently. The Canadian encounter with the land otherwise termed 'Canadian Collision' reverses the traditional British portrayal of an embalmed and ennobling nature. John Moss terms it 'garrison mentality' and attributes the reason to the 'fragile' and 'precarious' state of a man balanced against the vast and hostile North-American environment. D.G. Jones maintains that the difference of outlook and treatment between the English and French Canadian writers is conditioned by their respective cultural and historical development and writes:

> "Compared to their English Canadian counterparts, many French Canadian writers have themselves been more deeply infected by the garrison mentality and that mentality has been reinforced by the weapons of western culture that French Canada has traditionally emphasized for use against a hostile world, namely, the spiritual weapons of detachment, of mortification and renunciation. English-Canadian culture has generally placed more emphasis on the material weapons for transforming the world, on technology and scientific technique" (Jones, 1979: 9).

Both the English and French Canadian literature tends to be sterile due to their extremity of attitude and have been criticized by writers like Leonard Cohen in his *Beautiful Losers.*

In comparison to their English and French counterparts, the South Asian Canadian writers have treated man-nature relationship in their works from a completely different perspective. Particularly, for these writers hailing from a warm country like India, the Nature in the mountainous region is considered to be more human-friendly than in the arid and desert region. As such Eastern attitude toward Nature is based more on caring and sharing. But the influence of the western culture especially their emphasis on technology and development has become the chief cause for the environmental degradation and ecological crisis in a country like India. Such ecological crisis in the South-Asian countries demands an altogether different approach with a view to deal with the destructive effect of modernization based on consumerism and industrialisation and the consequent existential crisis. Among the current brood of South Asian writers in Canada, Rohinton

Mistry has dealt elaborately with this aspect of ecological and environmental crisis in his fiction.

In his novel *A Fine Balance* Mistry has portrayed a few characters' relationship with the Nature around them with utmost sensitivity and depth. Most of these characters belong to his own Parsi Community, which is an ethnic minority in a predominantly Hindu India. Thus the existential crisis which they confront in their personal, social and national life constitutes the central concern of the novel. The protagonist Farokh Kohlah happens to be a victim of History, namely, the partition of India in 1947, a ruthless and selfish imposition of the British coloniser:

> "A foreigner drew a magic line on a map and called it the new border; it became a river of blood upon the earth. And the orchards, fields, factories, businesses, all on the wrong side of that line, vanished with a wave of the pale conjuror's wand" (*AFB* 205).

Despite the loss of the vast family fortune, Farokh along with his wife Aban and little son Maneck continue to relish their life in the foothills of the Northern mountain in India meeting out their needs from the small left out general store. In addition to this Farokh had been handed over a secret soft drink formula by his father, popular as Kaycey and quite a rage among the small town people. Though his wife's people living in a city by the sea beseeched them periodically to leave the mountain and move over to their place, Farokh and his family continue to live in their home in the hills praising always, "The air and water is so pure, the mountains so beautiful." Like his father, son Meneck too loves his home in the mountain to such an extent that his temporary departure for the city for education makes him nostalgic. Even a steaming bowl of water in the bathroom brings to his mind the vision of the dreamy mist that would be hugging the mountains in the morning:

> "[...] at this hour it would be swirling fancifully, encircling the snow-covered peaks. Just after dawn was the best time to observe the slow dance, before the sun was strong enough to snatch away the veil. And he would stand at the window, watch the pink and orange of sunrise, imagine the mist tickling the mountain's ear chucking it under the chin or weaving a cap for it (*AFB* 201).

Though Farokh had lost one of his eyes in an accident while bottling Kollah's Cola and wore an eyepatch on it, on his long evening walks though the hillside forest he would put it in his pocket and admire for the umpteenth time the beauty of the place. His wife Aban too enjoyed the magnificent view of the valley from the back of the general store. Not only for Farokh and his family, but for his friends like Major Grewal and others also the mountain was a part of their life, like a living intimate persona as if they lived together side by side. However their harmonious relationship with the nature was soon disrupted by the government's plan to connect the hill town to the cities. They who never dreamt of leaving the mountain were shocked to find the mountain leaving them. Mistry's subtle and veiled criticism is candid enough to target the self-styled messiahs for the development of the nation:

> "These were to be modern roads [...] roads that would hum with the swift passage of modern traffic. Roads wide and heavy duty, to replace the scenic mountain paths too narrow for the broad vision of nation builders and World Bank officials" (*AFB* 215).

Threatened by the forces of modernization and urbanization which would eventually destroy the green mountain and the environment of the hill-town, Farokh and his friend Major Grewal organize meetings to condemn "the flawed development policy, the shortsightedness, the greed that was sacrificing the country's natural beauty to the demon of progress" (*AFB* 215). They sign petitions and lodge their protest with the authorities, and wait. To their utter dismay, the authorities, those messengers of development equipped with the western ideas of technology and urbanization turn a deaf ear to their fervent appeal. The road continue to inch upwards, swallowing everything on its path. The invasion of technology is presented by Mistry quite evocatively:

> "The beautiful hills by its side become gashed and scarred. From high on the slopes, the advancing tracks looked like rivers of muds defying gravity as though nature had gone mad. The distant thunder of blasting and the roar of earth-moving machines floated up early in the morning and the dreaminess of the dawn mist turned to night-mare."

More than anybody else Farokh Kollah is shocked to the core of his heart. He feels as if he has been displaced from his dear land once again. The devastation of nature around him makes him depressive and terrified. His mental state is captured in the following touching lines:

> "Mr Kollah watched helplessly as the asphalting began, changing the brown rivers into black, completing the transmogrification of his beloved birth place where his forefathers had lived as in paradise. He watched powerlessly, while, for the second time, lines on paper ruined the Kollah family. Only this time it was an indigenous surveyor's cartogram, not a foreigner's imperial map" (*AFB* 216).

Ironically enough, the nation's plan primarily deprives him of his family fortune but holds out the promises of increased business in the second place. But in its promises lurks the venom of modernization which would deprive him of the family's name and his sense of identity. He complains to his wife bitterly that "the noxious exhaust from the lorries was searing his nostrils and the ugly throbhing of their engines was ripping his eardrums to shreds." Along with the pollution of air and noise, which is the primary cause of ecological imbalance, the so-called modernization brings in hordes of job-seekers who live in shacks and shanties by the slope of the hill and defile the environment through defecation and devour the forest for fire-word. Farokh is shocked by a permanent stench of human waste that hung in the mountain air and to see "bold patches upon the body of the hill." As though, corresponding to the protagonist's feelings of convulsion and anguish, the nature too reacts sharply against the technological invasion unleashed upon it, as Mistry notes:

> "Then the seasons revolted. The rain which used to make things grow and ripen descended torrentially on the denuded hills, causing mudslides and avalanches. Snow, which had provided an ample blanket for the hills, turned skimpy. Even at the height of winter the cover was ragged and patchy" (*AFB* 217).

Farokh felt a perverse satisfaction at nature's rebellion. It was a vindication of sorts: he was not alone in being appalled by the hideous rape of the environment. But the seasonal disorder continued year after year only to break him deep down inside. Talking a walk in the hills, the long solitary rambles which were the greatest pleasure to invigorate him, now seemed like a death watch. Haunted by the continual loss of the trees and rocks of the dearest mountain where he belonged, Farokh desperately looks for them:

> "Coming upon a favourite tree, he would stop under its branches a while before moving on. He would run his hand along the gnarled trunk, happy that an old friend had survived another day" (*AFB* 217-18).

The menace of modernization causes ecological imbalance and consequently, an existential dilemma for Farokh. While the people's comments about the disillusioned protagonist, "Mr Kollah's screw is getting a little loose. He speaks to trees and rocks and pats them like they were his dogs" brings out his mental state, it also impresses upon us his desperate search for his old place in the lap of nature. At this juncture Mistry's portrayal of the protagonist is that of a knowledgeable, sensitive and spiritual person based upon idealism and traditionalism, while the generation of people around him stand out in stark contrast as ignorant, insensitive and materialists charged with spirit of modernization and change.

Finally, it was a heartrending vision of the sunset during his walk in the hillside that conveys Farokh the inevitable message he was so desperately waiting for:

> "Suddenly he noticed that dusk had fallen: the sunset was forfeited behind the pall. And the entire scene was so mean and squalid by the twilight, so utterly beyond his ability to accept or comprehend. He felt lost and frightened. Waves of anger, compassion, disgust, sorrow, failure, betrayal, love-surged and crashed, battering and confusing him. For what? Of Whom? And why was it? If only he could..." (*AFB* 218).

Unable to make out the myriads of confusing emotions, Farokh feels a tightness in his chest, then his throat constricts as if he were chocking. He weeps helplessly, and silently venting his emotions. The meanings that this vision gives him is too new and terrifying for him to explore. There is no place for escape and he realizes that "his dreams had succumbed, during their collision with the passing years. He had struggled, he had won, he had lost. He would keep on struggling [...]" (*AFB* 219).

A further bout of displacement catches him unaware, through modern material force of consumerism. Their technique of 'hard-sell' and cut-throat competition targets to overtake the sell of his family softdrink, Kaycey forcing it to the brink of close-down. Though his son Maneck, being modern generation young man welcomes the idea of change and improve the general store, Farokh looks for his identity in the restoration of the past. He has an honest and touching reply about the consumerist culture and its garbed language like 'hard-sell':

> "What kind of a language is that? Sounds absolutely undignified. Like begging. Those big companies from the city can behave like barbarians if they want to. Here we are civilized people" (*AFB* 220).

The modern generation has no place for such traditional and old fashioned men and no honour for their sentiment. By his resistance to modernization and change, Farokh loses both his son and his own place in the scheme of a transmogrified home-land.

The final wish of Farokh after his death speaks volume about the intense shock and anguish he had undergone by the invasion of modernization and its accompanying forces like consumerism and technology. Disillusioned by the way his dearest home-land in the hills was devastated and defiled, he wishes to be cremated and to get his ashes scattered in all the difficult places and terrains of his dear hills. Primarily, his wish for cremation was an outraging one as his religion Zoroastrianism prescribes the disposal of dead body by feeding it to vultures. Anticipating that any left out part of his body might further defile the land, he even dares to violate the sanction of his religion. Further more by the consummation of his final wish with scattering of his ashes over the hills and the valley, Farokh seeks his lost identity through complete assimilation with his dearest trees, rocks and hills.

Man interacts with nature through the medium of culture. It is the culture, which provides the values and knowledge for man-land (Nature) interaction Mistry's message in this regard is quite candid and radical. So long as the cultural values are sensitive to ecology, man's relationship with Nature remains harmonious and cordial. But when we adopt cultural values alien and unsuitable to our environment lured by its superficial and glamorous façade, a vicious circle of destruction and decay is unleashed, whose swift currents wash down the life-sustaining elements of nature. "Modernisation and development through technology and science," a concept of the western culture is not an unwelcome idea. Rather, Mistry seems to suggest that its mindless execution without proper introspection and planning, would adversely affect the Nature, thereby creating ecological and existential crisis. Through his elaborate and sensitive presentation of man-nature relationship. Rohinton Mistry stands out as another spokeperson of Ecological movement.

WORKS CITED

1. D.G. Jones. *Butterfly in the Rock* (Toronto: Univ. of Toronto Press, 1970).
2. Rohinton Mistry. *A Fine Balance* (London: Faber, and Faber Limited, 1996). Cited as *AFB*.
3. John Moss. *Patterns and Isolation* (Toronto: Mc Clelland and Stewart Ltd., 1974).

8

Passion and Devastation beneath Ethnic and Polytropic Identities in Michael Ondaatje's *The English Patient*

RASHMI GAUR

Born in Colombo, Sri Lanka in 1943, where his family owned a tea plantation, Ondaatje immigrated to England, at the age of nine, and then to Montreal, at the age of nineteen. He has written poetry, fiction, criticism as well as screen plays (Elliott 800). *The English Patient* is his best known novel, which won the Booker Prize in 1992, the very year of its publication, and also a number of other awards. The cinematographic version appeared in 1996, produced and directed by Anthony Minghella, with the cooperation of Ondaatje and received seven Oscars (Tötösy 2). The novel has been analysed from various angles: its colonial context, introduction of fragmented cultural identities, ethnic issues, sub-textual richness, poetic weaving of the past and the present, and above all, its treatment of history have always attracted critics—towards the novel, as well as towards the film. The present paper discusses these themes briefly and tries to analyze how these are ultimately linked with the dominant theme of complex human passions and devastation of internal and external landscapes.

The colonial context is present in *The English Patient* not only as a force of political change but at a subtler level also, as a vehicle of gradual yet permanent socio-cultural shifts. This aspect is unobtrusively presented by the explorations arranged by the British Royal Geographical Society during the two Wars. The English patient recalls it "Look at a map of the Libyan

Desert and you will see names. Kemal el Din in 1925, who, almost solitary, carried out the first great modern expedition. Bagnold 1930-32. Almasy-Madox 1931-37. Just north of the Tropic of Cancer" (*EP* 137). Leaving their "civilized" societies these adventurers go to a desert and face its primitive challenges. These exploits echo the natural scientists' dream of mapping the unchartered desert and also the colonial argument for political expansion of power, as the desert was soon to become the strategic arbiter of military wins. The pure scientific attitude is represented by Madox who, unable to accept the cruel realities of the war, commits suicide in a Suffox home—"Someone's war was slashing apart his delicate tapestry of companions" (*EP* 241). The scientific aspect of explorations is soon replaced by the camouflage of agents like Clifton whose motive is to exploit scientific knowledge for colonial expansion. "He was not just an innocent Englishman [...]. As far as the English were concerned, he was keeping an eye on your strange group in the Egyptian-Libyan desert" (*EP* 252). Against these circumstances the Bedouins are also unable to retain the unperturbed innocence of their tradition and learn to save a burning pilot for trading his skills. Western forces used the Bedouins for their "military aims and often infiltrated them," forcing them to shun their friendly and hospitable ways (Paula 45).

The representation of fragmented cultural identity is as acute in suggestivity as the colonial context is in the novel. The characters in *The English Patient* do not have a well-defined cultural identity. The characteristics are overlapping and mixed and a "plural notion of identity that belongs to different cultural spaces" has been presented (Corina 75). Juxtaposed against it is the awareness of race and ethnicity codified as an indicator of behavioural responses during the significant moments of national loss and gain. The war makes the ethnic divisions more conspicuous. The characters' response to the atomic bomb illuminates the extent to which ethnic identity conditions and generates reactions. Kip realizes it after the bomb, "You and then the Americans converted us. With your missionary rules. And Indian soldiers wasted their lives as heroes so they could be *pukkah*. You had wars like cricket. How did you fool us into this? Here—listen to what you people have done" (*EP* 283). Ethnic and racial awareness becomes a way of focusing larger issues within a particular perspective. W.E.B. Du Bois has rightly suggested that race "as a socio-cultural construct was the battleground for the delineation of a modern self within society" (*The Souls of Black Folk,* 1903, quoted by Elliott 413). The concept of racial inferiority was developed as a debilitating weapon to subvert the potential development of societies, and is central to the unraveling and decoding of the true history of the 20th century. Du Bois further states, "The history of the world is the history, not of individuals, but of groups, not of nations, but of races, and he who ignores or seeks to override the race idea in human history ignores and overrides the central thought of all history" (*ibidem*). The bomb startles Kip into a sudden awareness of the commonality of Asian aspirations and he aligns himself to the vision of his brother.

The colonial context, ethnic insecurity and alienation are vividly present in Kip's portrayal. Nonetheless, along with other major characters of the novel, his personality can also be termed as "polytropic." The word itself can be interpreted as "having 'many ways of being,' always turning in various directions and multiplying the ways of his nature" (Corina 75). The English patient has a "hybrid of identities" (*ibidem* 3). He is an enigma, a mystery, the despairing Christ of Hana. He compares himself to Kip, calling him an "international bastard" (*EP* 176). He does not want to belong to anyone, to any nation, and uses the multiplicity of his identities to transmit different versions about himself. Similarly, Hana moves around in an alien territory trying to look within herself and find her true self. She also does not possess any fixed identity. She cannot relate herself to the ravages of war. Sick of Europe, she does not want to go to Canada either. War has changed this innocent youth into a disillusioned being. The patient identifies it. Hana goes into a withdrawn self-imposed exile in the villa and like a nomad keeps on searching for oases. She prefers to be "nomadic in the house [...] living like a vagrant" (*EP* 13). Caravaggio too is a traveller with multiple and polytropic identities—the thief, the double agent, the drunk, the lover, and the uncle. He systematically reawakens the memories of a pleasant past in Hana—dance, music and the Marseilles. The polytropic identities are clear in Kim too, despite his ethnic background. Away from his country, he is constantly on movement, sweeping land in different countries to detect unexploded mines. He does not share nostalgic reconstruction of the past with other characters and seems to be rooted in the present. Like the burnt patient he too sees "reason in everything" (*EP* 84).

The English Patient has the discernible presence of three books which illustrate and heighten the significance of the different contours of the novel. The most quoted book is Herodotus' *Histories*, which provides the framework for the desert explorations of Almasy and others. The English patient's copy of *Histories* also doubles as his diary in which he jots down notes and pastes photographs. It also occasions many memories and constantly acts as a reference point for him, "This history of mine," Herodotus says, "has from the beginning sought out the supplementary to the main argument?" What you find in him are cul-de-sacs within the sweep of history—how people betray each other for the sake of nations, how people fall in love [...]" (*EP* 119). The connections between Herodotus and the novel are "more than just the sum of a number of references" as the structure and themes of the ancient treatise are echoed in the novel (Harrison 1). *The Charaterhouse of Parma* discusses Napoleon's invasion of Italy and is a parallel discourse on the occupation of the same territory by aggressors. Rudyard Kipling's *Kim* is an artistic counterpoint to the sapper's life. The intertextuality and historical references impart a sonorous depth to the non-linear presentation of the story. The weaving together of the past and the present creates a multilayered poetic richness of suggestivity which could not be realized through traditional methods. It is enhanced by Ondaatje's method of fictionalizing the historical figures and events. Without going into a debate on whether he was aware of the history of some of his characters or not, it can be safely stated that many of the characters in the novel poses real life parallels, and their real story is selectively translated into the fictional mode. The English patient Almasy himself is a sketch of the Hungarian aristocrat, cartographer, explorer and military officer of the same name (Tötösy). The details of the real life match with the fictional representation of the personality. The real Almasy had discovered the legendary oasis Zarzura in the Libyan desert and the prehistorical paintings in the caves of the Uweinat mountains—these facts have been retained in the fiction. However, this curious overlapping of history and fiction is not maintained as closely in the case of other characters—*viz.*, Katharine, Kip and Caravaggio. Katharine is modelled on Lady Clayton, but the fictional representation is not truthful to the real individual (Tötösy 5). It is mentioned that Kip is a portrayal of Lt. General Inder Singh Gill, who died recently. Lt. General Gill had served in Italy during the Second World War. Trained initially as a sapper he was linked with the bomb disposal units. Not much evidence has been unearthed about this link, though strong parallels exist. Caravaggio is not modelled after any historical person, but his name points to the Italian Renaissance painter, Caravaggio, whose painting "David with the Head of Goliath" is referred to by the English patient as an illustration of his attitude towards Kip. It is assumed that "the face of David is a portrait of the youthful Caravaggio and the head of Goliath is a portrait of him as an older man, how he looked when he did the painting [...] I think [...] that Kip is my David" (*EP* 116).

Ultimately, however, these themes seem peripheral in comparison to the depiction of the deepest and most turbulent passions of human life and the suggestive rendering of the devastation littered in the internal and external landscapes of the contemporary world. Ondaatje has depicted the intensity of human passion and love which has always intrigued mankind. The love he describes is laced with struggles, disillusions and suffering, and its treatment reminds us of Turgenev's stories, particularly "Asya." Set against turbulent times of war and a presentiment of an impending catastrophe, it throbs with an alarming rhythm. The destruction and devastation wrecked by warring nations is matched by the inner desolation and tragedies of the characters. The polytropic and ethnic identities of the characters are significant pointers to the development of their attitudes, but beneath these identities a story of desperate passion, longing and devastation unfolds before us, leading us to the denouement that human beings should preserve, and not violate the sacred life and its emotions.

The English Patient is a story about trapped people—people who are trapped in their past casting its shadow on their present, and struggling to somehow possess a hold over life. Almasy is trapped in his past, reliving it constantly to escape the pain of the present. Hana too does not have the freedom of mind and is yet to overcome the loss of her lover, child and father in the war. She retreated from everybody around her except the child with whom she shares everything in her mind (*EP* 82). She wanted to go home; unable to do so she opts for the next possible action-stepping outside the war and staying with a patient, "[...] she hardly talked during the war. She needed an uncle, a member of the family. She needed the father of the child [...]" (*EP* 85). With determination she creates a barrier of silence around her, using her experiences as nurse, using even the hammock and the shoes of the dead (*EP* 47) to live and underline the determination of not falling apart "at this" (*EP* 48). She "would have nothing to link her, to lock her, to death" (*EP* 50). What Ondaatje has presented before us is a picture of life pitted against death which is duplicated by the setting of the Tuscan villa. Mined and ruined, its surroundings are littered with death and devastation. In sharp contrast the villa itself is painted—each room with a different season, as if in celebration of life. Inside the villa Hana is brought back to life once again by the English patient in whose presence she "could turn away from being an adult" (*EP* 52), and Caravaggio, who brings back her past to her. Hana's journey towards life completes with her passionate love for Kip. Their friendship starts with a functional note and soon develops into an intimacy—"As they grow intimate the space between them during the day grows longer" giving them a private energy (*EP* 127). Though intimate, their passionate relationship is rather unsure and tentative. Kip does not allow himself "to be beholden to her, or her to him" (*EP* 128). The psychological depth of his passion again reminds us of Turgenev's handling of similar themes. Kip realizes that "he could never turn and inquire of her what deepest motive caused this relationship. He held her with the same strength of love he felt for those three strange English people [...]" (*EP* 197). Kip, who remains a foreigner to others (*EP* 105), is able to overcome his colonial background in his relationship with Hana, till the tragic occurrence of the Bomb. Their passion for each other is suffused with a lyrical note, as the love they have known remains with them forever.

The passionate and rather tragic love story of Hana and Kip is paralleled by that of the patient and Katharine. The patient had noted down on his copy of the *Histories*, "A love story is not about those who lose their heart but about those who find that sullen inhabitant who, when it is stumbled upon, means the body can fool no one, can fool nothing [...]. It is a consuming of oneself and the past" (*EP* 97). Katharine's reading of Candaules' story becomes the first errant step towards their mutual passion (*EP* 233). Helplessly they are drawn towards each other, unable to decide whether it was betrayal of those around them, or the desire of another life (*EP* 238). Madox gives a warning signal through a paragraph from *Anna Karenina* which is strengthened gradually and Katharine ultimately returns to her husband, "From this point on, she whispered, we will either find or lose our souls" (*EP* 238). Their intense passion for each other draws them together once again in the final moments of Katharine's life. She is left in the "Cave of Swimmers" while Almasy goes to seek help, is captured and comes back after three years. The passages describing their ardent love throb with a passionate intensity which is relived constantly and repetitively by the English patient. His constant speech which fills every waking minute reconstructs his love and also enacts barriers—as Hana's silence has done for her—around him and his love. His pain, separation and suffering compel him to look within and find solace in vocalized memory.

The passionate concern for each other in these relationships is ultimately thwarted by war. Ondaatje has captured and presented the intensity and the rhythm of passion by presenting disjointed mental process in the non-realistic convention of the poetic novel. The failure of individual sensibility and passion in those times which justified all sorts of cruelties in the name of reason has been polemically presented by the author. The spirit of war broods over the novel and images of death and devastation permeate its world. The desolation is clearly present in the surroundings of the villa. Retreating German forces mine the houses (*EP* 11) using every conceivable object—wooden boxes, pipes, vehicles. "Italy was worse than Africa [...]. As Sappers entered cities they walked along avenues where corpses were strung from trees or the balconies of buildings [...]. Some of the hanging corpses were mined and had to be blown up in midair" (*EP* 275). We have images of death, diseases and senseless devastation: typhus epidemic breaking out, people bombed inside tunnels and ships freshly mined underwater, Madox kills himself in silent protest against war, Almasy is arrested and cannot reach Katharine with help in time, Hana withdraws within herself, Caravaggio's thumbs are cut off and Kip lives by defying the bomb wire. These images are intensified in the ultimate expression of devastation, *i.e.* the bombs dropped on two Japanese cities. The colonial context once again becomes dominant as Kip recollects that his brother had advised him not to turn his back on Europe, "The deal makers. The contract makers. The map drawers. Never trust Europeans, he said" (*EP* 284). Caravaggio also feels that such a bomb can never have been dropped on a white nation (*EP* 286). Once Kip leaves the villa Girolamo he does not look back. The atmospheric devastation has swallowed up his passion. Yet the love is never forgotten, the passion remains and sustains life. The patient lives through the memories of Katharine and her love, and in the same manner Kip harbours Hana's love in the centrality of his existence. Ethnic and polytropic identities and the difference therein do neither mitigate the intensity of passion nor soft-pedal the introduction of devastation as an overpowering reality of their day.

Thus we find that the thematic rendering of *The English Patient* possesses a multiplicity. The core story develops and unfolds as a tale of intense passion and complex sensitivity, which burgeons amidst chaotic, meaninglessly acute and immediate devastation. Despite the overpowering oppression, Ondaatje has been successful in communicating the message that passionate love imparts meaning and purpose to life despite constraints, and is capable of creating some permanent transcendental vision within the self amidst the haze of pathetic diablerie.

WORKS CITED

Corina Ana Anghel. "Polytropic Identities in Michael Ondaatje's *The English Patient*." *Journal of Indo-Canadian Studies*, Vol. 1, No. 2, July 2001, 73-86.

Emory Elliott. *The Columbia History of the American Novel*. New York: Columbia University Press, 1991.

Michael Ondaatje. *The English Patient*. New York: Vintage International, 1992.

Paula Garcia-Ramirez. "The Colonial Context of Michael Ondaatje's *The English Patient*," *The Atlantic Literary Review*, Vol. 2, No. 1, 42-49.

Steven Tötösy de Zepetnek. "Michael Ondaatje's *The English Patient*, 'History,' and the other." http://clcwebjournal.lib.purdue.edu/cclweb99-4/Tötösy 99-2html.

Thomas Harrison. "Herodotus and *The English Patient*." <http://www.ie/~classics/98/Harrison 98.htme.

9

Resisting Cultural Genocide: Beatrice Culletin's *In Search of April Raintree*

B. INDIRA

> White Man, to you my voice is like the unheard call in the wilderness [...]. When you first came, most of our tribes began with peace and trust [...] we were willing to share with you our vast wealth [...]. For our efforts we are labeled savages [...]. We turned to treaties. And [...] we ran into your cunning trickery [...] we lost our lands, our freedom [...] we are held in contempt [...].
>
> [...] you say that we are a people without dignity [...]. We cannot accept a life, which has been imposed on us.
>
> You say that we are drunkards [...] drinking is a way of dying. Dying without enjoying.
>
> [...] we are Indian people, we are still dying.
>
> [...] our wisdom is dying [...] if Indian wisdom dies, you, White Man, will not be far behind [...]. (*In Search of April Raintree* 169-70)

Beatrice Culletin's *In Search of April Raintree*, the present text under consideration is a moving account of two Metis sisters, April and Cheryl, born to a father of "mixed blood, a little of this, a little of that and a whole lot of Indian," and a mother, part Irish and part Ojibway. The two sisters are surrounded by squalour, despair, promiscuity throughout their lives and especially in the process of growing up from childhood to adulthood they confront a series of tragedies placed as they are in a racist white culture that ostracizes them for their Metis roots.

The novel has been an important teaching text in all the school and college courses in literature, women's studies and native studies in Canada. C.H. Mountford's review of the novel says that "students will respond to the strength of her [the novelist's] emotions." Joanne Peters considers the novel a "central text in Native literature." The novel appeals to one as an artistic fractionalizing of cultural displacement of the Metis in Canada, generally referred to as a "combination" off the concepts of "civilization" and "savagery" by non-native Canadians. Canadian novelists have always used Metis/half-breed characters to illustrate civilized-savagery point of view (Emma Laroque).

Euro centric definition of civilization refers to only those literates who understand the White man's language and culture. Europeans have obliterated several native cultures all over the globe as part of establishing political, social and cultural hegemony. In today's postcolonial and multicultural societies the issue of native identities have occupied most of the postmodern and postcolonial debates, as natives of the colonies are the original inhabitants of the land.

Art of any form—visual, performing, literature—is vital to the identity of the Fourth World. "Of these," says Adam Shoemaker, "indigenous writing is the most fascinating," and he further says that the native voice is "more full of passion and persuasiveness than Government inquiries or Royal Commissions" (245).

Nancy Burke in her essay on the native peoples' voice quotes Agnes Grant to define Native literature as "native people telling their own stories, in their own ways, unfettered by criterion from another time and place."

Natives in Canada, Australia and New Zealand—Canadian Indians, Inuit, Aborigines, Torres Strait Islanders, and Maoris—share a common history, of violence, of rape, of exploitation, of dispossession and death. Rightly so, their writings provide an "unparallel view of indigenous histories as lived experiences" (A. Shoemaker 246). Since 1990 it has been firmly established in all these countries that the indigenous voice can no longer be silenced. Because of their common histories, "the flesh-and-blood genre of historical and family realism is very strong in (the literatures of) all the countries" (A. Shoemaker 246).

A writer's world-view is sharply determined by his or her historical and cultural roots and experience. Talking of the inseparable link between the study of literature and history Edward Said says that "the study of literature is not abstract but is set irrecusably and unarguably within a culture whose historical situation influences [...] a great deal of what we say and do" (xxxi). To him, by concentrating on empty humanism while interpreting literature we are eliminating "any mention of transnational experiences such as war, slavery, imperialism, poverty and ignorance that has disfigured human history" (xxxi).

Beatrice Culletin along with other writers of the Fourth World identifies herself with the "vision and objectives of other postcolonial writing: the quest for personal and social, cultural identity, the belief that writing is an integral part of self-definition, the emphasis on historical construction" (Elleke Boehmer, 228-29). Metis writing reflect a new race that is a combination of white and red. What should have been the best of both worlds, the Metis became a worst nightmare for either, thanks to the discriminating policies of the government. These "road allowance people," (Maria Campbell's term for Metis) are a "soft spot in the psyche of the aboriginal writing as well" (E.F. Ted Dyck). Products of two mixed traditions Metis commanded both European and Indian languages. By late 1800s as their numbers increased, they married amongst their own creed and a new aboriginal culture that is neither European nor Indian came into existence proclaiming a new tribal identity. Each of these groups is unique by itself for it has its own language and lifestyle depending on the specific Indian roots they belong to. However, all the communities share a collective consciousness determined by their historical circumstances. And as they became more concentrated and endogamous, Metis' group consciousness grew. In 1982 the Canadian Government finally acknowledged the right of Metis to exist as a separate people.

Euro centric socio-cultural stance however, still looks down upon Metis with contempt. The term Metis—a French word meaning to mix or combine—continues to be used as a derogatory racist label attached to a group of non-conformists who resisted the genocidal operations of the Whites thereby separating them from the other aboriginal/native population.

In spite of their active participation in Canada's battle against American annexation no Canadian history book never mentions Metis' contribution to what Canada is today. They have been pushed into oblivion labeled as rebels.

Cheryl Raintree one of the two central characters of *In Search of April Raintree* raises in protest against a distorted version of history in a white racist class at school:

> "This is all a bunch of lies [...]."
>
> "I'm going to pretend I didn't hear that," the teacher had said calmly.
>
> "Then I'll say it again. I'm not going to learn this garbage about Indian people [...].
>
> If this is history, how come so many Indian tribes were wiped out? How come they haven't got their land any more? How come their food supplies were wiped out? Lies! Lies! Lies! Your history books don't say how the white people can do is teach a bunch of lies to cover your own tracks [...]" (57).

Acclaimed as an "*exceptional Metis*" Cheryl gets strapped for the outburst yet maintains her native pride and tells her sister:

> "I think it's important we know our own history."

for revival of culture plays a privotal role in asserting native identities. Native cultures are always distorted and exploited by the colonial power in exerting and establishing its authority over the native subjecting the native to forced-assimilation into the white culture. Distortion of history, damaging the source of food supplies, forceful evacuation from their lands and many such activities are part of the white man's strategy of assimilation. This tantamounts to genocide with no bloodshed which in other words is death to a cultural order, in this case the Metis.

Prof. R.J. Rummel rightly points out that the "near universal assumption that war is mankind's foremost killing machine is wrong [...] genocides have caused four times more deaths than all the wars in history [...]" (*The Hindu*).

Not only direct killing even causing serious mental or physical harm to members of a target group or deliberately inflicting any condition that may destruct a group even partially or imposing birth control mechanisms or forcibly transferring children of the group to another group amounts to genocide according to Genocide Convention's definition (*The Hindu*). Thus genocide need not necessarily be aimed at killing as many people as is possible.

A close reading of the novel, *In Search of April Raintree* reveals to us the several steps governments take to obliterate a certain group in an attempt to rewrite its history. The novelist gives vent to the pathos of living as a Metis in a white society through the lives of April and Cheryl. The artistry of the novelist lies in presenting to us two divergent view-points of the same problem from an insider's point of view: April, a conformist detests to be identified as a Metis and would even go to the extent of evading Cheryl whose appearance is pronouncedly native. Cheryl on the other hand takes pride in her roots and goes to the extent of fantasizing her ancestral roots to proclaim herself what she is, a true Metis. Though at the end there is an ironical reversal of views, most of the insights into a Metis' life are provided to the reader through Cheryl's consciousness. What is interesting to note is that the novelist herself was raised in white foster homes like the protagonists of the novel and her two sisters committed suicide drawing a close parallel to that of Cheryl's suicide in the novel.

At the beginning of 20th century Canadian government developed a policy by which native children are taken away from their families in order to *civilize* them on the pretext they would be safer living away from the alcoholic parents. That the parents were turned into alcohol-dependents by the state is beside the point.

These children are largely used as domestics by white families in return to the food and education given to them constantly posing threat to their native pride. In spite of the sub-human life of poverty, alcohol, drunken brawls, promiscuity back home, April still prefers to live with her parents. She wages a silent rebellion against her foster mother who welcomes her with "*I know you half breeds, you love to wallow in filth*" (38) and pushes her into a "cold room that smelled mouldy." Being a half breed to her is to be "*poor and dirty, being weak and having to drink, being ugly and stupid, living off white-people.*"

The native identity that gets robbed in the process of

civilizing these natives never gets even partially substituted. In stead they are offered negative stereotypes. When the two sisters decide to run away from the foster home unable to put up with the bullying of getting separated from each other they get caught mid-way. Their social worker, Mrs Semple gives them a taste of what they are going to make of their lives accusing them of developing "native girl Syndrome" not bothering to check the sub human fare provided to them in the foster-home:

> [...] and you girls are headed in that direction. It starts out with fighting, the running away, the lies. Next come the accusations that everyone in the world is against you. There are the sullen uncooperative silences, the feeling sorry for yourselves.
>
> And when you go on your own, you get pregnant [...] can't find or keep jobs [...], start with alcohol and drugs [...] into shoplifting and prostitution and in and out of jails [...] live with men who abuse you [...] [finally] living off society [...] (67).

Drugs, prostitution, shoplifting, are beyond the comprehension of their young Innocent minds. But that does not prevent the social worker from drafting their future for them:

> "Now you're going the same route as many other native girls [...] end up in the same place as they do. *Skid row*!" (67)

Ironically Cheryl, the younger of the two, the more compassionate of the two, the more committed to the cause suffers from cultural shame and gets pushed into the same direction by circumstances.

She finally jumps to death from the same bridge her mother jumped herself to death when she could no longer to stand the separation from her children, a drunken husband, ill-health crumpled as she was under the weight of a faceless existence. The suicides prove that *civilized* White society has very little to offer these half-breeds in terms of a succour as a substitute to what has been robbed off—their identity.

Evacuating natives from their land and providing them with cheap houses under the government housing programmes is yet another facet of assimilation that we find in the novel. Of these houses, Cheryl tells April:

> [...] cheaply made, no planning, no sewer system [...] those housing programmes were thought up by Indian Affairs, which means only Treaty Indians get any of the supposed benefit [...] Non-status Indians and Metis get welfare [...] [for] employment was hard for them to come by (174).

The following extract further bears testimony to the impoverished lives of Metis in Canada:

> [...] the way they live in winter [...] [they] have to walk miles and miles just for their water. They roll up newspapers inside their jackets for extra warmth. Cardboards and plastics replace broken windowpanes. Their furniture is wooden crates and blankets on the floor [...] (174).

A study of the novel shows that the promulgation of the several *welfare schemes* has given the world a distortion of facts for the schemes succeeded only in transforming full-blooded human beings into automatons responding only to alcohol and welfare doled out by the government. Their women are easy targets of rape by the white men. It takes a brutal gang rape of herself and the suicide of her sister for April to realize that all along she has been denying a basic part of herself by trying to gain access to white social ladder to evade her Metis-identity.

The novel concludes on a mixed note of pathos and hope. Cheryl who writes to her sister a parting note yearning to have a real family—"All my life I wanted for us to be a real family [...] I couldn't even mother my own baby [...]"—leaves behind her son, Henry Liberty Raintree whom April readily takes into her fold to make Cheryl's dream come true. April, resolves:

> [...] there would be a tomorrow. And it would be better. I would strive for it. For my sister and her son. For my parents. For my people (228).

It would be fitting to conclude the paper with Cheryl's words exuding incurable optimism:

"All life dies to give new life."

* * *

Excerpts from Maria Campbell's letter to the novelist:

> [...] You have written an important story, one that should be read by all Canadians, Indian and White [...]. It is a

powerful story because, with gentleness, it deals with the sickness in our society and our people. It is the kind of writing that will begin the healing of our people and help a dominant society understand and feel the lives of a people it almost destroyed [...] (*In Search of April Raintree* viii).

WORKS CITED

Anonymous. *Genocide and Assimilation: Canada's Aboriginal Peoples' Experience, Ethnic Cleansing—Canadian Style.**

Boehmer, Elleke. *Colonial & Post Colonial Literatures*, OUP, 1995.

Burke, Nancy. *The Native Peoples' Voice—Expressing Identity in Canadian Literature.**

Culletin, Beatrice. *In Search of April Raintree.* Winnipeg: Pemmican, 1985.

Gould, Carolyne. *A Little, Very Little, Native American History.**

Laroque, Emma. *The Metis in English Canadian Literature.**

Mountford, C.H. *A Review of April Raintree.* Cm archive book review, vol. 12, No. l, 1984 Jan.*

Peters, Joanne. *Ibid.*, No. 4.*

Said, Edward W. *Reflections on Exile.* New York: Penguin, 2001.

Shetty, K. Ashok Vardhan. "When war exterminates mankind," *The Hindu Magazine*, September 16, 2001.

Shoemaker, Adam. *Paper Tracks: Indigenous Literatures in Canada, Australia and New Zealand.* Bruce King ed. *New National and Post Colonial Literatures.* Oxford: Claredon Press, 1998.

Ted Dyck, E.F. *The Places of Aboriginal Writing 2000 in Canada: The Novel.**

(*Source Internet)

10

The Treatment of Love in *Savitri*: A Decolonized Indian Perspective

DIPANKAR CHAKRABARTI

Sri Aurobindo took to writing in a period when the colonial India, probably, could not have even thought of an effort of decolonizing English Literature, as it is today. But this enlightened Yogi of India, though attained a very high watermark of excellence in European thought and means of expression, did not compromise with his Indianness. The struggle for liberation by the Indians from the imperialistic Britishers had temporarily converted him into the extremist of the extremists but his conception of 'liberty itself was ultimately dictated, as it appears, by his vision of permanent peace. On ultimate analysis it may be prognosticated that the absolute serenity of his mind created a divine urge in him for invoking the great Indian Muse. The divine Muse, in response, was pleased to award him a life of rare creativity. He was, now free to philosophize events [...] from politics to the eternal Indian mythology, for hiring a better life on the Earth's crest.

The entire literary bulk of Sri Aurobindo is, basically, a reframing of the Classical Indian thoughts. With this eternal Indian thoughts, what he added, probably, was the blending of his ascetic knowledge about the essence of Integral Yoga. His was the notions typically Indian and their judgement can only be apt, if the criteria is fixed to be the "Decolonized Indian Perspective." My assumptions may be critically illustrated with reference to his famous epic *Savitri* [...] though, I confess, I know very little about this grand epic. As regards the periphery of my discussion, I would like to highlight Sri Aurobindo's treatment of the theme of love in *Savitri,* and how it attains an uniqueness *vis-a-vis* the European standards. *Savitri* is a divinised and reconstructed love-legend of prince Satyavan and his wife Savitri. The basic framework of the story is taken from the *Mahabharata.* Sri Aurobindo worked on this ambitious epic for a period of more than fifty years to write 23,813 lines, still some parts of this *magnum opus* remained unfinished. It is a story where pure love empowers Savitri to defeat mortality. Sri Aurobindo utilized this story to symbolically preach his philosophy of Man's realization of making life divine on this earth. In his own words *Savitri* is a "spiritual poetry cast into a symbolic figure" (Sri Auronbindo: 750). The external framework of the story is not much changed from its original, except in few cases as in Aswapathy's Yoga, Savitri's penance and her confrontation with death. The significant changes are there at the level of internal action. The internal action of the epic is directed unidimensionally to tell about the power of love [...] where love is considered as the divine scaller, riding though which man gains heavenly qualities and becomes as powerful as the Almighty. The major external change of Savitri's confrontation with death is made nearly tenfold to its original for enabling the poet to impart his spiritual message. This deliberate spiritualization lends a symbolic possibility to the epic, where Savitri is "The Divine Word, daughter of Sun. Goddess of the Supreme Truth, who comes down and is born to save [...]." Satyavan is explained as "the Soul carrying the Divine Truth of Being within itself, but descended into the grip of death and ignorance," and Aswapathy completes his penance of eighteen years to 'concentrate energy of spiritual endeavour' which assists man "to rise from the mortal to the immortal Planes (Sri Aurobindo: 265). The story of *Savitri* as is clear, is purely Indian in origin and treatment. The evaluation of such an episode of mystic Indian love may prove to be alien to the European standard. However, an analysis of the main story, in brief, may help us penetrate the underlying classical Indian faith in humanity.

The eternalized love story of *Savitri* starts on the fateful day when Satyavan is to die. The first three Books of Part-I narrate the quest of an earthly Yogi for the salvation of human beings.

To his philosophy, salvation is not possible until the World Soul gains Absolute knowledge. Not satisfied with the personal salvation, he continues his ardent asceticism to let the Divine Mother lovingly promise [...]. 'One shall descend and break the iron law/ change Nature's doom to the lone Spirit's power.' The happy Yogi returns and finds this earth a fit place for the fruition of the blessing. It was an intrinsic love for humanity, not for any particular individual, so ells away from the reach of sage Durbasa's curse as was in Abhijnan Sakuntalam.

The opening volumes of Part-II (Books IV to VII) narrate the stories of Savitri's birth and her upbringing, her search for a life partner, almost in the manner of a flash-back. In spite of the Divine Sage Narada's warning, she finds her dream-mate in the person of Satyavan ('I know that thou—only thou art he'). The concluding Book of this section describes Savitri's Yoga for strengthening herself for the ensuing encounter with Death. Her internalized quest for self-realisation provides the power to deglamourise Death. Towards the last part of this quest she meets her 'Secret Soul' in the last chamber of a mystic cave and 'They rushed into each other and grew one.' This in turn provides her a superior consciousness to defeat the forces of Negation by passing through a divine instrument called worldly sufferings. Here in this epic though the love-story starts in the worldly manner it is ultimately elevated to the level of spirituality.

The first three books of Part-III describe the confrontation of Savitri with Death—the character which makes the soul of deceased Satyavan captive. The labourious debate between Death and the 'Dark-browed Sophist' did not have a bearing on the adamant spirit of Savitri. The proof of Savitri's Divine Truthfulness makes Death flee. As a result Satyavan returns to life. In Book XI, Death is also transformed into a Being of Light to show its true colour to the worldly people. Refusing the temptation of a married life in heaven, she comes back to the earth, 'to change the earthly life to a life divine.' In the final Book of this epic, the happy couple comes back to 'the many-voiced human world' in the evening, while Night in her bosom nurses a greater drawn. Here also Savitri's Love for humanity makes her happy to create a paradise on this earth.

The theme of love and love-relations are also illustrated by the English poets, like William Shakespeare, John Donne,

Tennyson, Keats, Browning etc. In Shakespearean sonnets, we find an elevated conception of love's ever-lastingness and love's power to have a victory over Time and Death. This feeling, in Shakespeare, plays the most dominant role so far as the Dark-lady affair, *i.e.*, man-woman relationship was concerned. The usage of platonic conception of love by Jonne Donne and other Caveliar poets and the Romantic love of Tennyson and Browning could not dive deeper to unfold the manifold layers of love. But in *Savitri*, the word 'love' has a multiple layer of meanings. The story of love is related to various levels [...] man-women (as in Savitri and Satyavan), father-daughter (as in Aswapathy and Savitri), God-disciple (as in Divine Mother and Aswapathy), individuals-Society (as in Savitri-Satyavan couple and the earthly people), Soul-Oversoul, the world Soul and Supreme Soul, lastly the human soul and its 'Secret Soul' as was witnessed in the mystic cave. So Sri Aurobindo's vision of love has greater credibility and mobility. In this context, it may be hypothesized that the classical Indian society, after a prolonged experimentation, could come up with a working realisation about the means and end of 'love' and 'life,' whereas the European Community is still experimenting with the nature of both. 'Love' in classical Indian meaning may be compared to a sun-beam whereas its Western thought is only one of the scattered rays through a fine prism.

According to the modern theory of Eugenics, originated and advanced in European soil, all love affairs are guided and regulated by a force. In 'elan vital,' Bergson defined it as Life Force. The conception of life force had been modernized several times by the philosophical thinkers like Samuel Butler, Neitzche, Schopenhauer, G.B. Shaw etc. According to European thoughts, not only the beginning, but also the end of all successful love affair is the progenitor of a new generation which is more advanced in all respects from the earlier one. The mutual attraction for the opposite sex, in any love affair, is initiated by the urge created by the unborn body. Here also the conception of biological love, European in origin, is deeply rooted in body wisdom. The latest development in this field tells that the force works in the process of trial and error. The guiding force in love is not the God, or Almighty, but a compulsive Life Force striving to be so. But in Sri Aurobindo, the force seems to be enormously powerful and works to the dictates of the Omniscient. Here the earthy process of trial and error is of no use and hence the wastage of unsuccessful experimentation is nullified. The Western philosophy of life force, seems to have, produced the incarnation of a diety which is God defying. This force, at times, appears to be a representative of self declared god between a Jusus and a Jesus. But God in any classical faith does not tolerate blasphemy. God is habituated to see His devotees peer-handed. According to any religious faith the root of all satisfaction is the absolute surrender to Him. Even in love affair, as directed by Life Force, there is no compensation for the unsuccessful experimentations. This may produce evil which will definitely be a hindrance to the progress of godliness. But Sri Aurobindo's faith, as it appears, in the power of man for creating a God's world is firmly rooted in the heart of goodness. He believes in a God who is the Absolute Donor. The classical Hindoo religion in Sri Aurobindo's faith provides a better substitute for it, in the form of a never-dying Omniscient. His has the belief dominated by love. To him love is the quality common in man and God. So love is the factor which can convert God into man or man into God.

In *Savitri,* it seems that, Sri Aurobindo takes the assistance of a well-known love legend to rejuvenate the element of goodness which is already there in the heart of the present generation. Here the Savitri-Satyavan Couple, symbolically, becomes the progenitor of a new Indian generation where love is the guiding force to banish "barrenness" and "unfirtility" of love from human life. Probably, Sri Aurobindo believed that, to end spiritual anarchy for regenerating humanity, a holocaust is not required. His had a firm faith in killing the badness rather than the badmen. With the 'down' of good sense, faithlessness and frustration will be eliminated from our minds. The World-soul, devoid of all ugliness, will be able to commune with the Oversoul. In this process, *Savitri* becomes an inner epic of love between soul and Oversoul. The process of attaining salvation, in this religious epic, tells about the conception of Sri Aurobindo's Integral Yoga, according to which, 'God must be born on this earth and be as man/ than Man being human may grow even as God.' So, it appears that, the epic was written with a purpose [...] the purpose of elevating the mortals to the level of divinity. He took upon himself the task of transforming this earth into the God's world, where love is the guiding principle. To usher a newer world of humanity, he clings to the Hindoo views of life, reinforced by his own philosophy of Yoga. His had a firm faith that, if man becomes godly, earth because heaven. So, the classic story of Savitri and Satyavan is aimed at giving birth to a heavenly generation which will convert mother Earth into Heaven.

WORK CITED

Sri Aurobindo. *Sri Aurobindo on Himself,* Sri Aurobindo Birth Centenary Library. Vol. XXVI. Pondicherry, 1971: 265.

Sri Aurobindo. *Letters on Savitri,* Sri Aurobindo Birth Centenary Library. Vol. XXIV. Pondicherry, 1970: 750.

Naik, M.K. *A History of Indian English Literature,* Sahitya Akademi, 1989 (reprint). All the poetic lines are quoted from this book.

SELECT BIBLIOGRAPHY

Gokak, V.K. *Sri Aurobindo: Seer and Poet.* New Delhi: Abhinav Prakashan, 1973.

Gupta, Rameshwar. *Eternity in Words: Sri Aurobindo's Savitri.* Bombay: Chetna Prakashan, 1969.

Iyengar, K.R. Srinivasa. *Sri Aurobindo: A Biography and a History,* 2 Vols. Pondicherry: Sri Aurobindo International Centre of Education, 1972.

Nanda Kumar, Prema. *A Study of Savitri.* Pondicherry Aurobindo Ashram, 1962.

Sethna, K.D. *The Poetic Genius of Sri Aurobindo,* Pondicherry: Sri Aurobindo Ashram, 1947.

11

The Devil's Wind: A Critical Appraisal

P.N. SINHA

The Revolt of 1857 was a momentous event in the history of India. It marked a turning point in the history of British imperialism. Its significance as a decisive event in the British rule in India has been adequately recognized by Englishmen in a series of historical accounts. Compared to the historical work on or about the Mutiny, imaginative literature on the same theme has not been much less in bulk. S.D. Singh says in the Preface to *Novels on the Indian Mutiny*, "There exist not less than fifty novels written by Englishmen and women about the Indian Mutiny."[1]

The British historians have presented the history of the Indian Mutiny from their point of view in their books. As they were more interested in perpetuating the British rule in India than in the objective interpretation of the facts of Indian history. It was necessary for that purpose to disparage the Indian leaders and throw a sort of blanket over the valour, determination and aspiration of the Indians. So they glorified the British valour and projected the British officers as heroes but depicted the Indians as murderers and cowards. The British historians have given their own side of the picture and have consciously ignored the Indian point of view about it. The observation of Jawaharlal Nehru is quite relevant in this context: "A great deal of false and perverted history has been written about the Revolt and its suppression."[2] The same playing up of British valour and heroism is to be found in the English novels written by British authors on Indian Mutiny. That is why, Malgonkar does not agree with the view that John Master's *Nightrunners of Bengal* is "the best historical novel about the Indian Mutiny."[3] In course of an interview with James Y. Dayanand he says:

> He (John Masters) writes about the rebellion as though it were a mutiny, he writes about us Indians as the enemy, and he wanted naturally, the British ruler of the companies to be perpetuated, whereas my view-point is so opposite in this novel (*The Devil's Wind*) at all times, that there was no possibility of any agreement, on our viewpoints, at least.[4]

Malgonkar does not agree with the view of the British authors that the 'revolt of 1857' was a 'mutiny' and it was confined to the sepoys only, who rebelled only because they were afraid of losing their caste and religion because of the newly introduced greased catridges. Nor does he agree with their view that Nana Saheb, one of the principal heroes of the revolt, was a "monster of ferocity"[5] and a murderer of women and children. As several princes, queens and even some 'sadhus' and 'maulvis' had taken active part in the revolt. In Oudh, even common men came to the forefront to drive the English away from their land. Nana Saheb says in *The Devil's Wind* about Oudh "Here even they could not camouflage and degrade the revolt by calling it a 'mutiny,' for their opponents were not restricted to their ex-sepoys."[6] Jawaharlal Nehru holds similar view about the revolt: "It was much more than a military mutiny and it agreed rapidly and assumed the character of a popular rebellion and a war of Indian Independence."[7]

In fact, it is a question of viewpoints, occidental against oriental, imperial against national and realistic against emotional. If Nana Saheb was a "monster of ferocity" and murderer of women and children from the British point of view, the British officers because of their acts of savagery and atrocity during and after the 'revolt' were worse than Timur and Nadir Shah from the Indian point of view. Speaking about the general massacre of the inhabitants of Delhi by the British, Nehruji says: "The days of Timur and Nadir Shah were remembered, but their exploits were eclipsed by the new terror, both in extent and the length of time it lasted."[8] But the Indian point of view about the 'revolt' was consciously kept out of the printed pages. Nehruji says: "What the Indian thinks about it (the revolt) seldom finds its way to the printed page."[9]

Sawarkar was the first Indian to present the 'revolt' as the first war of Indian Independence in his book *The History of the War of Indian Independence*, but his book was promptly banned by the British. Malgonkar felt the need for the reappraisal of the 'revolt of 1857' and the character of Nana Saheb from the Indian point of view. As the British historians and the novelists could not rise above their national interest and subdue their racial prejudices in interpreting the facts of Indian Mutiny. Moreover, they have betrayed their utter lack of "imaginative understanding"[10] of the mind of the then Indians. Carr says: "History cannot be written unless the historians can achieve some kind of contact with the mind of those about whom he is writing."[11] With "stern accuracy in inquiring," Malgonkar gathers facts about the Revolt of 1857 and Nana Saheb and presents the history of the 'revolt' and the story of Nana Saheb from the Indian point of view in his novel *The Devil's Wind*. Malgonkar shares the view that "facts are sacred"[12] and so he does not take liberty with facts. Malgonkar's book *The Devil's Wind*, as he himself puts it, "is fiction, but it takes no liberty with verifiable facts or even with probabilities."[13]

Like Edward Bulwer Lytton, Malgonkar utilizes his historical novel *The Devil's Wind* for the re-evaluation of the Revolt of 1857 which has been "carelessly dismissed"[14] as Mutiny by the British and the character of Nana Saheb who has been "hitherto looked upon unfavourably."[15]

With the exercise of his scholarly accuracy and "bold imagination,"[16] Malgonkar gives the lie to the observation of Edward Thomson, a great friend of India, who said out of sympathy, for the Indians:

> Indians are not historians [...]. They are not likely to displace our account of our connection with India. Thcy are not able to arrange their knowledge so as to gain that first essential towards a favourable judgement, a hearing.[17]

The words 'devil's wind'[18] were first of all used by G.O. Trevelyan in his book *Cawnpore* for the Indian Mutiny. The very use of the word shows the British attitude towards the Revolt of 1857. From the British point of view the Indian Mutiny was a 'devil's wind' which started from the Meerut cantonment and spread with the speed of wind all over the north India and turned their own sepoys and guns against them.

The title of the novel *The Devil's Wind* symbolizes rebellious ideas and anti-British feelings which swept over the country with the speed of wind and sparked off revolt from cantonment to cantonment and from one capital to another. The whole of North India, especially from Bengal to Delhi, and areas in the central India began to burn. Massacre grim and galore the order of the day. Only Bombay and Madras regiments did not revolt and the Sikhs remained loyal to the British.

From the Indian point of view, the title alludes to people's belief in the dying pronouncements of *Satis,* widows who cremated themselves on their husband's funeral pyres and the prophecy of saints after the defeat of Indians in the Battle of Plassey. They had predicted, "When the hundred years had elapsed, the company's rule would end. The Devil's Wind would arise and unsackle Mother India."[19] One significant fact about the title of the novel is that Patricia Wentworth, an English authoress, also wrote a novel on the Indian Mutiny in 1912 and titled it *The Devil's Wind.* It may be just a coincidence that Malgonkar also titled his novel on 'the revolt of 1857' *The Devil's Wind* or he may have borrowed the title from Patricia Wentworth as Malgonkar's novel was published only in 1972. Despite the similarity in the title and subject-matter of the two novels, both present more a study in contrast than in comparison in the treatment of the subject-matter.

The Devil's Wind by Patricia Wentworth is more a story of love than an appraisal of the Indian Mutiny. The mutiny forms a functional background for the sake of enhancing the value of the tale of love. S.D. Singh says: "Patricia Wentworth in her *The Devil's Wind* produces realistic and human pictures because she keeps the emotional life of the characters in the forefront, and the mutiny in the background."[20] The fictionalization of history demands a romantic situation to go along side the historical situation and Nana Saheb, the central character in *The Devil's Wind* by Manohar Malgonkar, does fall in love with Eliza Wheeler. But he restrains himself and does not let anybody, not even Eliza, know about it. Despite his immense love for Eliza, her presence in the Entrenchment did not influence his slightest action. He says: "I, who had been accepted as a sort of king by one side, has no business to be in love with the daughter of the enemy king."[21]

Nana Saheb never allows his emotion to cloud his reason. In *The Devil's Wind* by Malgonkar the emphasis is on the appraisal of the 'revolt of 1857' and the revelation of Nana Saheb's motive rather than on the element of love in the story. Like *The Princes, The Devil's Wind* is also both an epic and an autobiography. As an epic, *The Devil's Wind* describes the fall and decline of the Maratha Confederacy right from 1796 to the complete destruction of Bithoor, the vestigial kingdom of the Peshwa in 1857. It also describes in depth the social and political condition which led to the outbreak of the revolt in 1857 and the principal participants in it.

The Maratha Confederacy, which, before the British came, had ruled the greater part of India, was headed by the Peshwas or Prime Ministers. The Peshwa had usurped the Maratha King's position and ruled in reality. Bajirao II, the adoptive father of Nana Saheb, sat on the prestigious 'guddi' of the Peshwa in 1796 and was proved the last among the Peshwas by his own misdeeds. He was cruel, callous and coward. He delighted in humiliating his feudatories and seizing their estates on the flimsiest of pretexts and, above all, he often cast his unholy glances upon their women. He was a sexual pervert and had "a fetish for observing beautiful women undress and titivate themselves."[22] That is why, even his powerful hereditary chieftains were often up in arms against him. He had no natural qualities of leadership, least of all valour. Despite the fact that he was a descendant of Bajirao, his grandfather whose name he bore and who was India's most talented military genius of all times, he dreaded the very sound of gunfire and could not face his enemies in the battlefield. It was because of his cowardice that people called him "Running"[23] Bajirao.

Once he had run to the British for protection against one of his principal feudatories, the Holcar. The British took it for a wind-fall, as the fountainhead of the Maratha power, the greatest in the land, had gone to them for shelter and their aid. They restored him to his 'guddi' in Poona, the seat of the Peshwas and stationed a permanent force there for his protection.

Bajirao II had to cede a large portion of land to them for the expenses of the escort. He ruled as Peshwa for another sixteen years but he was no better than "a British dummy calf."[24] During the years, the British isolated him from his feudatories so much so that he was bereft of all his supporters and despised by his own men. "By 1817 the boil was ready to burst, the mango ripped for plucking."[25] The British deposed Bajirao II as the Peshwa at Poona in 1818 and banished him to Bithoor. He was kept on pension and allowed to retain his title. The novel presents the end of an epoch in Indian history.

The novel also brings to life in very human dimensions the turbulent period in India before and during the 'revolt of 1857.' While dealing with the historical situation, Malgonkar does not make departure from the factuality of history. The dates of historical events such as the date of the liquidation of Maratha Confederacy, the outbreak of revolt and the annexation of Oudh and also the names of historical personages who headed the Maratha Confederacy and those who participated in the revolt are the same in history and in *The Devil's Wind.* In *The Princes,* Malgonkar describes the historical event and condition with the help of fictional characters. In *The Devil's Wind* he reverses the order. He describes the historical event and condition with the help of historical persons. He also adds some fictional adventures and puts into the mouth of Nana Saheb, the principal hero of the revolt, words for which there is no documented evidence.

Even then one cannot agree with G.S. Amar who says: "*The Devil's Wind* is more history than novel."[26] To talk of *The Devil's Wind* as a document of history is to tell the half truth about it. As it is not just a description of a historical event nor is it a recreation of the social and political condition of a period. It is also a thrilling, exciting and heartrending story of the invincible spirit of Nana Saheb who lost every thing he loved, yet he never accepted defeat. Nor could he be arrested by the British, the greatest military power of its time. He wrote a letter to Queen Victoria: "You have no enemy more determined than myself. So long as I live, I shall fight."[27] Moreover, a historian deals in causes. He marshals the events of the past in an orderly sequence of cause and effect. E.H. Carr says: "The study of history is a study of causes."[28]

The historian takes no notice of the motive of the historical personage. Nor does he focus his attention on the private life of the historical personage. But a novelist focuses his attention both on the public and private life of a historical personage. He looks at and beyond his action to the motive and craving in his heart. Malgonkar describes the public life of Nana Saheb on the basis of documented facts. But he puts emphasis on the depiction of his private life and on the revelation of his motive behind his every action in his novel *The Devil's Wind.*

The private life of Nana Saheb is not adequately documented elsewhere. As "the most homely and intimate and personal things slip through the hands of the historian."[29] Surprisingly enough, even the last days of Nana Saheb are still shrouded in mystery. Malgonkar adds some fictional adventures to complete the story of Nana Saheb which is half-told in history. With his artistic imagination he recovers some of the irrecoverable things in history, and these are the close, intimate personal things, what might be called "the human touches."[30] He turns history into a story. H. Butterfield says: "History is full of events and issues out of which a story could be made [...] it is not wanting in incident, but these things are not stories, they have to be transmuted into story."[31] With the help of his creative imagination, Malgonkar fleshes in the "dry bones"[32] of history and turns the history of Nana Saheb into a thrilling "drama of hearts and homes"[33] and love for motherland. He puts Nana Saheb in some of the fictional situations to enable him to reveal his motive himself behind his every action. Even G.S. Amar says: "The accent throughout is on the clarification of his motives."[34]

Nana Saheb says before participating in the 'revolt' that his intention was pious. He wanted to liberate his country from the foreign yoke with the minimum of bloodshed. He says that he had hoped to go down in history as a man "who had helped his own people to achieve freedom from foreign conquerer with only the minimal blood-letting."[35] He had believed that he would be "the voice of reason"[36] in the drama of murder and rape. But all his hopes were belied and contrary to his intention and expectation he was declared the "villain of the century,"[37] by the British. E.H. Carr has rightly said: "There is something in the nature of historical events which twists the course of history in a direction that no man ever intended."[38]

It is the quality of Malgonkar's artistic imagination to portray the private life of a historical personage which is irrecoverable in history and to reveal his hidden motive, which raises him above the historian and lends him a place of distinction among the creative writers of his day. The success of *The Devil's Wind* both at home and abroad, no doubt, is due to his skill as a story-teller and to the fertility of his imagination. Despite the fact that the story is old, the readers are always kept in the state of suspense and are anxious to know what happens next. But the significant fact about *The Devil's Wind* is that "the fictional element is rigidly restricted to the depiction of the inward life"[39] of Nana Saheb and especially in regard to determining his motives, like the historical novels of Bulwar Lytton. So like *The Princes, The Devil's Wind* is as much a document of history as a work of conscious literary art. It is both fact and fiction. But the fictional elements have been used to "fill in the lines where history is inadequate"[40] or to "elucidate facts."[41]

Both themes of the decline and fall of the Maratha confederacy and the outbreak and the failure of the revolt of 1857—have been skilfully interwoven with the personal story of Nana Saheb. *The Devil's Wind* is also an autobiography because Nana Saheb narrates his story since birth in the first person. Malgonkar makes use of the first person narrative as an artistic device to reveal the motive of Nana Saheb behind all his actions both in public and private life. He says: "This, then, is Nana's story as I believe he might have written it himself."[42]

Like Abhayraj in *The Princes,* Nana Saheb, the first person narrator, is the central character in *The Devil's Wind.* He is seen both as an actor and as a narrator, describing his experiences in retrospect but "in character." The story begins quite in the primitive way of story-telling technique. He was born in a conservative Brahmin family at Bithoor. His parents had named him "Dhondhu" which means a stone, a worthless object in order to exorcise a family curse of child mortality. As his horoscope predicted that he was destined to become a king, a respectful suffix was added to his name and he was addressed Dhondhu Pant or "Stone Esquire." The then deposed Peshwa Bajirao II was attracted by the prophecy about the child and adopted him as his heir in 1827, while he was only three years old. Thus he became the Peshwa's heir. Nana Saheb says: "In me he saw someone destined to win back what he had lost."[43] He named him Nana Saheb after one of his Peshwa ancestors. So all his life he was known by two names: Dhondhu Pant and Nana Saheb.

Malgonkar describes the childhood of Nana Saheb in the background of social and political condition of that time. Belief in the supernatural power and the practice of adopting heir particularly among the princes was the salient features of the social and political life of that time. Bajirao II took special care of Nana Saheb's education and training as a prince. He was taught English, Hindi, Persian, Urdu and more particularly Sanskrit so that he might read the Hindu scriptures in original. He was given training of riding, fencing and swimming from his very childhood. His fencing teacher was Tantya Bhat who later emerged as one of the greatest heroes of revolt. Mani was one of the several children of Bajirao's family who attended the riding and fencing school with him. She was Bajirao's goddaughter, whom he was bringing up to be Nana's wife. Despite the fact that Bajirao II took special interest in Nana Saheb's upbringing. Nana Saheb had nothing but contempt for him. Like Abhayraj in *The Princes*, he was ashamed of his father's private life. He says about his father, "Religion was one of the Bajirao's two major obsessions, the other being sex."[44]

His life was sickeningly filled with sex during the hours of darkness and with religion during the hours of day light. But his inclination towards religion was more because of fright than because of faith and devotion. As he was haunted with an ancestral ghost who would torture him with curses at night. The ghost used to say that his life would end with his successor. If the successor co-habited with his wife, she would die. Bajirao wasted a log of money on religious works to exorcise the ghost. But the ghost stayed with him all his life. As his successor could not have marital relations with his wife.

Bajirao changed his mind and got Mani married to the ruling prince of Jhansi. This was the first shock which Nana Saheb experienced in his life. He says: "I experienced a sudden sense of loss as though something to which I had been grafted was being severed, leaving a raw wound that would remain with me all my life."[45] As a compensation to her, he was presented with his first concubine, Champa. He was initiated into the world of sex by her and had revealing experiences of life in her company. Though Champa was not married to him, she was sincere and devoted to him. It was because of her sincerity that she became a partner, of his joys and sorrows, a nurse during his illness and a jester during his ill humours. She became the mistress of his household. She bore him a daughter whom he called Gangamala. Even his second concubine was no less sincere to him particularly in his public life. She took the sword during the revolt and went the martyr's way. He says: "Fated to be unlucky with the women I married, I have been singularly fortunate in my mistresses."[46]

He was always grieved at heart as his personal life was not happy, at all. His entire life had been warped because of the family curse. For it happened as the ghost said it would. The first two women he had married did not long survive the marriage. He had no desire to marry the third. As he was too kind to kill an innocent woman for a successor. But Bajirao's thirst for a successor was insatiable. And he had to give way to his pressure and marry Kashi, a south Indian girl. But he never lived as a husband to her. She reminded him of "a crow brought to a snake house for a python's meal."[47] Only during ceremonies and festivals they would sit side by side as man and wife and offer prayers together. He says: "She was married to me, but she was no more than a piece of furniture in the wada—something to be put on display on public occasions."[48] Though she looked like another Maneka on the earth, he always looked upon her as "a serpent in the closet"[49] and guarded against taking her to bed. Yet she was obedient and serviceable to him. "It was almost a master and slave relationship"[50] between them. He would often squire with guilt at her unswerving loyalty and could not understand whether he was saving her from death by not sleeping with her or by the same token killing the woman in her. He was tied to this problem with no solution by his father's excessive and unnecessary concern for a successor, as there was nothing worth succeeding to it.

This and several other misdeeds of his father had debased and defiled his life. That is why even his death did not cause him grief. He knew that he had to inherit a bundle of his father's sins which was greater than his worldly possession. He had no love and respect for him but he never showed disrespect to him during his life or even after his death. He went through the full ritual of mourning. He even announced that he would make a 'mahadana.' But he was shocked to learn that he could not give away the required land for the sacred purpose because he himself did not possess any. Even the land on which the 'wada' stood belonged to him only for life. Then he realized "what Bajirao had scuttled when he had run to the British merchants for protection."[51] Despite the fact that he did not accept the offer of land by Raghunath Vinchurkar whom Bajirao had humiliated more than honoured, impoverished more than enriched, he was overwhelmed with his greatness. He saw the glimpse of that other India in him, "which, for all its turmoil and misery, had yet been a richer, nobler land."[52] He was equally shocked and disappointed at the revelation of British pretentious generosity. The so-called "honourable company bahadur" rejected his claim for his father's pension and titles.

Lord Dalhousie, the then Governor-General of the East India Company, was an ambitious man. He seemed determined to clear India of Indian rulers. Like Rahu and Ketu, "Our mythological moon eaters,"[53] he went about swallowing kingdom after kingdom on the basis of 'the Doctrine of Lapse' and maladministration. The Doctrine of Lapse was an instrument of confiscation. The right of the Indian rulers to adopt heir was severed by this doctrine. It was in the light of this doctrine that Nana was not recognized as the legal heir to Bajirao II. The Rani of Jhansi was not allowed to rule for the adopted heir, and her principality was annexed. Even Delhi was faced with similar problem. The Doctrine of Lapse created panic and rage among the Indian rulers. Zeenat Mahal, a prominent Mogul queen, was determined to teach a lesson to the British. She got the help of Ahmadulla Shah, Moulvi of Fyzabad who came to be known as "Mad Mullah." He spread and fanned rebellious ideas against the British both among the Hindus and the Muslims by the circulation of "Chapatis" (baked cakes). The annexation of Oudh on the flimsy ground of maladministration was proved to be the last straw on the camel's back. It left no doubt about their malicious intention against the Indian rulers. The policy of annexations followed by Dalhousie resulted in political unity among the Indian rulers against the British. Revolt emerged as the only remedy for the political malady.

The introduction of a new cartridge which was to be bitten to break open before loading adding fuel to the fire. It was believed or rumoured that the cartridge were coated with the fat of pig and cow. It hurt the religious prejudices of the sepoys and united both the Hindu and Muslim sepoys against the British. The cruel suppression of the sepoys in Barrackpore for their refusal to accept the cartridge further infuriated the sepoys elsewhere—It "provided the match which lit the fire."[54] On the 10th May, 1857, the sepoys in Meerut went on revolt and killed their officers. They broke open the bungalows and butchered their wives and children. Then they set for Delhi. Thus the Devil's Wind started from Meerut and soon it swept over Delhi, Lucknow, Benaras, Allahabad and Kanpur.

At that time Nana Saheb was in two minds. By temperament he was non-violent. He shrank from the very idea of violence that lay ahead. As he believed "that all life, human, animal, even insect life—was part of a great single divinity and therefore sacrosanct."[55] Besides, he had more friends among the whites than among his own kind. He says: "Apart from my own retainers, Englishmen were the only people I had any intimate contact with. I did not wish them ill."[56] But at the sametime he was fully convinced that the British had no moral right to enslave India. He was torn between his love for his country and his love for his English friends. He says: "My loyalties were hopelessly intermixed, and my hatred far from pure."[57] But his love for motherland triumphs over his love for friends. At once, like Brutus in *Julius Caesar* he decides to kill all his caesars for the liberation of his motherland. As freedom of motherland is far more sacred than friendship and even human blood. He says: "Lest my motives be misunderstood, let me make it clear that even at the time I was, as I am now, wholly convinced that we were morally right."[58]

He could not remain a silent spectator to the drama of national struggle for freedom. He joined hands with the sepoys and led them to the liberation of Kanpur within a few days. All the white families took shelter in the Wheeler's Entrenchment. He had no animosity against the English and did not want to harm particularly the women and children who were facing misery and starvation in the Entrenchment. He planned to dispatch them to a safe place across the Ganges. Despite all his precautionary measures, the disbanded soldiers of Allahabad and Benaras regiments opened fire at them and excepting some, who escaped, most were massacred at Satichaura ghat. Despite his best efforts, Nana Saheb could save some wounded women and children whom he kept as prisoners at the Bibighar, Nana Saheb was installed as the Peshwa, the Viceroy of the Emperor in Kanpur as well as in Poona on June 30, 1857. Once again the saffron banner of the Maratha was unfurled. The return of the freedom was celebrated all over the city. The English had been driven away from Poona, Delhi, Satara, as from Kanpur. But happiness proved to be a very brief episode in the drama of his life of sorrow, suffering, struggle and sacrifice. As the British soldiers under Havelock's command had the advantage of overwhelmingly superior fire power and experienced generals. With the new rifle, the Enfield, they could shoot at Nana's troops long before they came within the range of their weapons. He and his troops could not fight on equal terms. Besides, Azim says: "They also had the contingent of diseased minds formed by the "loyal sepoys."[59]

The Sikhs who fought on the side of the British tried to be more brutal against their own countrymen to prove their loyalty to their masters. Nana Saheb was deeply grieved to see his own countrymen "shedding their blood in order to assist in the mechanics of Mother India's revishment."[60] On July 17, 1857, the British flag once more flew over Kanpur. He (Nana Saheb) was fully convinced of the fact that "if the Ferozpure contingent had fought on Havelock's side and if the Indian camp followers had not vied with each other to tow his guns through the mud or to bring his ammunition and food in headloads I, not Havelock, would have come out as the victor in the battle for Kanpur."[61] He was more grieved to learn that the women and children held prisoners in the Bibighar were slaughtered by butchers one day before the fall of Kanpur. It was Hussainy Begam who wreaked vengeance upon the white families for the acts of savagery and brutality of Neil and Havelock.

But there was no time to think and regret. As he had lost the battle. But he could not lose hope in victory. As the Rani of

Jhansi, Tantya Topi and Begam Hazarat Mahal, the queen of Oudh, had still been fighting vigorously against the English. He had a lurking hope in the return of the tide in his favour. He took 'Jal-Samadhi' in the eyes of all but went, in fact, across the Ganges to Chaurasi. On his way to Chaurasi he did save Eliza Wheeler, one of the victims of Satichaura ghat, from the cruel clutches of Nizam Ali's wife. Within a few days he could gather a large number of troops and once again forced the British soldiers to retreat. Kanpur remained under his control for a few days. But he could not retain his victory for long. The fall of Delhi had already weakened the morale of his troops and the native soldiers, the so-called 'loyal sepoys,' played a decisive role in the British victory. He was filled with anguish and disgust to see that, "Slaves were assisting their masters to conquer their own motherland and thus perpetuate their slavery. No country could live down such degradation of its people [...]."[62]

Kanpur fell to the British for the second time. He was declared an outlaw with a price of one lakh of rupees on his head. He had no alternative but to take refuge in Nepal, the only free and neighbouring country. During the period of hide and retreat he was shocked to learn that he was held responsible for Satichaura massacre and the Bibighar tragedy. He was declared "the greatest villain of the century."[63] He was himself grieved at what had happened at Satichaura ghat and in the Bibighar. He did not want to whitewash the cruel acts of savagery by means of excuses. He says:

> Satichaura and Bibighar are monuments to our brutality. Look and be ashamed, the world will forever admonish us [...]. So long as the sun and the moon go round, our noses will be rubbed in their drags.[64]

But at the same time he wants that the said acts of savagery must not be separated from their causes and examined in isolation. As both were a form of primitive retaliation against the savagery of the advancing column and have to be viewed in the same frame, as composite pictures. He says:

> If Daryaganj and the other villages had not been burned down as guilty villages, Satichaura might never have happened; and if Fatepur had not been destroyed merely as a follow through to a victorious military action, Bibighar might never have happened.[65]

But the blindness of the English to their own shortcomings may be said to be proverbial.[66] Nana Saheb says: "What the British did to Lucknow cannot be balanced against a hundred Satichauras, cannot be washed away by banning all mention of it from history books [...]."[67]

But history sings the lore of the victors. The victors do no wrong. The responsibility for all death and destruction lies with the vanquished. Nana Saheb had to leave his country as an outlaw and take refuge in Nepal only because he had demanded freedom of his country. Malgonkar realizes the anguish of his heart and lets the world hear the cry and cravings of his anguished heart in his novel *The Devil's Wind.*

Jang Bahadur, the then Prime Minister of Nepal, proved meaner than even the village 'maang,' the lowest among the untouchables in India, who preferred to be bitten by a mad dog rather than divulge the secret about Nana for winning even one lakh of rupees. Nana Saheb had to lose his wife to him and pay one thousand rupees for each day of his stay in Nepal by selling his ancestral Naulakha necklace. He was extremely grieved at the infidelity of his wife, Kashi, who preferred "to be in the glitter of a great King's Court, not in a hermitage"[68] with him and "disgraced every single one of the Peshwa wives."[69]

But the shock he had experienced at the deceit of his wife, was overcome by the warmth shown by Eliza Wheeler who preferred to lead the life "of a hermit, a sadhu"[70] in his company rather than return to her fold. He was blessed with a daughter in her company, whom he named Mani after the Rani of Jhansi. He led a fully contented life for fourteen long years like Ram and Sita during their exile. He says:

> This surely was *nirvan*, a state of being freed from the coils of life. Once again there was a woman to love and a child to address me as father [...]. I led a richer, more satisfying life than I had as the master of the wada at Bithoor [...].[71]

He came back to India because of political instability in Nepal and performed the *Sradh* of his father on his death anniversary. He was recognized by the priest Kashiram Pande who gave him unexpected love and respect. He visited the places of historic occurrences in Kanpur where the British had erected memorials for their own dead. He was grieved to read his name inscribed on the marble tablets as the murderer of the women and children. He was held responsible for the acts of savagery of some berserk men and women. On the same principle, he feels, that Queen Victoria should have been held responsible for the acts of savagery and atrocity of the British soldiers. But history is written for the victors and by the victors. The voice of the vanquished never gets room on the pages of history. Nehruji says about history and Kanpur: "History is almost always written by the victors and conquerors and gives their viewpoint [...]. There is no memorial for the Indians who died at Kanpur."[72]

With the help of Jayaji Scindia of Gwalior, Nana Saheb leaves for Mecca with the hope that some day someone will erect a memorial for the Indian deads. *The Devil's Wind* is a step in that direction in the field of art with the help of creative imagination, Malgonkar creates a memorial, as it were, to Nana Saheb and gives tongue to his point of view in *The Devil's Wind*. It is also a souvenir to a man who laid down all he had on the altar of his country and yet he was forced to lead his last days far beyond the bounds of his country in Constantinople. G.S. Amar says: "Malgonkar performs a useful task in representing the mysterious and controversial figure of Nana in the Indian perspective."[73]

The Devil's Wind has close associations with Kanhoji Angrey, a historical biography of the Maratha Admiral, in which Malgonkar gave the lie to the views of the British who labelled him as a pirate. He presented him as a great national hero from the Indian point of view in his book. In the same way *The Devil's Wind* gives the lie to the view of the British who held Nana Saheb as the "villain of the century" and presents him as one of the heroes of the 'revolt' against the British rule. Despite the fact that the novel is in autobiographical form, Malgonkar does not whitewash his lapses. He presents him "as a rather mixed-up human being, like most of us are."[74] But Malgonkar has succeeded in restoring to the image of Nana Saheb its humanity and Indian identity.

Malgonkar presents the story of Nana Saheb in the authentic social, political and mythological background of India. Nana Saheb often alludes to the Hindu scriptures in course of narrating his story. He recites the "gayatri mantra"[75] whenever he is in trouble to derive strength like a common Indian. He compares himself and Eliza to Ram and Sita, during their exile (*The Ramayan*). His curse about his marriage reminds us of the curses of Pandu in the Mahabharat.[76] He alludes to the Indian myths and legends and compares Lord Dalhousie to Rahu and Ketu, "our mythological moon eaters,"[77] and also presents Heill and Renand as Ahi and Mahi, "our twin mythological moon eaters."[78] It lends credibility to his narrative and restores to him his Indian identity.

Despite the fact that the story of Nana Saheb has been narrated from the Indian point of view, Malgonkar shows no favour to Indians and bias against the English. With the characteristic detachment of an artist, Malgonkar presents both the Indians and the English in his novels. If he decries the British for their acts of savagery and atrocity, he also decries the so-called loyal sepoys who "were more brutal than their masters."[79] If he compares Dalhousie to Rahu and Ketu and Neill and Renand to Ahi and Mahi, he also praises Hillersdon and Wheeler as their "opposite numbers" among the English and, above all, presents Michael Palmer as godlike creature on the earth. He prays to his gods to accept "this new God as their peer."[80] He gets heavenly bliss in the company of Eliza and compares her with Sita, an ideal of Indian womanhood. Bias and prejudices have been consciously kept out of the novel.

Apart from describing the historical event and the historical personage of Nana Saheb, he also expresses what he perceives in and conceives of life in this novel. While he fully endorses the truth of "Satyam-eva-Jayate": truth alone triumphs[81] and also, 'Yato-dharma-Stato-jaya': the right cause always wins, he also adds his own vision of life and says: "The right also had to have battalions and guns more powerful than its enemies; truth could never triumph merely because it was the truth, not unless it had resources greater than those possessed by untruth."[82]

The story of Nana Saheb illustrates his vision of life. *The Devil's Wind* depicts a struggle between freedom fighters or the householder on the one hand the pirates and slave traders or the robbers on the other. Victory should have sided with the freedom fighters or the householder. But in *The Devil's Wind*, victory sides with the aggressor or the robber. The novel illustrates and proves that truth alone is not enough for victory. Truth needs strength and resources greater than the holders of untruth, for victory. Thus, *The Devil's Wind* is more than a history-book, as it reveals the novelist's vision of life. It belongs to "the literature of power" and is far superior to a history-book which belongs to "the literature of knowledge."[83]

NOTES

1. Sailendra Dhari Singh, Preface to *Novels on the Indian Mutiny.* (New Delhi: Arnold Heinemann Publishers, 1980).
2. Jawaharlal Nehru. *The Discovery of India.* (London: Meridian Books Ltd., 1956) 236.
3. John Cotton. "Masters John," *Contemporary Novelists,* Second edition. (London: St. James Press Ltd., 1976) 915.
4. James Y. Dayanand. "On Authors and Books," Interview with Manohar Malgonkar. *The Literary Half-Yearly,* 16, 2 July, 1975, 103.
5. Manohar Malgonkar. *The Devil's Wind, op. cit.,* 253.
6. Malgonkar 242.
7. Nehru 324.
8. Nehru 326.
9. Nehru 326.
10. E.H. Carr. *What is History?* Pelican Books, 1968, 24.
11. Carr 24.
12. Carr 10.
13. Malgonkar x.
14. James C. Simmons. *The Novelist as Historian* (The Hague: N.V. Publishers, 1973) 41.
15. Simmons 1973: 37.
16. Simmons 1973: 39.
17. Edward Thomson. *The Other Side of the Medal* (London: The Hogarth Press, 1930) 83.
18. G.O. Trevelyan. *Cawnpore* (London: Macmillan and Co., 1863) 49.
19. Malgonkar 116.
20. Singh 193.
21. Malgonkar 169.
22. Malgonkar 18.
23. Malgonkar 19.
24. Malgonkar 20.

25. Malgonkar 20.
26. Amar. *Manohar Malgonkar* (New Delhi: Arnold Publishers (P) Ltd., 1973) 135.
27. Malgonkar 279.
28. Carr 87
29. H. Butterfield. *The Historical Novel* (Cambridge: The UP, 1924) 15.
30. Butterfield 21.
31. Butterfield 21.
32. Simmons 39
33. Butterfield 20.
34. Amar 125.
35. Malgonkar 139.
36. Malgonkar 139.
37. Malgonkar 251.
38. Carr 51.
39. Simmons 45.
40. Butterfield 29.
41. Simmons 45.
42. Malgonkar x.
43. Malgonkar 17.
44. Malgonkar 18.
45. Malgonkar 32.
46. Malgonkar 49.
47. Malgonkar 50.
48. Malgonkar 238.
49. Malgonkar 238.
50. Malgonkar 51.
51. Malgonkar 54.
52. Malgonkar 56.
53. Malgonkar 212.
54. Singh 15.
55. Malgonkar 87.
56. Malgonkar 128.
57. Malgonkar 87.
58. Malgonkar 87.
59. Malgonkar 242.
60. Malgonkar 242.

61. Malgonkar 244.
62. Malgonkar 244.
63. Malgonkar 252.
64. Malgonkar 219.
65. Malgonkar 219.
66. Singh 11.
67. Malgonkar 246.
68. Malgonkar 271.
69. Malgonkar 271.
70. Malgonkar 277.
71. Malgonkar 284.
72. Nehru 287-325
73. Amar 125.
74. M. Rajagopalachari. *The Novels of Manohar Malgonkar* (New Delhi: Prestige Books, 1989) 69.
75. *Regveda*, Mandal-3, Sukt-63, Mantra No.10, Sarvdeshik Arya Pratinidhi Sabha, New Delhi, 1946.
76. *The Mahabharata*, Part 1, Chapter 17, Sloka No. 27, Translated by Pandit Ram Narayan Dutta Shastri. Gorakhpur: Rama, Gita Press, Sambat 2025.
77. Malgonkar 69.
78. Malgonkar 212.
79. Malgonkar 183.
80. Malgonkar 260.
81. *Mundkopnishad*, First Part, Mantra-6, 222 (Estadi Nine Upnishad) (Gorakhpur: 9th ed., Gita Press, 1981).
82. Malgonkar 184.
83. Thomas De Quincey. "Review of the Works of Alexander Pope," (1847). Quoted in *The Pelican Books of English Prose*, Vol. V, Edited by Kenneth Allott: 271.

12

POLYPHONIC JOURNEYS: GUR CHARAN DAS'S *A FINE FAMILY*

K.M. PANDEY

The paper makes a critical study of Gur Charan Das's *A Fine Family*.[1] The first part locates, in brief, the centrality of journey—physical, metaphysical, psychological or spiritual—in the life of human beings as well as literary texts. The second part discusses the literal journey which takes place in the novel due to a variety of factors. The third part takes up the psychological and spiritual journeys. The last part of the paper picks up the findings and makes necessary generalizations.

I

From times immemorial, journey has been an integral part of the lives of human beings. It has provided multidimensional knowledge regarding the human existence upon this earth. The centrality of journey in the literatures of both the East and the West has been unquestionably significant. Both of the *arsha Kavyas* of India, *The Ramayana* and *The Mahabharata* abound in journey, spatial as well as metaphorical. *The Ramayana* traces Rama's journey from Ayodhya in the north to Lanka in the south and also his return journey from Lanka to Ayodhya. Likewise, *The Mahabharata* Charts out the journey of the Pandavas during their *Vanavāsa* period and by the end of the epic they reach the place from where they had begun it. Kalidasa's *Meghdoot* is another outstanding example of journey poem which describes Yaksha's mental journey from the Himalayan region to Ujjayini.

Likewise, the western epics, *The Odyssey* and *The Aeneid* are developed around the theme of journey and separation. The same can be said about Milton's *Paradise Lost* which traces the journey of Adam and Eve from the Garden of Eden to the earth. His other epic *Paradise Regained* is built around Christ's journey from the earth to the heaven.

In recent times, our Indian sub-continent has witnessed the historic and traumatic dislocation of 1947 and the event has inspired many an Indian novelist to portray the event in fiction the modern counterpart to epic. K.A. Abbas' *Inquilab* (1955), Khushwant Singh's *Train to Pakistan* (1956), Manohar Malgonkar's *A Bend In The Ganges* (1964), Chaman Nahal's *Azadi* (1995) and a host of other novels are written around this theme.

II

Gur Charan Das's *A Fine Family* is built around the theme of partition and the metaphor of journey is central to its plot. The novelist has portrayed the three generations of a Punjabi family which has suffered the onslaught of the terrible blow of partition in 1947. The novel is divided into three parts which relate to three different places in India. Part one revolves round Lyallpur in Punjab. The second part is about the incidents taking place in Simla. The last part has Bombay as its locale. The time span of the novel is about sixty years, beginning in the '20s the period of the Non-Cooperation Movement and ending in the '80s when Indira Gandhi retrieves power.

The protagonist of the novel Diwan Chand, often referred to in the novel as Bauji, is an advocate. He is a man of western learning and his leader is Gopal Gokhale, a lawyer himself and a moderate. His distaste for Gandhi, "particularly his 'bazaar politics'" (17) is well-known in the family. To find out a suitable husband for his daughter Tara, he goes to a Guru's Ashram where the would-be-son-in-law Seva Ram, an engineer by profession, lives. He undergoes humiliation in the train. "At the railway station Bauji did what he had done for years: he bought a first class ticket and went and sat in a second class carriage" (24). He does so because he is "afraid of a chance meeting with an Englishman in the first class coach" (24). He remembers the incident in which he had been insulted like

Gandhiji in South Africa and had filed a suit against it which ended with "a frivolous inquiry" (25) but vindicated his faith in the British law. It brought him fame and success as an advocate. "Thus a personal injustice, which might have radicalized him and pushed him into the nationalist camp, in fact reinforced his faith in the impartiality of the British Raj" (25).

When he reaches the Ashram, he hears the Guru teaching his disciples to "look upon this world as a passenger on a train looks at a wayside stop" (28). He does not like the idea at all but keeping his own interest in the mind lies suspended between the two worlds for the time-being. Ultimately he succeeds in marrying his daughter Tara to Seva Ram. His rumination at the time of his daughter's marriage is that of a typical Indian father who is worried about the journey of the daughter's married life:

> Did he give her all his love and care for the past twenty years so that she should go away from him just like that? It did not seem right. Yet it was the way of nature. Birds did it. Animals too. So why not people? Perhaps it *did* make sense to live like a passenger on a train (67).

Meanwhile, India gains freedom and before that Bauji has to leave his place of birth as it is also to be divided in the historic event. In this newly evolved situation Lyallpur goes in Pakistan's territory. So he leaves Lyallpur on August 12, 1947 and the unwanted journey commences. His psychological condition is well represented by the novelist:

> His humiliating journey had begun. Bauji was taking his family and a few belongings out of Lyallpur. The Tonga was on its way to the railway station. He was vanquished and sore, like the defeated horse leading his tonga (101).

But the family never reaches the railway station. "As they approached they heard the sound of bullets and found Hindus pouring out in the hundreds from the direction of the station. Many were fleeing across the railway tracks. They learnt that the Muslim guards had taken over the station under the leadership of the Superintendent of Police, and they were indiscriminately shooting at anyone who tried to get unto a train" (105). Unable to decide what to do Bauji's family join the escaping Hindus who form into a *Kafla* and are heading out by the only road leading east towards Lahore. The Odyssey of the millions of people is passionately portrayed by the novelist:

> On the road, where millions were marching, there was no relief. The train of humanity ploughed along noiselessly, sinking to the hub of wheels, straggling through the soft, stifling, heated dust that did not settle even at night. A part of this dust impeded the movement of feet and of wheels; the other part rose in the air and hovered like a cloud of dust.
>
> By eight in the morning, the body was wet with sweat, clothes were soaked, and the mind sapped by the fear that it would grow even hotter. The sun looked like a purple ball, dazzling blindingly. Not a breath of air stirred, and the human beings suffocated in the quiet atmosphere. Those who survived filed past, column after column, miles and miles of tramping feet. They trudged along, covering their noses and mouths. If they passed a village, they rushed for the wells. They fought for water, and drank every drop till nothing but mud was left. But often what greeted them in the villages was a faint hot smoke that bore the smell of burnt bodies. With terrified eyes, the refugees would return the convoy with desiccated thoughts. They had to choose, whether to die of thirst or from the Muslim's sword (109-10).

Within this short passage the novelist has suggested the troublesome journey imposed on the people. The partition thrust an unprecedented transfer of population which rendered about ten million people homeless. It is also ironical that the partition of the country takes place to provide "a homeland for the Muslims" (116) but results in making millions of people homeless, both Hindus and Muslims.

If, on the one hand, this journey shows the communal killings (There is even a situation when there are more people to be killed than are the killers), looting, mass-massacre and rape, representing man turning into beast, it also shows, on the other hand, the redemptive power of love shown in the form of the Muslim tonga driver, Mr Hamid and Anees. The tongawallah tries his best to save Bauji and his family by entering into different lanes. Hamid takes Bauji to his own house and looks after him.

There is another side of this journey. It turns out to be "a testimony to the human spirit" (167) as Bauji tells Tara years later. He recalls the difference in the attitude to life adopted by those who were influenced by the partition directly and those who were only familiar with it:

> After having fallen in the abyss, the refugees had pulled themselves out from the depths, made a new life of their own and risen up again. In many ways they had shown more initiative than the people who were not refugees, that is, the people who were already living in the towns and villages to which the refugees went. That is because they had to work harder to pull themselves up than their more fortunate brothers who had been of right religion on the right side of the line which Radcliffe had drawn. And for this the refugees were naturally resented (167-68).

It is a common human experience that a man does not know his own strength until he has met with adversity, the stern, rugged nurse who nurtures patience and wisdom.

The partition does not affect Tara and Seva Ram in the way it had affected Bauji. Both of them reach the safe pale of the Ashram before facing any untoward situation. Since Seva Ram is a government employee, he is transferred from Lahore to Simla, the new capital of the Punjab. Tara feels elated at the thought because a visit to the Himalayan capital of the British Raj was considered to be an unbelievable stroke of good luck.

The train Tara and Seva Ram with their son Arjun take remains standing at the Jullunder station for six hours. "There was chaos at the station since no one knew to what schedule the trains were running" (139). When a train comes from Delhi, the Sikh boys start firing at it. Soon an "elderly Sikh gentleman" (140) forces his way into the compartment. He narrates the horrifying incident in which all his family members were killed and he simply watched the whole drama of brutality in which even his son was killed but before being killed the "poor brave boy hurled an axe" (140) at the strangers and died. And this gentleman(?) had the only thought of escaping with his life. Somehow, he manages to enter a Punjab force truck and reaches the train compartment. He says, "And here I am now, shamelessly alive with nothing to call my own in this world, waiting to go wherever this train will take me" (141).

The life of Tara and Seva Ram in Simla passes without much furore and from the eighth section of the second part of the novel Arjun, now eighteen takes over the novel as its central character. He gets a job in Bombay which is "a miniature India" (244) and his journey to the metropolitan city symbolizes a common man's journey with a dream of earning money and then going back to the city whence they come. But the city never fulfils the latter part of the dream and whosoever comes to it begins to call it his home. It is in this city that Arjun meets his beloved Priti, marries her and lives with many ups and downs which open up unknown territories for him.

III

The spiritual journey is suggested by the Guru and his followers. His Ashram represents arcadia or the golden world of innocence free from the hustle and bustle of the world. The Guru's character has not been fully developed by the novelist but his views are significantly interwoven in the texture of the novel. When Bauji visits his Ashram, he is delivering his routine speech. In this *dharmopadesha* he draws upon the metaphor of train journey to illustrate his philosophy of life to his disciples:

> Look upon this world as a passenger on a train looks at a wayside stop. On the train journey the traveller makes an acquaintance with fellow passengers. Some passengers get off earlier, some later; some have a short journey, some have a longer one. But no one makes deep friendships because they all know that each one has to get off. This is how you must learn to live in the world. Do not imagine for even a moment that your parents, children, friends are going with you. They are all passengers (28).

It can be added here that the Guru is saying what has been told by the Upanishadic sages of the hoary past:

> *Kurvanneveh Karmāni jijivishechchatam samāh*
> *Evam tvayi nānya thetosti na karma lipyate nare.*[2]

Always performing works here one should wish to live a hundred years. If you live thus as a man, there is no way other than this by which Karman (or deed) does not adhere to you. Lord Krishna, too, says the same thing in a different way:

> *Karmanye vādhikaraste mā phalesu kadāchana.*[3]
> Do thy duty; reward is not thy concern.

The only difference between what the Guru says and what the quoted lines say is that he uses a modern and concrete analogy to elaborate his viewpoint. The analogy disturbs Bauji because of the past incidents which had taken place in his life in the train. Moreover he wonders what the world would be like if all relationships were as casual as those of passengers.

Later, talking to Seva Ram Bauji again says that he is a man of the world who likes being involved. He says, "I like this world with all its imperfections. I don't want to give it up" (54-55). He also tells Seva Ram that he "wouldn't want to live in this world like a passenger" (54). If opting for the spiritual world meant giving up the world, or living in it like a passenger, then he might as well choose the imperfect one. But the analogy never leaves him.

Seva Ram, the true disciple of the Guru, explains human brutality in philosophical terms. He attributes the killing and the hate to the imperfection of the phenomenal world. According to him, the catastrophe is an enactment of god's moral justice, which mere mortals cannot hope to fathom. He feels no anger or outrage but rather compassion for the suffering people, who are misguided by organized religion and its priests. He visualizes true religion as man's private relationship with god, as the Atman's submersion in the Brahma, which could be perfected in privacy through meditation.

Priti's relationship Arjun shows another dimension of the spiritual journey. In her teens, she elopes with Karam, a nationalist leader. After a short period, there is a drift between the two. When Arjun is in Bombay, she meets him after about ten years and the old relationship is renewed. Arjun has his individuation through Priti and the two decide to marry but he discovers Priti's restlessness and unhappiness. He comes to know that "she was seeking to find some kind of truth about them. She was searching in each life for some general principle which she could apply to her own life" (258).

Even after marriage Priti feels swayed away by some thoughts. She is unable to decode what these thoughts symbolize. But slowly and slowly her inwardness grows. The novelist narrates her mental make up as follows:

> All the time deep inside her, Priti waited for something to happen. She was quite clear in her mind that it was not another man that she desired. But what was it that she wanted? She did not know. Every morning she would wake up and hope to find it there. She looked out of the window, listened to every new sound, but nothing would happen. At sunset, she would grow sad and wait for the next day (304).

Priti remains in this situation for a long time. Before Arjun could do any thing for her, he gets involved in a business clash with Guba, a trade union leader, and is put behind the bars during the emergency period. He, too, has to turn inward and realize some truths about life. One day, during his evening walk, he is attracted by a stone in a quiet corner of the jail compound. Each day the stone in freshly decorated with red powder and flowers. He comes to know that it is a weaver in the next cell who worships the God. One day the jail authorities remove the stone, but it makes no difference. The weaver finds another stone and anoints it. The event leaves a lasting impact on Arjun and the novelist effectively portrays his reaction to it:

> Arjun was shocked. Slowly he realized that any piece of stone which his neighbour anointed became God for him. What mattered was the faith, not the stone. Gradually he began to understand how the weaver's mythical imagination directed his inner life. In his simplicity the weaver had kept alive the ancient way of perceiving the world, which was similar to the sages of the Vedas at the dawn of civilization.
>
> Arjun was fascinated and disturbed. One part of him dismissed the weaver's world as superstitious; it was precisely this kind of obscurantism, he felt, which kept the country backward and perpetuated an unjust caste order. Another part of him was attracted to the weaver's daring subjective world, which enabled him to see organic connections between the animal and human worlds and all of nature surrounding him (318).

The same kind of view is expressed by the noted Kannada writer U.R. Ananthan Moorthy who says that the weaver's reaction represents the complex pattern of ancient Indian thought and its daring subjectivity which is unaffected by the narrow confines of western scientific rationality. He further observes, "In his simplicity the peasant still keeps alive the mode of thinking and perception which at the dawn of human civilization revealed to the sages of the *Upanishads* the vision that Atman is Brahman."[4]

The efforts of Priti bring Arjun out of the prison but her growing inwardness disturbs Arjun. She wants to be away from him so that she can see the Guru in the Ashram where she had lived with her in-laws when Arjun was in jail. Arjun is sobered by the thought that her quest is bigger than himself and bigger than the world. But he is also troubled, because he himself does not believe in any thing beyond the here and now. One evening when the two are alone, they talk about the problem:

> Priti was first to speak. 'The difference between the wise and us is that we flit around the world, absorbed by all the silly, distracting happenings around us. While the wise turn inwards; we turn outwards.'
>
> 'What do you mean "inwards"?' Arjun asked.
>
> 'Reality is inside us,' she said.
>
> 'What is reality ?'
>
> 'The Absolute. God,' she said boldly.
>
> 'What is God ?' he asked with sincerity in his voice.
>
> 'Pure consciousness,' she said. 'It is so pure that its knowledge of itself cannot be conscious knowledge—for that would imply two things, the knower and the known: the one which is aware and that which it is aware of' (332).

She explains God in terms of *Neti, Neti* and tells him that the only reality is god and to merge one's self with it is the only legitimate aim in life. Quoting the Guru she says that one should try to subdue his ego and his mind because the mind is an "unruly monkey prancing among branches of a tree" (333).

The Arjun-Priti dialogue reminds us of such dialogue between Ramaswamy and Madeliene in Raja Rao's novel *The Serpent and the Rope.* In that novel the pair symbolize two extremes the poles of which cannot meet and which ultimately results in the drift of their marital relationship. In this novel, however, we do not have that kind of extreme. Priti maintains her love for Arjun but sticks to her decision of going to the

Ashram despite Arjun's disagreement to the proposal. She says she would be back within two weeks but stays in the Ashram for one year. Her absence makes Arjun think about life in a new and more synthesizing way. When she is back in his life, he gets a new meaning of life. Now it is not only his personal self the welfare of which worries him but he starts seeking happiness through the welfare of others. The project started by him for the welfare of the Adivasi women symbolizes the widening as well as the enlightenment of his self.

IV

The foregoing analysis makes it obvious that journey is the central motif in the novel. Das has embedded several kinds of journeys into the texture of the novel. It should also be remembered that his novel makes a long diachronic journey beginning in the 1920s and ending in about 1980. The longer time span gives him greater freedom to include a variety of themes but often the novelist is allured by his wish to say some thing about everything which certainly weakens the plot. A small portion of the novel is undoubtedly patchy and journalistic in tone. The way Arjun is shown solving the strike problem in his company is very filmy in tone and seems unrealistic. But the portrayal of the journey of the three generations of the family of Bauji is effectively done.

REFERENCES

1. Das, Gur Charan. *A Fine Family.* New Delhi: Penguin, 1990.
2. *I'sa Upanisad,* mantra 2, in S. Radhakrishnan (ed.) *The Principal Upanisads* (New Delhi: Indus, 1994): 569.
3. *Bhagwad Gita* Chapter II, Verse 47.
4. Anantha Moorthy, U.R. "Search For An Identity : A Viewpoint of a Kannada Writer," in Sudhir Kakkar (ed.) *Identity and Adulthood* (Delhi: OUP, 1992).

13

'Black and White' in the Short Stories of Jhumpa Lahiri

STELLA

The discrimination prevalent between the Blacks and the Whites and the consequent pride of one and the prejudice of the other, seems to be deeply embedded in the sub-conscious mind of Jhumpa Lahiri, the expatriate. Hence, her short stories are the outcome of a conscious effort of the writer in question; her psychological perturbation finds unconsciously, an outlet through her handling of this 'contrast technique.' Of the nine short stories, I have taken up only three of those, in order to substantiate my view of the writer.

As a short story writer, she far excels others, in her narration of a series of incidents that happen in the life of the protagonist who is arrayed against antagonist or antagonists. Suspense is built up in the story, as the heroine is not in a position to choose between two undesirable courses of action. For example, in the "Treatment of Bibi Haldar," it is the psychotic trauma of Bibi Haldar. In "The Interpreter of Maladies" it is the psyche of Mrs. Das that is focused. *Sexy* is the psycho-analysis of the problem of a woman. Though they are psychological studies it is love and sex that form the embryo or the nucleus around which the stories are woven.

Finally, as the mark of a good short story, folly and remedy come from one and the same source. For instance, if mistake lies in one part of the society, it is being rectified by the remaining part of the society.

"The Interpreter of Maladies" deals with the problem of hidden sin. By a direct presentation of an American mother Jhumpa Lahiri indirectly contrasts her with a loyal and sacrificial Indian mother. Mrs. Das is always "lost behind her sunglasses" and is ever found polishing her nails only. She walks "past her children as if they were strangers." When she is interested in beautifying her nails, she does not offer "her puffed rice to anyone." Indian surrounding "gives her the creeps" and a travel by car around it only results in "an impatient sigh as if she has been travelling the whole life," Bobby's birth and her extra marital life with a Punjabi friend of her husband it kept in the dark.

Similarly an Indian like Mr Kapasi has "pressed his palms together in greeting" when Mr Das "Squeezed hands like an American." While his wife "flexed one side of her month [...] smiling dutifully without displaying any interest in him. Americans visiting India, find shirtless men with a dirty turban who walk barefooted. They are amazed to see the cart and bullocks.

Americans have never "seen monkeys outside of a zoo" according to them; drivers in India are "sitting on the wrong side of the ear." There, husband and wife are "behaving like an older brother and sister to children" and it appears "they were in charge of the children for the day." If Mr Das is considered representing American man, he is money-minded whereas his wife is comfort-loving. Curiously enough, a husband is "calling the wife by her first name." Being attracted by Mrs Das and her long legs "he was anxious to be along with her" yet "he felt nervous to walk at her side" as Mr Kapasi, unlike, Mrs Das is tradition-bound.

To Mr Kapasi, the interpreters job "was a thankless occupation. He found nothing noble in interpreting peoples maladies." While his wife "had little regard for his career she uses the phrase." "Doctors assistant" as if "the process of interpretation were equal to taking someone's temperature." If for Raj. "It was a tiresome one," "it was so romantic" to his wife.

A contrast is struck between the behaviour of Mrs Das and Mrs Kapasi towards their husbands. Mrs Das "did not behave in a romantic way toward her husband and yet she used the word to describe him (Mr Kapasi), her sudden interest in him (Kapasi) an interest she did not express either in her husband or her children," is revealed. Furthermore, she who has kept her illicit affair with another man a secret for eight long years confesses it openly to a total stranger, seeking his help to take her out of the quagmire in which she is in.

Kapasi is often found comparing his wife, with Mrs Das and discovering the contrast between them. "Unlike his wife she had [...] intellectual challenge." His attitude towards Mrs Das is indeed noteworthy. He is "pleased especially that it pleased Mrs Das." He imagines the days when they will discuss and share each other's opinion of India and America respectively. When she is close by "he could smell a scent on her skin and worried suddenly that he could smell his perspiration." The bickering the indifference and the protracted silences that exist between Mrs and Mr Das, make him wonder "if Mr and Mrs Das were a bad match just as he and his wife were."

Verbal irony ensue out of use of words like (but, yet) and phrases like 'humourless jokes,' 'Pleasant shock' 'delirious with relief' "spoke slowly, but thinking aloud" and "gaze fixed but drowsy." Irony of situation arises when Kapasi builds castles in the air, imagining Mrs Das, as his fiancée, whereas she "had thought of him only as a parent." Though only an interpreter of the maladies of the villagers of Konarak to doctors, he imagines himself to be interpreting to diplomats and dignitaries. Giving her his name and address, he dreams of the possibility of the letter being lost or the accidental reversing of the postal code and of the possibility of the relationship growing between them, for, according to his conjecture "Unlike the other woman, who had an interest only in the temple, Mrs Das had taken an interest in him." And as he has dreamed, so has he witnessed, "The paper fluttered away in the wind" and the passing fancy of his, came to a still. Rear view mirror and the Giant Chariot with pictures of topless women stand as symbols, "The feeling he had toward her, that had made him check his reflection." Similarly, the flash back technique is used by the writer, when he sees these pictures. He has never seen his wife fully naked neither has he ever admired the backs of his wife's legs the way that he now admires Mrs Das.

Kapasi's mind is fully occupied with Mrs Das and at that juncture, "her confession," regarding, her eight years' secret, "depresses him all the more." When he brooks secret love towards her, she confesses her secret love to a Punjabi, to him. White he dreams of being her fiance she finds in him, a mediator. She who has committed a blunder, wants a remedy. "Suggest a remedy to a woman who loved neither her husband nor her children; had already fallen out of love, wife, life." The problem that has been so long corroding her inner psyche has at last been resolved by her sincere effort.

If *The Interpreter of Maladies* carries a cynical view of love, *Sexy* gives a cynical outlook on love and sex. What the Protagonist considers 'Love' is not love in the real sense of the term, but it is lust. If lust is what it means to an adult, when he uses the term 'sexy' it conveys a totally different and innocent meaning to a smell boy like Rohin. The work, therefore, means and makes sense differently.

As the short story begins, we hear from Laxmi of her cuisine's plight. Her cousins husband, changes his course of flight, as he falls in love with a woman, sitting next to him on a plane. So, instead of getting down at Montreal, where his house is, he gets off with her at Heathrow. The traumatic experience undergone by her cousin, is narrated pathetically to Miranda, who ironically, is in no way better than Laxmi's cousin's husband. In Laxmi's cousin's husband's life, it is a conversation with her that changes his life.

The object common to almost all the characters, is the telephone. While Laxmi uses it, to cool down the temperament of her cousin, the people over there use it to ply the radio station with pledges. When these two use the telephone for constructive purposes, Miranda the hearer of Laxmi's complaint, uses it fix the place to meet Dev, a Bengali.

Irony plays a vital role in the development of the story. If Laxmi cousin's husband is wooing Ena—an English lady, Miranda, a foreigner expresses her love to Dev, a married man and an Indian. Extramarital relationship is what is common, in both the cases.

Mirror and the Taj Mahal stand as symbols. While Miranda is glancing at her reflection in one of the angled mirrors, Dev is glancing too, thus leading to their love affair. If Dev is a Bengali Laxmi's cousin's husband is half Punjabi and half Bengali too. Laxmi's cousin's husband falls in love with the English lady in his wife's absence so does Dev too. Spending nights and days together has become their daily routine. "Unlike the boys she dated in college, who were simply taller heavier versions of the ones she dated at school." Dev is the first to whisper her name again and again. He is the first to tell her, that her legs are long. While Laxmi discloses the secret of her cousins husband, Miranda keeps hers a secret.

'Sexy' is first uttered by Dev to Miranda while standing across the bridge, farther away from each other, "It was the first time a man had called her sexy, and when closed her eyes she could still feel his whisper, drifting through her body;" Dev will tell her stories about his childhood and question her on the number of her lovers. But "he entered her without a word" for twelve minutes, and then has slept soundly, unlike Miranda, who never sleeps after that. An internal change takes place in Miranda, at a particular moment "It shamed her now." Laxmi's cousin's life turns turbulent, her husband argues bitterly, and leaves Montreal, once and for all, seeking a divorce.

It so chances, that Miranda meets, Rohin, Laxmi's cousin's son. He is a brilliant boy, ever ready to give right answers, to anyone who questions him. When Miranda "looks at him feeling slightly depressed, Rohin didn't look depressed." Miranda hears the boy saying you are "sexy" when he helps her with the Zipper. Through Miranda is shocked to hear it from a small boy, in the manner Dev used to, "she knew it meant nothing [...]. Rohin probably referred to all women as sexy" but when "she thought she knew what his words meant, at the time they'd made sense." For Rohin "it means loving someone you not know" from the context of his father loving a stranger "Miranda felt Rohin's words under her skin, the same way she felt Dev's. Rohin's words bring Miranda back to senses, contrary to Dev's that makes her lose sense. Now she weeps bitterly but Rohin still slept."

From then on, she decides sensibly to leave Dev for ever, by giving one false excuse or another, "In spite of herself, she longed for him." It takes three weeks for Miranda, to relieve herself from his clutches. "Now the clear black sky is spread over the city."

"The Treatment of Bibi Haldar" is the story of a twentynine-year-old girl, struck by mental illness. Being an orphan, she is looked after by an elder cousin of hers and his wife. Despite her insanity, she is never given the right antidote but is exploited to the maximum, for their own purpose: "Bibi has caused enough worry, added enough to expenses, sallied enough the family name." In the name of treatment, innumerable suggestions and advises are given by many. The result is that her health deteriorates from bad to worse. Her own treatment, that of one of her neighbours and that of wise men help her a little, while the rest of the treatments, only worsen her condition.

It is nothing but necessary to note that an orphaned insane girl toils to earn a little for her existence. It is she who records inventory for the cosmetics shop, "listing labels and prices without promise of a future," "for her meals provisions and sufficient metres of cotton [...] to replenish for wardrobe." All that she is provided with are a pair of cracked plastic slippers and a housecoat reaching some inches below the knee. What the doctors prescribed to her is that "relations will calm her blood."

Quite contrary to the advice of the doctors, sundry suggestions are given:

Concerned members of the town "brought her holy water from seven holy rivers." Her wrists "were bound with ropes and stinging poultices pressed upon her." Some prayed for her while Christians with blind faith took her to holy places, in order to kiss the tombs of saints and martyrs. "Auspicious stones adorned her fingers" by gem therapists "amulets warding against the evil eye girded her arms and neck" by priests. Friendly circle advises her cousin, that she can be provided with a change of scene, at times they even rushed out of apartments to calm her. Many a time, they send their servants to summon her cousin. Fortunetellers consulted almanacs to determine a propitious hour. Spinsters of the nearby area rather passed their comments, "No man wants a woman, who dresses like a dishwasher." Fools and wise alike had their share. They advised her either to shun garlic or "consume bitters," drink green coconut water, swallow "raw duck's eggs beaten in milk" and pass her time in meditation. Some did their part of service to her, by massaging "eucalyptus balm into temples" and by steaming "her face with herbal infusions."

"Too many cooks spoil the broth." She is treated not by one but many. She was being "shuttled from specialist to another." The result of having consulted, allopathic, homeopaths and ayurvedics, was contrariwise. When one advised her to gain weight, the other advised her to lose weight. If one asked her "not to sleep beyond dawn" the other wanted her "to remain in bed till noon." While one suggested remedy through hypnosis the other suggested headstand. While the next suggested chanting of vedic verses. "X-rays, probes, auscultatics and injections" only complicated her psychological condition all the more.

While her father was alive, it was totally a different treatment. He firmly believed that "to every problem, there is a solution." Therefore, he wrote letters to doctors in England and spent evenings at libraries, reading casebooks. He gave up taking meat on Fridays, in order to appease his family gods. He gave up teaching as well for her sake and started tutoring from home, so that "he could monitor Bibi." He also "created a chart of her symptoms with directions for calming her "and then distributed it throughout the neighbourhood." These papers have by now quite pathetically "turned into sail boats or to calculate ledgers on the reverse side."

Inimically enough Bibi Haldar, though unanimously accepted as insane, is perhaps the most same person. For she is found treating herself, without making a hullabaloo of it. She "polished her toe nails," "softened her elbows" goading "others for recipes," "applied glycerine" and "resisted sweets to reduce her measurement," "stitched salwar kameez in the fashions" and also sought "opinions of tiara designs and locket setting." Further, her fondness for marriage, the apt remedy for her ailment, is revealed through her interest shown in "magenta Benares silk or turquoise one and one of the colour of marigolds."

"Black and white technique" is therefore the contrast technique, by which Jhumpa Lahiri has objectified her subject 'love and sex' that had greatly obsessed her. The series of incidents that are woven around the two main characters—mainly an

Indian and a foreigner also help to learn the contrast in relationships with children, appearances, lives, dreams, culture and manner, between the two different races, in the first two short stories. However, it is obvious that the white stand above the black and the maxim, "appearances are deceptive" come true only in the hypocritical lives of Indians, the Red Indians. This technique is befittingly followed in the last story too, as it deals with the contrasting treatments given to Bibi, by the so-called 'sane' to the 'insane.'

Jhumpa Lahiri, the inside-outsider and *vice versa*, as she was born in London, grew up in Rhode Island is now living in New York, is a keen observer who realistically portrays her observations of Indians and foreigners. No wonder *The Time* aptly says that "Lahiri has a gift for illuminating the full meaning of brief relationships—with lovers, family friends, those met in travel."

14

"I" AND "THEY": THE DIALOGIC OF KAMALA DAS'S "INTRODUCTION"

—RAMA KUNDU

K.R. Srinivasa Iyengar, the noted scholar of Indian writing in English, and a pathmaker in a way, sounds unnecessarily harsh as he briefly sums up Kamala Das's poetry and prose. The one paragraph in his voluminous book, which is devoted to the poet, is made of guarded observations which disclose more than once the critic's uneasiness about the poet. His dislike, remains, indeed, hardly concealed; and reservations spill through the chinks of polite sophisticated formulations.

> "Kamala Das won *sudden* recognition in 1965, and [...] she has *tried to stabilise her reputation as the femme fatale of Indo-Anglian poetry*" (emphasis added 712).

"Her 'Composition' is a sustained *exercise in self-exposure.*" Refined insinuations yield place to direct attack,—"but such promiscuous self-exposure has only made a sensitive critic like Vimala Rao feel [...]." The reputed critic cites a relatively obscure one in support of his argument: "Kamala Das finally appears to be a poet of decadence [...] a victim of the inadequacies of her life, failing to gain control over her art" (Iyengar 712). It is rather disturbing that Iyengar who is usually so generous to young talents in the field, should take even "sleuthing" into account in the present case.

> "Her autobiographical *My Story* and her experiments in prose fiction have further stimulated interest in the poet more than in the poetry. And now there is sleuthing after her Malabar antecedents, and M. Elias (*JIWE*, July 1978)

> concludes that, when Kamala Das speaks, it is 'rather the Nair maiden unburdening her collective nightmare;' and so her sexual philosophy is to be traced back to 'her own cultural heritage deriving from the South or Dravidian India'" (712-13).

Of course at the end of the paragraph Iyengar resumes his usual generous tone and praises some of Kamala's lines which he finds to be "beyond the monotonous self-exhibitionism, and the deadening sex and sensuality" (713); but the admission too exemplifies a way which can use praise but to highlight the blamable points once again.

Iyengar's book (*India Writing in English*) is fondly held and cited by the emerging and emerged writers in the field. He has done a lot towards giving respectability to the branch and introducing authors. Then why does he turn so against Kamala Das in particular, and in such an unexpected manner?

Bijoy K. Das, a later and younger critic of our times, looks at Kamala Das from another angle. Das tries to place the poet in the indigenous tradition:

> "Kamala Das too works out her emotional and sexual traumas in poems of unexceptionable frankness reminiscent of the medieval shaja (*sahajia*?) poets who espoused free love as a means of realizing oneself [...]. Kamala Das highlights with boldness the sexual permissiveness and unhibition rooted in her native culture and produces arresting effect on readers" (Das 21).

Bijoy K. Das is a bright scholar and perceptive critic. Yet he, too, perceptive though, seems to miss something vital about Kamala Das by highlighting only her "uninhibition" which had revolted Iyengar as promiscuous.

One can get nearer the crux of the problem—where does Kamala elude such sharp minds—if one turns attention to the dialogic of Kamala Das's poems. "An Introduction" may be taken as an example. The poem has often been considered a 'confessional' exercise, expressing dissatisfaction and discontent in morbid sexual terms. However what is more important and really remarkable is the way the poem introduces several voices. It, of course, starts with an "I," then goes on to include successively "they," "he," and "you." Several voices and utterances (including unvoiced ones) thus enter the texture of the poem to weave suggestions and create an extraordinary dramatic tension. These other voices provoke, mould, constrict, condition the utterance of the "I," and also by the very means serve to release "I" into the fulfilling joy of making a unique utterance; at the same time they come up from the writer's community,—its social-cultural ethos. The critics of Kamala's poems are but part and extension of the "they," and understandably the anguish and yearnings of the dissociating, nonconforming "I" elude them. "An Introduction," read between the lines, is basically about identity, like many other poems of Kamala Das. In the process of defining and asserting her self-identity the speaker envisions the challenge in a series of binaries: I-they; I-he; I-you; I-I.

From the very start the speaker seems to speak from the consciousness of interfering voices and she struggles against their attempt to impose any readymade or traditional construct upon her. As result the voice carries the intonation of fierce resistance and assertion. Thus the monologue is actually a dialogue. The "I" is engaged with "they" in a tense tussle.

For Bakhtin a literary text could be the typical site for such interaction:

> "In life, we do this at every moment; we appraise ourselves from the point of view of others, we attempt to understand the trans-gradient moments of our very consciousness and to take them into account through the other [...] in a word, constantly and intensely, we oversee and apprehend the reflections of our life in the plane of consciousness of other men" (1984 : 94).

The speaker's consciousness of "they," 'he,' and "you" and other "I"-s successively and synchronically affect her intonation. As Holquist says: "Intonation is a material expression of the shaping role the other plays in the speech production of any individual self" (61); or to put it better in Bakhtin's own words: "The commonness of assumed basic value judgments constitutes the canvas upon which living human speech embroiders the designs of intonation" ("Discourse in Life and Discourse in Art" in Holquist 61).

The shrill and sad, loud and subdued intonational shades

in Kamala Das's poem is the result of the speaker's desperate attempt to disengage herself from "they," "he," and even "you" in order to be able to ignore or overcome their judgment, their assault or their indifference. The speaker senses the reproach or indifference of the others and immediately puts on her armour of indignation which is accentuated by bitterness and moderated by sadness. The poet subtly posits the extraverbal context that makes the utterance a meaningful locution for the listener/ reader.

The poem begins with an "I" who rejects a political identity; instead she proffers a national card, and a colour brand which she proudly proclaims. But when "they" come to coerce her into accepting an exclusivist linguistic or cultural she refuses. She retains her right to "speak" as she likes, and winds up her description of her own language,—"all mine, mine alone"—with a challenge flung across the board: "don't you see?" The voice she has acquired is likened to both "cawing" and "roaring," gentleness and ferocity.

The language is the speech of the conscious mind, and sentience is necessarily painful. The self-consciousness has been a painfully achieved awareness,—a realization reached through hesitation, uncertainties, confusion, anguish. It has been a bruising, crushing experience that has turned her in fear from recognizing her physiological identity. By rejecting the traditional accessories of a woman she tries to forge her identity above gender definitions. "He" had traumatized her. No "they" try to categories. Their commanding and intimidating voice rises in a crescendo until they "cry" out to her telling her not to cry.

A sudden shift follows. Another "he" enters; from, the subdued almost wistful intonation it is apparent that this time it is a different impact that this "he" produces on the utterance of "I." She does not deny her womanhood any more. Still she goes on assessing her situation by means of comparison and contrast. It is not as two specific man and woman, but as "every man" and "every woman." And she is saddened by the contrast in which society holds them. The man is proud in proclaiming his identity.

"Who are you?
It is I."

That is considered sufficient answer from a male. He gets fitted into this world like the sword in its sheath. The repetition of "s" sound gives the feel of smoothness; sheath also protects the sword, and the sword easily cuts through things. The "one" anywhere and everywhere who calls himself "I" gets finely fitted into this world which shield him like the sheath. Everywhere the speaker hears them responding to queries with proud assertion of their place and status, the ego of the "I." The other "I" is contrasted to this male "I,"—"himself." The woman is also an "I;" but she is alienated, alone in her self-consciousness. This "I" tries to reach out but retreats shamefaced, and is finally annihilated alone. (The lonely death scene recalls the death of Ammu in *God of Small Things.*)

This woman "I" does not run like a river, but waits like the ocean; she is not the active but the passive role. The same passivity is indicated by the be-prefix,—"beloved" and "betrayed." In sad recognition she registers the different images that are attributed to her, images of sinner or saint; that is she remains an object, either to be despised or worshipped, but not an individual in her own right. In love too she gets reduced to this secondary role. Her joys and aches all revolve around him; because in love she gets completely merged her lover, and absorbs his feelings as her own. Still she does not surrender her identity. The phrase with which the poem is clinched seems ironical: "I too call myself I."

The binaries of the poem are comprised of pronouns,—nameless identities. The anonymity gives them a group/collective face. At the end the binaries appear to have disappeared as the two "I"-s overlap. But this is only illusory. The end posits two separate "I"-s,—one comfortably accommodated by the society, the other alienated, ignored, exiled, but desperately trying to wedge in.

Kamala Das's "I" at the end of the poem does not denote just the speaker's own self-hood. It is also a representative voice, and, therefore, nameless. As Holquist explains: "they (the utterances) exist only in the individual minds of particular people in particular groups" and "in dialogism, of course the 'I' of such individual minds is always assumed to be a function of the 'we' that is their particular group" (67).

For this "we" here, it is still going to be a long-drawn struggle and no wonder there is little recognition as yet.

WORKS CITED

Bakhtin, M. in T. Todorov, *Mikhail Bakhtin: The Dialogical Principle.* Minnesota UP, 1984.

Das, B.K. *Aspects of Commonwealth Literature.* New Delhi: Creative Books, 1995.

Das, Kamala. "An Introduction," in *An Anthology of Indian English Poetry.* Patna: Orient Longman, 1989.

Holquist, M. *Dialogism: Bakhtin and His World.* N.Y.: Routledge, 1990.

Iyengar, K.R.S. *Indian Writing in English.* New Delhi: Sterling Publishers, 1985.

15

Effulgence of Imagery in the Verdurous SAARC Poems

SUKA JOSHUA

"The image exists in a poem to excite, to stimulate, but it also must tranquilize what it excites and it is then that its position as the poetic image is justified, or else it is neither poetic image nor does it make a poem."[1] The SAARC poems are replete with such images that excite and stimulate a less curious reader and tranquilize an agitated or anxious reader. The poems selected for study and scrutiny proves the SAARC poet's skilful employment of images and how they could come up with delightfully surprising and unerring images. The use of imaginary is so artistically arresting that the readers are left with a lasting impression that SAARC poets, can be treated in a par with the native English poets. The images and various modes of poetic expression in South Asian poems show an essential unity of their culture and literary sensibility.

Love is the dominant theme of the SAARC poems. These poems abound in images drawn from nature, man and man-made objects. The images that get prominence are the images of a lost happiness, a lost lover or a never forgotten memory. Marghana Sharq, an Afghanistan poet in his 'In my lonely Room,' talks about the various thoughts and memories that jostle against his mind and dreams that came crashing down. He compares his flow of tears to that of monsoon rains. After a disturbed sleep at night, he wakes with some hope. The sunshine and birds' song seem to revive hope in the forlorn poet. In his 'Caravan' also the poet drawns images like the storm, the desert and the hot sun to picture the deserted girl who ruined 'her life for others.'

'The storm thundered
Everything was blown away
Her life was a desert
With the hot sun burning overhead
It burnt her desires, hope and faith

The imagery in this poem is suffused with the feeling of sadness, pathos and a sense of loss. Yet towards the end there is a note of optimism and the girl hopes a day would come when a caravan would take her away from the deserts and give her hope and life. "In many poems, even in the ones where there is a finality of the loss, there is an undercurrent of belief in some transcendental resolution—some renewal, a meeting again, a rebirth, or a perpetual, everlasting unity that is not shattered by temporal facts of birth and death."[2]

The poem 'Firs Love' by the Bangladesh poet Thomas Ansell concretizes the emotions of love and joy by drawing comparison from different objects of nature. The shy, blushing girl in her first experience of love is pictured through a beautiful image thus:

And the shyest primrose shelters
    under the hawthorn bough;
    there is no love like your first love
    And no time at all, like now.

In an eight lined, simple poem, 'A Scribbled Lyric,' the details of the different features of April assume greater force and clarity with the application of precise and contextual imagery. The details are given in succession thus:

My heart, be still!
April has returned with the daffodil
And the blackbird's note
Warbles deliriously in his throat
Already bowed in bloom
White lilacs shower tremulous perfume
And diamond rain
Scribbles a lyric on my window pane.

Alauddin Al Azad's 'Still-Life' succeeds in presenting the inner urges, feelings and railings of the poet in terms of concrete and concise images. The following lines are pathetic expressions of unfulfilled love, and hopelessness.

> That moment has fled away. I could not
> perceive that you will also go
> By treading the paths of fallen leaves
> and the boulevard
> With dreams in eyes and heart beats for the dead
> adorned with paper-flowers.

'Fallen leaves' and 'paper-flowers' are more than enough to communicate the poet's disappointments and lifeless love. We find similar imagery in Shireen Kazi's 'The Bakul Flowers.'

> My tears fall like Bakul flowers
> [...].
> I long to be happy but tears fall instead [...].
> Oh, that these flowers, so fallen had crowned you!

In yet another poem 'A Dream Remembered' the poet expresses heavy, lonesome feelings talking about darkness, dumb birds and mute peacocks. A page of prosaic description would definitely not have expressed the sadness so emphatically as these few images in these few lines:

> And now my path has lonelier become
> Sunlight no more, and all the birds are dumb
> And dance no more the peacocks on the lawn
> And darkness now may just as well as dawn.

Shamsur Rahman's 'Sorrow' is saturated with sorrow. The poet sees nothing but sorrow everywhere. He sees sorrow's signature all around his house. This is a highly imaginative poem. The cause for sorrow remains a mystery. Is it the loss of a dear one whose presence is felt everywhere or is it a financial loss due to which every aspect of life suffers? The resort is not explicit but the density of sorrow is reflected by the poet's handling of the images. The utter hopelessness of the poet is pictured through the image of the bird that has never seen a blue sky.

> Oh my hopes like the beautiful bird
> of that never-seen distant blue sky
> and tender silken wind
> in the soft hidden language of my heart
> sorrow writes her name.

It is believed that best poetry is born in grief. The few Afghanistan and Bangladesh poems we saw earlier prove this. Indian poets also delve deep into this grief. The images employed here brings out with a touch of nostalgia and plain sadness the themes of love lost. Mahasweta Baxipatra's 'Expression' seems to say that the poet is at a loss for words to express his love. This mundane thought which every lover at one time or the other would have expressed, becomes poetry in the hands of Baxipatra with the binding image woven through this small poem:

> My love lies in the folds of silence
> On the frills of inhibition
> All those golden dreams
> Woven amidst secret threads
> in a speechless chamber
> Forgive me,
> my love is mute.

Kamala Das's unfulfilled love finds its effective expression through the striking imagery of falling snow and migrating bird in 'Ghanashyam' thus:

> In love when the snow slowly began to
> fall like a bird I migrated to warm climes
> That was my only method of survival
> In this tragic game the unwise like children play
> And often lose in.

Her longing for the warmth of sincere love is rewarded with cold indifference. Like Marghana Sharq, Das also takes the image of the desert-sun to talk about her loneliness. In another poem, 'A Wound on My side,' Das talks about her genuine longing for her husband's love. She does not express utter dejection when there was no way to make him love her. Her hurt was healed when she could find that love in yet another man. When her longing was thus fulfilled, her husband "fell off like a scab." The grandeur of this simple simile, the image of a scab falling off a healed wound speaks volumes about Das's attitude towards love.

Das's husband becomes the topic of description in the poem 'The Stone Age' where she describes him as an 'old, fat spider.' In an act of defiance and an assertion of her freedom, she breaks away from the mundane chores of domesticity, goes to 'the other man' and quenches her desire. The lines spring to life with the energy of erotic imagery when she questions,

> [...] Ask me, everybody, ask me
> What he sees in me, ask my why he is called a lion,
> A libertine, ask me the flavour of his
> Mouth, ask me why his hand sways like a hooded snake
> Before it clasps the pubs. Ask me why like
> A great tree, felled, he stumps against the breasts,
> And sleeps [...].

Through such daring erotic imagery Das wants to convey the sense of eroticism that love offers her. Her images profoundly correspond to her beliefs and values and express her unusual honesty and ultimate vision of love.

Gauri Deshpande's poems on social themes are a product of her sensitive response to city life. On 'Workaday Women' she probes into the life of working women in Bombay. Life has become a monotonous routine and so bore has become tedious. Deshpande ironically notes that these women lose their natural sensitiveness to the touch of love because

> [...] the too solid flesh
> will refuse
> when he demands that it melt
> at a Saturday-touch.

Her imagery relies heavily on the traditional images of drawn from seasons. Like Deshpande, Suniti Namjoshi also draws amply from images of the sun, the sea and the elements related with it. She expresses her protest against the ruthlessly utilitarian attitude in the modern world bringing in the imagery of sea in 'Cyclone in Pakistan.'

> "Think of the loss" they said
> "Visualize in numbers"
> Sea-sodden corpses
> Are useful to no one.
> 20,000 eyeballs
> never to be grafted
> 100,000 heads of hair
> spoilt by sea-water.

'Red Flower' communicates the agonizing experience of

disappointment in love. The intensity of emotion is conveyed powerfully through the imagistic feature that is so pronounced. She could compress an utterance through a telling-image.

> The corpse of love, freshly picked
> And the juice still held in the petals

and thus conveys the agony of the deeply-felt shock of the lover's infidelity.

Like an artist with paint and brush, A.K. Ramanujan paints a word picture of river Vaigai by his skilful employment of imagery. The similes and metaphors shock us with the picture of a dry river. While earlier poets sang the glory of the wealth of Madurai and the flooding Vaigai, Ramanujan wonders why the sight of dry river bed had missed their notice. To highlight the fact that very often the river would be dry, he brings in certain striking comparisons,

> Every summer
> A river dries to a trickle
> In the sand...
> The wet stone glistening like sleepy
> Crocodiles, the dry ones
> Shaven water-buffaloes
> Lounging in the sun.

S. Sankara Kurup in his poem 'Revelation' sustains the religious imagery throughout the poem. He talks about the peace, tranquility and purity one could attain by a visit to Sachidananda's presence. Indian religious culture is impressively portrayed through the imagery of fragrant flowers lighted lamp, fount of love and so on. P. Lal's 'There was a Man Who Had a Love Affair' and 'Radha Waits for Krishna' abound with religious imagery. Adarsh Misa's 'Puri Beach' is a beautiful expression of momentary nature of life and promises expressed through the imagery of waves.

> The waves build up
> With promise.
> They roll into breakers
> In their hold
> ....
> All moments slide
> Most moments pass

With hardly a ripple
Into the mind.
A few are remembered
By their speckles of white

D.V. Krishna Sastri's 'Song of Freedom' makes free use of imagery from the free nature and the poet asks, 'Why not I do just I please?' The poet asserts his right to be free and says:

I shall float on the wings of singing birds
And like a star amidst the stars,
Vanish in the sweetness of my songs!

The poet's strong desire for freedom is expressed through a list of images. He wishes to sail on the skies along the clouds, flash like lightning, play hide and seek with the friendly moon, dance with the gentle flowers, jump with the little fishes, leap with the pearls, float with the blowing wind, hide in the branches of trees and 'Whisper the secrets of love.' The list of comparisons not only reinforce the poet's desire for freedom but kindle in the readers the same longing.

Nissim Ezekiel uses images sparingly, uses them not for decorative purpose but for serious functional purpose. Certain images are repeated in his poems and they acquire symbolic overtones and thus help the poet to make the abstract concrete. The woman, the city and nature are the recurring images in Ezekiel's poetry. The image of pagan woman and city symbolize defilement and corruption. In 'Urban' the total image of the city and the city-men who are lost, disillusioned and bewildered are expressed with a vigour of language. 'Morning Walk' presents city in all its horror and ugliness:

Barbarie city sick with slums,
Deprived of seasons, blessed with rains,
Its hawkers, beggars, iron-lunged,
Processions led by frantic drums,
A million purgatorial lanes,
And child-like masses, many-tongued
Whose wages are in words and crumbs.

Here the city images is vividly identified with the other allied images—slums, hawkers, beggars, processions, drums and purgatorial lanes.

Nature for Ezekiel is a manifestation of the greatness and glory of the supreme. In 'A Word for the Wind' the poet considers the wind as an essential element and inspiring agent. In 'Stone' be establishes a unique kinship with the objects of nature and grows rather Wordsworthian in his approach. In 'Morning Prayer' the poet brings the images of hill, morning breeze, trees and garden. The urban man could get no divine secrets from the gentle morning breeze. Further, he describes a garden on the hill whose hedges are cut to look like birds and mythic beasts. The image of the city is the symbol of degeneration and dehumanization while images of nature represent life and warmth. Thus he makes nature shine by contrast of images.

The Nepalee poets share a common consciousness with the poets of other South Asian countries by being similar in the choice of themes and images. Madhav Prasad Ghimire's 'Lady Everest' sublimes the lofty Everest and expresses the poet's desire to soar high. He paints a word picture and captures the grandeur of the Everest and the Ganges. He intertwines nature imagery and religious imagery to give a touch of divinity to the beauty of Everest and Ganges.

> The first flash of morning on this twilight peak descends.
>
> ....
>
> Upon this peak fair Gouri, her tresses black cloth sun,
> After a bath in milk-lake will descend at dawn,
> Then Shiva, bearing the Ganges on his matted locks,
> Fastens the crescent on his tangled knots.
>
> ....
>
> And the moving clouds bore love messages of lovers to their love.

The poem 'Vaisakh' is so rich with imagery from local floura and fauna that one reading of it will help us visualize the lustre of the land. The poem talks about not just the 'myriads of blossoms' of Nepal but also of the many tribes. The second stanza of the poem goes thus:

> The Gurung girl plucked the Guras flower to wear on her ears;
> The Newar girl wove the Muswan flower in her plaited locks;

The Bhotia girl tied the Berki flower in her apron strings;
The cuckoo sang the memories of new love in the woods.

The poems 'Annapurna' also gives a picturesque description of the flowing mountain streams of Nepal, the earth verdant with vegetation, the rich rice fields, the million waves of beauty, the breeze of fragrance from the sweet-smelling paddy, the moon-lit nights of autumn, the mountain hills and so on. It reminds us of Keats' 'Ode to Autumn,' a poem known for its sensuous appeal. These poems prove that "poetry is a rhythmic experience of the human surroundings in relation to the phenomena of nature."[3] The images employed in these poems give a vivid sensuous appeal and also stimulate pleasure.

"A shared code of constitution of meaning and of expression, common dominant genres, similar themes and similarity of attitudes make South Asia a single literary cultural unit which has its global norms while at the same time it articulates locally the specific, particular personalities within the region." Pakistani poets share similar themes, show similarity of attitudes and articulate the beauty of Pakistan through shared imagery. Ahmed Nadeem Qasimi, like many other poets turns to poetry as a means of cathartic release from the tensions of love. 'Mist' is an outpouring of the poet's dejection, depression and disappointment. The imagery in the last three lines of the poem:

Time walks on leperous feet.
Blotches even on radiant faces.
Leaves fall from the tree of love.

Uncovers the layers of obscurity and concretizes the poet's emotions. Fahmida Riaz's 'The Laughter of a Woman' pictures a girl who enjoys and values her freedom and satisfaction. 'The Singing Springs of Story Mountains' seem to 'echo the gentle laughter' of the freedom-loving dame. Liberty is so valuable that it can neither be bought or sold in the market. She wouldn't exchange her freedom for anything. It belongs exclusively to her and none can hear the sob of her ecstasy.' The last three lines rich is imagery describes her thus:

There she goes, her hair billowing in the wind
The daughter of the wind
There she goes, singing with the wind.

Like the metaphysical poets who are known for their unique comparisons, Taufiq Rafat in his poem 'The Time of Love' compares love to a 'Country with its own climate.' Yet spring (or young age) is considered to be more apt for lovers and rhymesters. This idea is conveyed poetically thus:

> If spring
> Has many significance
> It is for us,
> The rhymesters,
> Who need
> A bough to perch on
> While we sing.

"Poetry assumes significance only in so far as it says the unsaid, discovers the unexpected and reveals aspects excluded by other discourses that may one day turn out to be vital areas of collective awareness." Poems by Singapore poets may not have said the unsaid but still whatever subject they dealt with turn out to be vital areas of collective awareness. Low Koh Chungs 'Old Home Revisited' expresses the poet's nostalgia for his childhood days and childhood home. His nostalgia is expressed through the description of various aspects of nature—like the babbling brook, wild flowers, the guava trees and the play mates with whom he was associated. The employment of felt metaphors and images enhance the aesthetic delight of the reader, apart from making the reader share the poet's sense of nostalgia. Lee Sam Hong's 'Flowers in the Late Afternon' talks about the holiday spirit and enhances the joy and liberty one experiences on a holiday by involving nature also in the sport.

> The holidays' breeze
> is always so gently dumb
> Swaying between the scarlet orchids
> Weaving musical notes,
> Endlessly humming
> A wordless song;
> A bunch
> Of flowering seasons.

Loo Kee Pau's 'The Rainy Season of the Trees' personifies trees and even simple natural movement of the branches and leaves signify sincere feelings of sorrow and loss.

In the rainy season
The trees first shiver in the wind
Then weep.
Tears of ancient sorrow drip down
From the spaces between the leaves
But can never drip away
The loneliness of the quiet rainy night.

An inanimate object is thus humanized with a marvelous use of imagery.

The poet suffering from bitterness, loss and loneliness sees nature also as indifferent and hostile as we see in Lee Guan Poon's 'The Falling Leaves.' Apart from the precision and accuracy of images employed the poet also employs pathetic fallacy and says:

The flowers are beautiful
But they never smile at me
Clouds crowd in the distance
But I do not glance at them.

The poet employs his images not only by means of similes and metaphors but also by means of ascribing to them human capabilities, sensations and emotions. Personification of trees is found once again in the poem 'When the Trees Awake' by N.G. Heng Teong. It is a beautiful nature poem where the trees are pictured to be getting ready for sleep. Insects sing bullaby, mist cool the atmosphere and the trees sleep, holding the tender dark night with 'their thousands of hands.' When they wake at dawn among the bustling, chirping birds the trees discover:

That no longer is it the night
which their myriad hands embrace
but the dazzling sunlight.

This flash of imagery seems to convey the message that life is a mixture of sunshine and shadow, pain and gain. Lee Tzu Pheng in his poem 'Knowing That Time Withers' employs the literary motif Carpe Diem. He is aware of the fleeting time and wants to strengthen his bond with his lady and asks her:

[...] the earth in me
reaches for your roots
vaster than what I cannot see
Stronger that my dreams

will you grow to that loveliness
to which my whole soul turns?

The lover's longing for his lady is so uniquely compared to the earth searching for its roots. The poet who stands transfixed, caught up in the enchanting beauty of the evening juxtaposes the throbbing beauty of nature and the dying civilization. The evening is said to be robed in gold, the resplendent golden hues. The beauty of this imagery is sustained till the second half of the last stanza when suddenly the poet is reminded of the dead civilization which has no time to adore the serenity of nature and learn from it.

Basil Fernando, though a Srilankan poet, shares the same anxiety of N.A. Rahman, a poet from Singapore. In the poem, "Age Four Revisited" Fernando calls butterflies flying flowers and says

You squeeze them tenderly unto a finish
As you do to flowers
And you are satisfied.
When beauty has withered away
In your hands you are satisfied.
.....
Little human don't think that way.

This poem strikes a note of similarity with 'Old Home Revisited' by Low Koh Chung where he expresses his nostalgia for childhood days. The diction and the image, the poet employs act as a skeleton, as a structure to convey the poet's impulses. Images with their expressive power are adequately competent to convey the confusion and conflict in the poet's mind. The ironic function of these images create an agony of emotional tension. The image of the butterfly that is squeezed sets the tone of morbid gloom that permeates the poem.

The study of some of the South Asian poets reveal that these poets develop images from their own experiences. They see no need to look to Western literature for images. Their images are products of their own imagination, experience and environment. The concrete images verbalize their thoughts in compressed form avoiding verbosity. The delightfully surprising and unerring images have helped these poets to deal sincerely with their private humiliations and sufferings and their intimate joy and ecstasy without ever being sentimental. It is their originality that makes their images effulgent and their poems verdurous.

REFERENCES

1. S.B. Srivastava. "Imagery: Indian point of view," *Journal of English Studies*, Vol. I, 1993, 21.
2. S.K. Sareen and Kapil Kapoor eds. "Introduction," *South Asian Love Poetry* (New Delhi: Affiliated East-West Press Pvt. Ltd., 1994) XIV.
3. Sareen XIII.

BIBLIOGRAPHY

Sachidananda, K. ed. *Gestures: An Anthology of Asian Poetry*. New Delhi: Sahitya Akademic, 1986.

Sareen, S.K. and Kapil Kapoor eds. *South Asian Love Poetry*. New Delhi: Affiliated East-West Press Pvt. Ltd., 1994.

Srivastava, S.B. "Imagery: Indian Point of View," *Vikram Journal of English Studies*, Vol. I, 1983: 15-21.

16

K.S. Venkataramani's *Murugan, The Tiller*: A Portrait of the Gandhian Dream of Rural India

UDAY SHANKAR OJHA

Indo-Anglian literature of the pre-Independence era brilliantly focuses on the stupendous impact of Mahatma Gandhi in general and his ideal of rural reconstruction as a step towards winning swaraj in K.S. Venkataramani's literary debut *Murugan, the Tiller* in particular. Mahatma Gandhi, with his epoch-making impact leading to the far-reaching changes in the entire socio-economic construct, has been instrumental in persuading the contemporaneous writings of K.S. Venkataramani, Mulk Raj Anand, Raja Rao, Kamala Markandeya and many others "to make a conscious shift of emphasis from the city to the village"[1] or to show the superiority of rural modes and manners over the urban luxury and sophistication in their novels. Precisely but accurately Dr A.K. Prasad opines that "the works of K.S. Venkataramani, Mulk Raj Anand and Raja Rao would not perhaps have been possible if Mahatma Gandhi had not such a stunning impact on the life and letters of the Indian society."[2]

Theoretically speaking, K.S. Venkataramani, an impassioned advocate of Gandhism, appeared on the literary horizon with his tour de force Indian English novel *Murugan, the Tiller* in 1927, which is an authentic record of the zeitgeist of the early decades of the nineteenth century India. In addition to this, his next novel *Kandan, the Patriot* (1932): Jatadharan, a collection of stories; *The Next Rung*, a critique of modern civilization; *Paper Boats*, a collection of sensitive rural sketches; and *On the Sand-*

Dunes, a philosophical causerie in rhythmical prose are all replete with the precepts of Gandhian economics and politics, exploring and upholding the ideals of rural transformation and upliftment, and Satyagraha and Swadeshi and calling for the ndian masses to work for freedom and regeneration of the Indian nation.

Venkataramani's *Murugan, the Tiller*, which has rightly been called "Vignette of vivid village life in South India"[3] for there is none other novel besides *Murugan, the Tiller* which portrays so simply and realistically the social, political and economic problems of the village life and manners of the South Indians, further evinces his unflinching belief in the reconstruction and regeneration of the Indian villages based on Gandhian thought of decentralized economy and polity. Extolling the village life, Venkataramani rightly emphasises this point:

> The Indian village is a national asset, and it is the first duty of renascent India to revitalise the hundreds of Indian villages by reviving its old agencies which rendered the Indian village a little paradise on earth. This sacred duty is clear to one who knows the significance of an Indian village and its importance to the world.[4]

As an apostle of rural reconstruction, Venkataramani interweaves the centrality of the novel keeping in view the Gandhian ideology of a self-sufficient, morally and economically integrated village community as the elemental unit of the superstructure of the Indian society. Sociologically, the novel makes an ardent appeal to the common people to "go back to the plough for an honest life in the open farm and lift yourself to the higher virtues of evolution; gentility, humility and love."[5] This heart-moving urge might be treated as the sole song of Venkaramani and is the message of peace that runs through his entire creative output. Perceiving the soothing and sonorous impact of Gandhian ideology, one can come across with Iyengar's view that "the Gandhian impact on contemporary literature has brought about results at various levels and in various directions.[6] More particularly, in his palatable academic discourse on Indian English literature of the Gandhian age, M.K. Naik could not resist the vehement urge to observe the turbulent influence of Gandhi under the heading 'The Gandhian Whirlwind':

> [...] The works of K.S. Venkataramani, Mulk Raj Anand and Raja Rao would not perhaps have been possible had the miracle that was Gandhi not occurred during this period.[7]

However, the fiction of K.S. Venkataramani (1892-1952) is the most epoch-making expression of the Gandhian era in Indian politics. His two novels *Murugan, the Tiller* and *Kandan, the Patriot* are even structurally very significant for they are, contemporary history, an authentic and compact reproduction of the social make-up of the age.

Coming a bit close to the main story of the novel *Murugan, the Tiller,* we have a shy, retiring, meditative and introvert Ramchandran (Ramu), the owner of a little coconut garden and a plot of agricultural land on the bank of the river Cauvery, who has failed B.A. and has returned, rather unwillingly, from Madras to his home in the village Alavanti. With a heavy heart, he expresses his sorrows before his family servant, Murugan, "the God-anointed Tiller" and "the most valued of the hereditary tillers of the soil" (1). Murugan, like the Good Angel in a medieval play, consoles him and advises, "Give up the Madras education which has drained our little wealth, and settle down in the village and look after the lands as your forefathers did" (6). On maturer reflections, Ramu decides to settle down at Alavanti in his ancestral estate.

The perusal of the novel suggests that Kedari, as ambitious, adventurous and flashy materialist friend of Ramu acts like the Evil Angel and writes to him, "It is no use remaining in your village and preparing for the B.A. as a private candidate. It will destroy the unity and growth of your culture" (9). Ramu ultimately falls a prey to the temptation of the city, leaves behind his fertile soil to the care of Murugan and arrives at Kedari's lodging in Madras. Instead of studying seriously, Ramu against the will of Murugan, marries a city girl of Madras named Janaki and fails the B.A. examination once again. He, a doubly repentant man, returns again to his village.

When Ramu gets solace in the tilling of the soil, his mother in law, a city-bred and ambitous woman, Meenakshi, does not like such a lowly profession and convinces him to accept a job of camp clerk to the District Collector of Cuddapah for Rs. 35 a month. In his first introduction to Mr Cadell, M.A., I.C.S., he "recollected with pain that it was a first occasion in a period of three centuries when a member of his family was obliged to accept menial a job and stand in servitude before another" (84).

Very soon, Ramu is promoted to the post of the Deputy Tahsildar on account of his honesty and simplicity. Cadel is also promoted the first Member of the Revenue Board in Madras.

Strategically, the tapestry of the novel has been construed in such a way, that the author himself falls in the trap of the novel mechanism, when a kind of transformation, a kind of new birth takes place in the heart of Ramu and he resolves to devote his entire life for the betterment and well being of society. Ramu appears with a concrete welfare plan for a backward rural area *i.e.*, for irrigation of the area by renovating a lake. His cosy confidence in the methods of rural reconstruction based on the Gandhian ideology earns him a great name amongst the people as well as amongst the top government officials of Madras. Mr Cadell, too, starts believing in the methods of rural reconstruction and agrees with Ramu's creed, "I agree with your creed that in an agricultural country like India rural reconstruction is the primary thing" (171).

Another minor female character, Sita, who later becomes a widow and secretly harbours deep love and respect for Ramu, also, feels passionately:

> The village needs great reforming. But the best men, men with brains, have left the village and the idlers and the unfit alone remain here (201).

Venkataramani's bird's eye view finds fuller exploration when he pinpoints:

> It is the high time to make a change in the habits, ideals, tastes and outlook of the people from the exotic to the indigenous, from the luxurious to the simple, from the urban to the rural, from the raw new to the ancient old. Simple life should be fixed as the ideal for all time.[8]

Contrary to Ramu's ideals of 'plain living and high thinking,' Kedari, Ramu's friend, in *Murugan, the Tiller* is a victim of Macbeth-like ambition which ultimately ruins his career as a lawyer. He involves himself in the election of the council which makes him completely bankrupt. K.R.S. Iyengar rightly analyses

Kedari's success-oriented approach to life and comments that such persons are of a certain species who utter revealingly: "'Kedari is ME'—and, indeed, the species is found all over India, and not in Mylapore alone, or in the legal profession alone."[9] At the end, in a state of repentance and sorrow Kedari meets his old friend Ramu and finds consolation and new meaning to life. He comes to realise that life is always a misery unless it is plainly lived. "Mere cultivation of the mind is no good. Mind power which has no roots in moral and human ideals, in character and simplicity, is combustible and self-destructive. It will destroy others and itself. There must be a change [...]" (304).

Unlike Kedari, Murugan, is shown passionately attached to the land and like all peasants and farmers, he worships the Mother Earth with religious devotion. He feels that "[...] the evil is in the system, and not in the man." But he, too, becomes a victim of the self-destructive ambition and in turn becomes a victim of the village politics and the governmental machinery and eventually ends up with the gang of Nagalapuram dacoits as an escaped prisoner only to be rescued by his old ventor and benefactor Ramu of Alavanti. Here, we are reminded of the simple peasant, who is tempted, made corrupt and behave like animals in a marvellous short story 'The Imp and the Peasant's Bread' written by an eminent novelist, short story writer and not critic Leo N. Tolstoy. Like Murugan, the peasant in that story is also a 'Good Angel' and ploughs innocently in his field. But he is provided corn more than he needs and taught by an imp how to make vodka. This habit of taking vodka takes away all his angelic qualities turning him into a beast. Tolstoy, at this point of the story rightly moralises that the blood of wild animals is always in man, but as long as men have only as much corn as they need, it is kept under control.

In the structural analysis of the novel, we find that Murugan is also ruined by the toddy shop and the ambition of Thoppai. Thoppai, a combination of three traits intellect, ambition and combative energy mysteriously influences Murugan in opening a toddy shop in the village. This leads him to his involvement in a riot, gets his arrested and imprisoned along with Thoppai and others. These prisoners, however, escape from jail, led by a fellow prisoner who is a robber chieftain. They find their way to Nagalapuram hills to lead a life of outlaws consequently posing a threat to the government. Ramu, who has been appointed to investigate the courses and nature of the criminal activities of the outlaws of Nagalapuram hills, impresses all the dacoits with his affectionate mind and habitual simplicity. Thematically it has been criss-crossed that he, further, offers to them a rehabilitation plan if they agree to go back to normal life. Murugan, "The true salt of this Earth," along with the whole gang of dacoits makes a passionate appeal before Ramu:

> Give us each three acres of land and a cow. We will work day and night for the production of the true wealth of the world. We will grow oil-seeds, cotton and corn, and help to nourish the life of towns. We will grow fruits and flowers and most delicious things for you" (246).

Metaphorically, Murugan's eyes shine with 'the farmer's love and peace' and put a kindred beam in the chieftain's eyes. The dacoits agree to the settlement scheme of a little garden city there were every member will have a three-acre holding for cultivation and a garden site with a house. With the active help and cooperation of the outlaws (now made lawful citizens) and Ramu's "cosmic power," the dream of an ideal agrarian colony takes a concrete shape in the form of Meenaksheepuram.

Meenaksheepuram, a garden city now smiling with a new life is all set to prepare man for a higher plane of action, a simpler and more fruitful existence. Ramu, after the completion of this scheme, gets promotion to the post of a District Collector, but realising the fact that living too much in the crowd, he would become a mere twig in the sea without drive or initiative, resignes from government service and settles down in that new settlement.

This is how, Venkataramani portrays here an ideal man who will build the India of Gandhi's dream—a rural India where "work was light and play for everyone [...] for it was work for their own joy. None slaved for mother. And labour was the kind which nourished body, mind and soul. Life was simple and joyous, and man was happy in the lap of nature, like a babe in the bosom of its mother" (335).

In *Murugan, the Tiller*, Venkataramani concerns himself not only with the agrarian problems but through the character like

Kedari he has highlightened the evils of western education, the Rule of Law and the racial difference in the country.

The novel, however, does not reflect the Indian struggle for freedom except for one or two stray discussions which take place in the novel. For example, when Mr. Cadell asks Ramu, "But how could you aspire for full citizenship or Swaraj when things are yet so unripe?" (147), Ramu answers to this, "for they can never ripen without Swaraj. We can never learn to swim without getting into water" (148).

Unlike *Kandan, the Patriot*, this novel may not, appeal as a political novel but the author's insistence on the reconstruction of the national economy through the development of the economic condition of the villages, and his appeal for a love for the country's tradition, is quite obvious from the conversations of the characters.

In the opinion of Venkataramani, the village is the true essence of India as about ninety per cent of its population, about one-fifth of the human race live in the villages and "follow the profession of plough." Therefore, a change is needed and an unorganised lot of poverty-stricken peasants, who depend largely on the vagaries of nature and at the mercy of local zamindars and their agents, must enjoy the leadership of selfless and devoted farmers like Ramu and Murugan, who can be the precursors of rural revival and change every ordinary village into a new "Meenaksheepuram."

The summum bonum of the novel critically and categorically suggests that it is a novel depicting primarily the Gandhian ideal of going 'back to the village' and, secondarily, emphasising the need for the traditional Indian way of living. Venkataramani, as an avantgarde has endeavoured to "try and catch the colour of life itself" and provides his readers with an immense variety of richly textured commentaries on manners and morals of man's life in a rural society. Venkataramani's heroes, Murugan and Kandan who represent the rural society of the age, work for the humanity on the lines of the Gandhian ideology but with a difference. This difference is well perceived by K.R.S. Iyengar when he writes:

> Murugan is an exponent of Gandhian economics as Kandan is an exponent of Gandhian politics.[10]

Whatever be the aspects of Gandhian ideology, Venkataramani has expounded them beautifully in his novels but in all his writings, a common but prominent voice has always been heard *i.e.*, to regenerate and renovate the Indian villages through social and economical amelioration. For a staunch nationalist like Venkataramani, city life is destructive and deceitful; village life is integral with our Indian traditions and culture and fundamentally healthy and good. The simple villagers, for K.S. Venkataramani, are 'the hidden flower-buds' who can blossom out if helped properly by the educated and selfless young men of the villages.

If thematically, Venkataramani's *Murugan, the Tiller,* is undoubtedly a perfect and compact portrayal of Gandhian dream of rural India, stylistically, it reigns supreme because the author's power of telling the story with spontaneity and ornaments of gay, humorous comments and poetic metaphors also contribute to the success of the novel as a work of art. Indubitably, K.S. Venkataramani is a creative artist of towering persona.

NOTES AND REFERENCES

1. Iyengar, K.R.S. *Indian Writing in English*, New Delhi, 1962, 228.
2. Prasad, Anil Kumar. *The Village in Indo-Anglian Fiction.* (Patna: Novelty & Co.) 5.
3. Isvaran, Manjari, S. *Venkataramani: Writer and Thinker—An Appreciation.* (Madras: The People's Printing and Publishing House, 1932) 1-2.
4. Venkataramani, K.S. *The Indian Village* (A Ten Year Plan), Madras, 1936, 17.
5. Venkataramani, K.S. *My Ashram Plan for Rural Uplift*, Madras, 1.
6. Iyengar 278.
7. Naik, N.K. *A History of Indian English Literature*, New Delhi, 1982, 118.
8. *My Ashram Plan for Rural Uplift*, 16.
9. Iyengar 279.
10. Iyengar 228.

17

THE NATIVE VOICES: A CASE FOR THE SECOND TRADITION OF THE POST-COLONIAL THEORY

GAJENDRA KUMAR AND KULDEEP KUMAR

The Statement

In the present essay we wish to focus on the exclusion of the native voices in the canon of post-colonial theory which is produced, processed and propagated in the metropolitan west for the consumption of the underdeveloped (say, third world) nations. It is in this sense that the postcolonial seems to incarnate as the colonial post, thanks largely to the presence of a flourishing community of collaborators-well-entrenched in the Indian academy—"a class of persons, Indian in blood and colour, but English in taste, in opinions, in morals, and in intellect."[1] The colonial cousins, so to say.

The first part of the essay deals with the meanings of the much—(ab) used term—"postcolonialism" and its conflation with yet another postal term, "postmodernism." The neglect of the Indian tradition in the writing of post-colonial theory will also be highlighted. It will also be analysed whether the Indian thinkers have something important to say with regard to the post-colonial situation in India. In the second part, a few illustrations from the writings of Indian thinkers (Vivekananda, Gandhi, Aurobindo, Bankim Chandra, Lohia, Ambedkar, Ashish Nandy, Bhalchandra Nemade and Makarand Paranjape) will be discussed only to exemplify, that the Indian-chapter of post-colonial theory will be incomplete and irrelevant until the native voices are given their legitimate space in it.

The Post-colonial or the Colonial Post?

The Politics of Exclusion

Let us begin by asking the question—"What does the term 'post-colonial' refer to?" The term is said to cover "all the culture effected by the imperial process from the moment of colonization to the present-day" and the post-colonial literatures "emerged in their present form out of the experience of colonization and asserted themselves by foregrounding the tension with the imperial power and by emphasizing their differences from the assumptions of the imperial centre."[2] It is to be noted that the key to the meanings of the term, according to his view, lies in the "experience of colonization" and the resultant "tension with the imperial power" and the assertion of differences from "the assumption of the imperial centre." Isn't it ironical that the post-colonial derives significance or meaning only in relation to the colonial centre—either by resisting or collaborating with it? In this view, this is, however, made quite clear that the post-colonial experience, that starts from the comment of colonization, in most acutely felt by a native at the site of culture. Going by this explanation of the term, all the discourses of resistance that counter the structures of colonialism or oppression, irrespective of the languages in which these discourses are couched, should form the corpus of post-colonial theory or criticism.

In yet another explanation of the term, it refers to "a period (either that following the attainment of nominal independence from imperial control or to the entire range of colonial, neo-colonial and post-colonial participations since the eighteenth century), a subject matter [...] and a variety of interesting reading strategies designed to decolonise the mind."[3] The post-colonial critique has been a "theory of engagement concerned with creating agency for the marginalized and oppressed, with recovering lost histories and voices, and with opening up the academy to the world."[4] This theoretical rigour and sophistication notwithstanding, the term "post-colonial," has not yet gained general acceptance, particularly among critics working outside the metropolis. 'Post-colonial' is a "term either ignored or disparaged in large parts of Africa, in the Caribbean, in India [...]. Cultural and economic nationalism still seems to be the more important priority for these groups, which do not wish to sacrifice the specificity of their concerns to the more general term, post-colonial."[5] It is significant to remember that this view, at last, gives due cognizance to the indequacy of the term "post-colonial" as it is a construct of the metropolitan west with which it wishes to universalize the vastly different and differing colonial—post-colonial experiences or histories of the people of the third world.

As it is evident from both these explanations of the term 'post-colonial,' it may legitimately be said that all those indigenous voices (or discourses) that resisted the ideological as well as political invasion by the colonial power(s), in the interest of the oppressed—subjected to enslavement and violence, should form the chunk of post-colonial criticism. If that be so, how can we account for the wilful exclusion of such leaders, thinkers, activists, writers as Rammohun Roy, Vivekananda, Aurobindo, Gandhi, Tagore, Subhash Bose, Rammanohar Lohia, B.R. Ambedkar, as others whose writings offer a valuable record of how the Indians encountered the impact of colonalism in different ways and prepared their own narratives of resistance? These are only few names randomly picked—in fact, the entire period of Indian freedom struggle is full of such visible and invisible voices of protest against the colonizing powers. It is, perhaps, high time we included these native voices in our version of post-colonial theory. This is how decolonization of theory may start in India.

II

The Nexus Between the Post-colonial and the Postmodern

I will quote a few examples in order to show the collusion between both the discourses—postmodernism and postcolonialism. Of all the major critics or theorists of the current postcolonial theory, the names of Gayatri Chakravorty Spivak and Homi Bhabha stand out by virtue of their acceptance and recognition in the west as the radical interpreters of third world post-colonial realities. In the textualization of their discourses, both these writers employ the jargonised post-structuralists, deconstructive strategies which inevitably end up diverting the attention of the reader from the pressing post-colonial texts or contexts to a futile and tiring word—play (called deconstructive method)—availing nothing! For example: Spivak's analysis of Mahasweta Devi's famous short-story "Draupadi"[6] (which Spivak herself translated) shows the violence done to a highly socially relevant text wilfully subjected to the post-structuralist critical tools. The story is about the Naxalbari Movement of the 60's which was led by the agrarian and tribal communities in West Bengal, Bihar, M.P., Orissa, and Andhra Pradesh against their massive exploitation by the landed aristocracy in collusion with the state. Mahasweta tells a tale of brutal violence and exploitation inflicted on Dopdi Mejhen, Dulna Majhi and their comrades—all tribals, by the authority—which acts an inhumane, and despotic power-structure. Dopdi or Draupadi is gangraped in the police-station; but she remains firmly dedicated to her cause—a radical change in the present oppressive social system.

It is, however interesting to see that all the tribal leaders who had to resort to violence in opposition to state terrorism, are killed in an unequal battle. Mahasweta understands the futility of violence as a means of social-change. In a significant scene, she makes the tribals refer to Gandhi as king Gandhi (*In Other Worlds*, 189). Had the Indian-state followed the Gandhian vision of gram-swaraj (*i.e.*, self-rule from below), the present scenario of unutterable violence and exploitation could have been avoided. Mahasweta's stories call for a radical social reconstruction of Indian society. This meaning is lost in the babble of postmodernistic jargon applied by Spivak in her critique.

What makes Gayatri's analysis interesting to a reader, situated in the metropolitan west because of an avowedly deconstructive method in which terms such as poverty, hunger, squalor and people are not even mentioned in the entire analysis, creates all kinds of problems of reading to an insider (or a reader) situated in a third world Indian community who also wants a radical change in the present socio-political structure and considers "Draupadi" as a resistance-narrative. Even elsewhere too, Spivak dilutes Mahasweta's stories (like "The Hunt," "Douloti The Bountiful," "Pterodactly, Puran Sahay, and Pirtha")[7] in the Derridean/Foucauldian discourse-stripping these text of an urgent message of social-national-reconstruction. The second example comes from Homi Bhabha's *The Location of Culture*[8]—

a collection of his essays on the post-colonial situation of the Third world communities involving such issues as nation, national identity, colonial discourse, culture, transculturation and hybridity. A la Spivak, Bhabha also marshals his awe-inspiring vocabulary and usage pertaining to the meta-linguistic, meta-critical, deconstructive language. In most of his essays, which attempt to analyse 'nation' and 'culture' under the impact of colonialism, he draws upon the western epistemology—Derrida, Barthes, Foucault, Lacan, Freud, Lyotard and other poststructural critics are the most quoted names. The native voices are conspicuous by their (manufactured) absence in the sections that pertain to the Indian post-colonial situations in the discourses of Bhabha and Spivak. They, in this manner, act as the interpreters of the unequal exchange between the first world and the third world. They represent a new tribe of metropolitan third-world writers/critics who write the native societies in their (western) critical idioms—ignoring the already available body of indigenous discourse in a post-colonial society.

It is worthwhile to reflect a little on the Rushdie-phenomenon also in this context. Salman Rushdie's recognition in the west as a post-colonial writer primarily rests on this nexus between postmodern or post-structuralist theory and the postcolonial realities.[9] The postmodern theory discounts the nation, the national and nationalism as authoritarian constructs that have outlived their utility after the two world wars and the unprecedented encorachments of the global capitalism in the third (and second) world societies. That's why, Rushdie, considers India as a myth, an imaginary construct the sign of which, in the form a country—"that vast, metamorphic, continent-sized culture that feels, to Indians and visitors alike, like a non-stop assault on the senses, the imagination and the spirit."[10] That's why, Kanishka Chaudhary aptly underlines this nexus or affiliation between the postmodern and the postcolonial discourses "Another salient example of the limitation of Western critical discourse on the subject of postcolonial literatures is the postmodern narrativization and subsequent (re)appropriation of the "other."[11]

It is because of this trafficking in postmodern discursive practices that Rushdie brushes aside the entire corpus of native language-literatures of India produced during the post-independence era as insignificant *vis-a-vis* the works of Indo English fiction.[12] Moreover, he completely erases the native language-literatures of Indian by using Indian Writing as a synonym of "Indian Writing in English." Hence the title of his anthology, that deliberately excludes the native writings (save Manto's "Toba Tek Singh"), "The Vintage Book of Indian Writing" (1947-1997).

III

The Native Voices: A Case for the Second Tradition

We now move on the third and concluding part of the essay which attempts to tackle the questions—"Do the native or indigenous discourses have any relevance to the understanding of the postcolonial situation, particularly in the context of India? If yes, it is of utmost significance to prepare our nativised versions of postcolonial criticism including the ideas of the native thinkers such as (tentatively listed) Rammohun Roy, Sir Syed Ahmad, Gandhi, Coomaraswamy, Aurobindo, Tagore, Vivekananda, Iqbal, Bankim Chandra, Subhash Bose, Dr B.R. Ambedkar, Ram Manohar Lohia, Jaya Prakash Narayan, Iravti Karve, Ashis Nandy, Nemade, Namvar Singh, Nirmal Verma, Makarand Paranjape, Partha Chatterjee, Asghar Ali Engineer and others. This may be considered our second tradition of post-colonial theory. The first tradition is too "sanskritic" (in the sense of being over-refined and over sophisticated) and too west-centred to allow us to think freely as it emerges from the grids of metropolitan, western epistemology. The second tradition is empowering and enabling as it does much to decolonise the Indian (native) mind and give us a handle to negotiate the external as well as the internal colonisation.

We shall cite only a few instances to prove how effective the (inclusion) of native voices in the postcolonial canon may be. For example, Gandhian vision exploits in his notions of truth, non-violence, swaraj, critique of modernity, nation, communal harmony, critique of orthodox Hinduism, sarvodaya (Universal Welfarism), satyagrah (truth force), noncooperation and gram-swaraj can be of great importance to a modern reader or a post-colonial subject. Vivekananda, Aurobindo, Gandhi, Tagore, Ambedkar, J.P. and Lohia, were sufficiently exposed to the west before preparing their critiques of the colonising powers. Those who are afraid of being labelled as "die-hard traditionalists" by using the insights of these native thinkers should ponder over what Gandhi says: "It is good to swim in the waters of tradition, but to sink in them is suicide" (*Collected Works*, Vol. 27, 308). What is even more remarkable is the often-mutually-complementary nature of their discursive practices (which may appear "contradictory" if seen from an academic point-of-view). To understand the internal colonisation it would be worthwhile to put Gandhi in the company of Ambedkar—who prepared a counter-discourse. Or it is interesting to see how Lohia, J.P., Nandy and Makarand revise the Gandhian praxis in the context of new post-colonial realities. Gandhi's sarvodaya and Tagore's internationalism can be studied together in order to reach a deeper understanding the connections between the local, the national and the global. It will be interesting to study Vivekananda's call for a massive social reconstruction implicit in his vision of dharma. Aurobindo's idea of Indian culture placed with the voices of the minorities (composite, syncretic culture of India), will benefit the readers immensely in their understanding of the post-colonial situation in India. Similarly, in recent time, we see how Nandy, Bhalchandra Nemade, G.N. Devy, Nirmal Verma, Makarand Paranjape, Partha Chatterjee and a host of others are engaged in extending the frontiers of Indian critical tradition—by writing a self-conscious, self-critical post-colonial criticism that critiques structures of power and powerlessness both. Thus, the second tradition will not be nationalistic in the negative sense. It will not overlook or neglect the profundity of the literary productions of various Indian languages. The second tradition of postcolonial theory will not be anti-west or insular to the noble ideas coming from the outside world. But it will make one say—"I want the cultures of all lands to be blown about my house as freely as possible. But I refuse to be blown off my feet by any."[13] We can be the critical insiders in our culture and the preservation of one's own culture "does not mean contempt for that of others, but requires assimilation of the best that there may be in all other cultures."[14]

NOTES

1. T.B. Macaulay, *Macaulay, Prose and Poetry*, Ed. G.M. Young, Cambridge, Mass. Harvard UP, 1952, 729. This is the famous quotation culled from Macaulay's (infamous) "Minutes"—which aptly sums up the agenda of

British colonialism in India. What is surprising is Macaulay's farsightedness as most of the nationalist elite who took over from the British in 1947 turned out to be Macaulay's distant, if not near, cousins—in their firm rejection of the indigenous ideas of the national reconstruction (Gandhi, Tagore, Vivekananda, Subhash Bose, Lohia, Ambedkar, Jaya Prakash Narayan and other prominent leaders who understood the Indian ground realities, were ignored by the Congress under Nehru) and their wholesale acceptance of the western paradigms of development, culture education and technological dependence on the west.

2. Bill Ashcroft, Gareth Grifith and Helen Tiffin. *The Empire Writes Back: Theory and Practice in Post-Colonial Literature* (London: Routledge, 1989), 2.
3. Eugene Benson and L.W. Conolly (eds). *Encyclopaedia of Post-colonial Literatures in English* Vol. 1 (London: Routledge, 1994), 282.
4. Eugene Benson and L.W. Conolly 282.
5. Eugence Benson and L.W. Conolly 283.
6. Gayatri Chakraborty Spivak. *In Other Worlds*. London: Routledge, 1989, 179-95. Darshan Perusak wrote an interesting article "Post-colonial Realities, Post-Structural Diversions. An Unamused Exchange" (*Economic & Political Weekly*, January 29, 1994, 243-49) in which Spivak's deconstructive reading of "Draupadi" was justifiably attacked. This also proves how native literature translated into English gets co-opted in the postmodernist discourse.
7. Gayatri Chakravorty Spivak. *Imaginary Maps*. London: Routledge, 1995.
8. Homi K. Bhabha. *The Location of Culture*. London: Routledge, 1994. See "Introduction: Locations of Culture," 18, "The other-Question: Stereotype, discrimination and the dicourse of colonialism" 66-84 in the same book.
9. See Arun Mukherjee. "Whose Postcolonialism and Whose Postmodernism" in *World Lit. Written in English*, vol. 30, No. 2, 1990, 1-9.
10. Salman Rushdie. "Introduction," *The Vintage Book of Indian Writing: 1947-1997*, Ed. Salman Rushdie and Elizabeth West (London: Vintage, 1997), IX.
11. Kanishka Chaudhary. "Theoretical Confrontations in the study of Postcolonial Literatures" in *Modern Fiction Studies*, Autumn 1991, vol. 37, No. 3, 611.
12. Salman Rushdie. "Introduction" *The Vintage Book of Indian Writings*, IX-XXIII. Rushdie's pronouncement on Indian Literatures drew flak from the leading Indian writers and intellectuals. But his valourisation of the literary work produced in English over the ones written in native languages proves the "bias" inherent in the metropolitan discourse of postcolonialism.
13. M.K. Gandhi. *Young India*, June 1, 1921.
14. Gandhi, Sept. 1, 1921.

18

PATRICK WHITE'S *VOSS*: THE SELF-EXPLORED

KH. KUNJO SINGH

Patrick White (of Australia) is well-known for his powerful dramatization of human isolation. He is concerned with the private life of the individual who, dissatisfied with society, runs away from the actual sphere of life to seek solace in his self-conceived world of the imagination. He delineates characters who, like cyclopes, are sensitive to the life's reality but apprehensive of its subtlety. The mind's eye has enabled them to mediate between the life within, (that is, the cerebral) and the life without (that is, the quotidian). White's characteristic strength is defined by the aggressive and imposing quality of these characters.

Patrick White's *Voss*[1] (1957) is the product of the common experience of human suffering and isolation. The setting of the novel, Colonial Australia, which is used as the climatic metaphor of the human psyche is the launching ground for a mythical voyage of exploration into the vast space of the human self. Voss is a half-crazed German explorer who is aggressively romantic and unrealistic about human limitations in the world with too noble a conception of himself, resisting even a momentary lapse into normal humanity. He has rejected the choices of salvation and fulfilment offered by religion and society to every human being. He bluntly rejects the healing forces of love and faith in realities of life as weakness. He is ambitious of achieving the Absolute. To him exploration is inevitable. He wishes to exemplify his life by acting his endurance power to assert his ambition throughout the torturous journey in the desert.

Voss has admiration for the Australian desert which also

conjures up the German nostalgic feelings of his childhood. He feels the inevitability about his exploration. Replying to Frank Le Mesurier, a companion in the expedition, Voss states:

> "Yes," answered Voss, without hesitation. "I will cross the continent from one end to the other, I have every intention to know it with my hearth. Why I am pursued by this necessity, it is no more possible for me to tell than it is for you, who have made my acquaintance only before yesterday."[2]

So faithful and honest he is, his shocking immersion in his private world brings him daemonic powers towards self-humiliation and the humiliation of their relations.

Voss assumes superhuman qualities and expect others to admire him in the process of realizing his ambitions. For Voss, humility is detestable, repentance, a weakness. He claims that one's will is his destiny. Voss attempts a justification of the exploration when he speaks to Frank Le Mesurier of the exercises of *Genius* (*Voss*):

> Every man has a genius, though it is not always discoverable. Least of all when chopped by the trivialities of daily existence. But in this disturbing country, as far as I have become acquainted with it already, it is possible more easily to discard the inessential and to attempt the infinite.[3]

He asserts himself in his reply to Laura, on another occasion:

> "Your future is what you will make it, Future," said Voss, "it will."[4]

Voss undergoes future transformation of his personality. His inner exploration, metaphorically represented by "the terrific journey through the desert" is complimented by outside forces which act as catalysts in bringing the ultimate self-recognition. These are categorised into human and elemental types. The first category includes the influencing relationship between the protagonist and the other characters, especially the love-link between Voss and Laura. The second type contains the force of climate and landscape, *i.e.*, the Australian desert. These forces, human and elemental, act on the rapidly shrinking selves of Voss and lead them through a series of epiphanies to the final denouement.

Voss's relationship with his companions in the expedition is diverse. Palfreyman whose suspicion of his own faith are mocked by Voss, gives lessons of humanity to the leader of the exploration even in his death. Voss learns the strength and value of humility from this honest ornithologist. Frank Le Mesurier, who is also the *alter ego* of Voss carrying the evil demon of ambition keeps Voss's conscience alert and mirrors the disastrous future of Voss's ambition. It is through his symbolic world that recognises himself and the destructive demon inside him. Judd, the ex-convict who is seen by Voss as a potential rival, and whose physical strength and rationality and logic are seen as a threat to Voss's leadership, reminds him of the human limitations. Besides these, there are Turner, Harry Roberts, Sanderson, Boyle, who all educate Voss in the futility of isolation and bring him nearer to the realization of his "human inheritance." In fact, Frank Le Mesurier is the conscience keeper of Voss.

Frank's prose-poems give a shocking self-revelation to Voss. As a man sharing the common daemon with Voss, Frank is inspired to write and record the progress of Voss's journey from the beginning of the ambition to the ultimate possible destiny. In *conclusion*, Frank records the four phases of Voss's questful story. In the first section of the poem describes how man turns himself into God through sheer intellect and ambition:

> Man is king. They hung a robe upon him, of blue sky. His crown was motten. He rode across his kingdom of dust which paid homage to him for a season, with Jasmine, and Lilies, and the visions of water. They had painted his mysteries upon the rock, but afraid of his presence, they had run away. So he accepted it. He continued to eat distance, and to raise up the sun in the morning and the moon was his slave by night. Fevers turned him from Man to God.[5]

This is the picture of Voss at Sydney with all his restlessness and ambition. Voss assumes divinity with all the dignity and superiority of a leader of the historical expedition. The second section records the arrogance of the man who acknowledges his own divinity:

> I am looking at the map of my hand, in which the rivers rise to the North-east. I am looking at my heart, which is

> the centre. My blood will water the earth and make it green. Winds will carry legends of smoke, birds that have picked the eyes for visions will drop their secrets in the crevices of rock; and trees will spring up to celebrate the god-head with their blue leaves.[6]

Voss is shown at the height of his arrogance as he starts from Sydney by the repeated use of "I" and the self-centred approach. At that time, when Mr Bonner questions whether he consulted the map, Voss replies arrogantly that he himself "will first make it." He feels that he can "lead an expedition across this continent."

In the third section of the "poem" there is the transformation of man by accepting "the visions of love" and the power of humility:

> Humility is my Brigalow, that I must remember: Here I shall find a thin shade in which to sit. As I grow weaker, so I shall become strong. As I shrivel, I shall recall with amazement the visions of love of trampling horses, of drowning candles, of hungry emeralds. Only goodness is fed.[7]

This shows Voss's acknowledgment of the powers of love and humility. It covers his journey from Rhine Towers to Jildra and into the desert.

The fourth section is the most important and prophetic one, since it projects Man as accepting his own humanness and praying to God for redemption:

> O, God, my God, I pray that you will take my spirit out of this my body's remains, and after you have scattered it, grant that it shall be everywhere, and in the rocks, and in the empty water holes, and in the true love of all men, and in you, O God, at last.[8]

Voss protests against this poetic estimate of his own character and destiny, since he is not yet convinced of his "successful" failure. But his self-assertion and self-pride are deeply affected after this self-revelation. He accepts love and humility in the visions of love but his "will," the "royal instrument," is yet to be freed from the delusions of divinity. In the loss the silent Frank writes poems which strike and lead Voss towards self-recognition.

The most interesting and important thing in Voss is his love-relationship with his beloved Laura. It is this love-relationship that saves Voss from losing his human identity. Laura is intellectual and is provided with a rare insight into life. She realizes the rocklike ambitions of her counterpart and prepares herself to save him even risking her own identity. She senses the arrogance of Voss who is a step closer than her towards damnation through intellectuality, and converts herself into a love-force to heal him and redeem his soul from the fires of hell.

In Sydney Laura performs the rituals of spiritual union between herself and Voss away in the desert towards harmony, and fulfilment through the restoration of love, humility and faith in Voss. Ironically enough, though Voss rejects love, in the beginning, it is the visions of love, in which Laura participates as a faithful companion, that bring him closer to realization and thus nearer to salvation.

The second and the most important influence, namely the elemental, is evidently couched in the major symbol in *Voss*, the Great Australian Desert. In the novel the Australian desert transforms itself into an abstract concept—a symbol of man's harmony with the infinite cosmos. Indeed, it serves as an emotional accompaniment, an indicator of mood and atmosphere throughout the questful journey of Voss, the explorer. The Australian experience of the novel deals with a German's discovery of Australia for Australians, its mineral splendours, its monstrocities as well its subtleties. Using "the psychology of the explorer as the metaphor of man," White transforms Voss's Australian experience into the legend of an individual's self-realization. Squirming in the flux of time represented through the transformation of the objects, the scene and the "being," Voss undergoes the rites of exorcism in the desert.

Voss becomes increasingly aware of his limitations and thus regains his human impulse when he is unable to solve the Black mystery, which allures him throughout.

Voss is prophetic novel combing epiphany and apocalypse. It not only presents an ecstatic fulfilment given tortured, humbled soul of an individual but also prophesies the ominous future of the scientific civilization. Behind the romantically exaggerated aspirations of a maniacal man, Patrick White exposes modern man's existential crisis. In a way, Voss is the summation of man's intellectual aspirations, doubts, convictions and the extremity of self-pride in isolation. White's intention is to exemplify Voss as an answer to this prevailing negation, turbulence and doubt. The grotesque figure of Voss, whose destructive expedition is like a pagan ritual, and whose ironic ambivalence embodies the restlessness of rational wisdom, represents the extreme phases of the individual's alienation. Governed by his glorified selfhood, Voss, the mystic, starts his quest with a devastating false step. In the beginning an exalted romantic individualist, Voss could evade the real by seeking refuge in the unassailable anatomy of his self. For him the laws of religion, and moral and spiritual conventions are mere outside forces acting on man to devaluate his stature. But, in the end, the same man moves towards a position of deep humility, accepting the mystery as not only inevitable but also redemptive.

To conclude, Patrick White takes the opportunity to caricature the Australian Philistinism, the insensitivity of the "Second-hand Europeans," as A.D. Hope called them. In a way the myth of the land enables the novelist to objectify his experiences and comment upon the obnoxious social mones as against the more prototypical experiences of the individual. Besides, the symbolic isolation of the individual, and the ordeals of his self-exploration confer on this novel the intensity and the subtlety required of masterpieces.

REFERENCES

1. White, Patrick. *Voss*. Harmondsworth: Penguin Books, 1979.
2. *Voss* 33.
3. *Voss* 35.
4. *Voss* 68.
5. *Voss* 296.
6. *Voss* 269.
7. *Voss* 297.
8. Ken Goodwin. *A History of Australian Literature*. London: Macmillan Education Ltd., 1988.

19

Cultural Contestation in Australian Aborigine Women Autobiographies

JYOTIRMAY TRIPATHY

My attempt in this paper has been to show a constant cultural negotiation and mediation in the Australian aborigine women autobiographies. For my study, I have taken up Sally Morgan's *My Place* and Ruby Langford's *Don't Take Your Love to Town* which throw away the image of a fixed indigenous identity predicated on purist and essentialist notions that seek to fix aborigine identity. These texts are the products of a space hyphenated by black and white cultures, a third space "where the negotiation of incommensurable differences creates a tension peculiar to borderline existences" (Bhabha 218, *The Location of Culture*). They are the sites of cultural contestation where none can help being caught between two cultures in the post-contact period. To think aboriginality in terms of pastness and an Edenic moment is a futile enterprise as the kooris have already lost that moment. To fix koori identity, as essentially different from those of the gubbs is a mythologisation of that uncontaminated period which can lead to the construction of koori identity in terms of "past" and "lack." The two autobiographies of our discussion show that acculturation (as distinguished from assimilation) is a necessary practice in the formation of subject positions as every subject is subjected to the discursive practices.

*　　　*　　　*

In the era of postcolonial theory and literature, there is nothing more humiliating than being spoken for. Given the

Australian aborigine literary scenario, the subaltern has started speaking; she might be mediated by language as everybody else is, but certainly not by a language using mediator. The hegemonic discourse and the discursive practices are not always repressive, they are also collaborative, and this collaboration upsets the binary of black and white and stresses the ambivalence of each position. About *My Place* Alice Walker says, "this sad and wise and funny book is of inestimable value in comprehending the relatedness of the global community [...]" (blurb to *My Place*). There is also ambivalence in Langford's position that does not totalize or close black experience.

> I had a longing for the relaxed tribal sense of time and of looking after the earth, but I knew I enjoyed luxuries like not having to boil the billy for a cup of tea, or having to make a fire to do that—and the hot shower and watching TV. I'd become soft in the modern world. (Langford 236)

So, the texts of our study are bicultural documents and appeal to two apparently different, yet cross-pollinating cultural codes. One code is that of black culture and is characterised by particular reservations or tribes. But the authors are educated, usually half-bloods and are unable to speak a tribal language. Sally Morgan does not know her native language; her mother Gladys has the same problem; Daisy (Nan) knows but fears/hates to use it and Arthur's use of the language is sparse. Morgan teaches and was taught in the alien language and is a product of the dominant discourse, being brought up in suburban Perth. Langford was born in a mission and lived in a world divided between black and white cultures, read Whitman, Shelley, Tennyson and other white poets, enjoyed the comfort of white life, yet retained her aborigine identity. So, the world and life these writers live is a highly ambivalent one, having lost that originary moment, yet not fully belonging to the present one.

The other code is the dominant white world which is also an ambivalent one. This is the world which decimated black tribes, their language and their culture. Yet, it is the same world that gives the writers their education, literature, publishers and to a large extent their readers. Both *My Place* and *Don't Take Your Love to Town* are published by white farms, the former in collaboration with the state of Western Australia. The black author does not know the native tongue, and the readers are principally white.

One possible solution will be a multivocal discourse; to write as an ethnic representative whose ethnicity is negotiated in a plurality and multiplicity of voices. He/She should not or cannot exhume his/her roots, a tradition he/she has never experienced and any attempt to do so will be a craving for a lost moment that is practically unlivable. Sally Morgan's quest for her real place is an ambivalent one because after all the inquiries and searches (which she brands a pilgrimage), she comes back to her suburban life and re-lives the lost moment in her mind. This notion of place or nation is a highly romantic one and conforms to Bhabha's critique of nationalism: "Nations, like narratives, lose their origins in the myths of time and only fully realize their horizons in the mind's eye" (Bhabha 1, *Nation and Narration*). The title *My Place* is an intriguing one, caught between dream and reality, the dream of an essential and pure place and the reality of living in a global community. But in spite of all this, she does not polarize ethnic/tribal life and experience. Towards the end of the book she says (through Daisy) about white people, "I am not saying they was all bad. Some of them was nice. You see nice people anywhere. Trouble is, you get the other ones as well" (Morgan 415). Or look at what Langford says about whites, "Some white people you could not knock, but you had to find out who and where they were" (Langford 268). So, both the writers deny an authoritative narrative voice and sublimate their repressed feeling of marginality.

The liminal space occupied by these writers, therefore, negates the binary of the oppressor and the oppressed and opens new possibilities for what Renee Green, using a term from architecture, calls "stairwell." Bhabha interprets this concept in a novel way; the stairwell "prevents identities at either end of it from setting into primordial polarities" and opens up a space "of cultural hybridity that entertains difference" (Bhabha 4, *The Location of Culture*). This hybrid position, Bhabha says elsewhere, is a "space of negotiation" and that "its articulation may be equivocal" (Bhabha 56, "Culture's In-Between") and this ambivalence rejects the binary representation of two different cultures. Both Morgan and Langford are caught in this interstice.

> I tell you, it made a wedge between the people. Some of the black men felt real low and some of the native girls with a bit of white in them wouldn't look at a black man. There I was, stuck in the middle. Too black for the whites and too white for the blacks. (Morgan 415)

The same ambivalence is expressed by Langford,

> I knew when I finished this book a weight would be lifted from my mind [...] because it may help better the relationship between the Aborigine and white people. That it might give some idea of the difficulty we have surviving between two cultures, that we are here and will always be here. (Langford 269)

This position emphasizes the composite over the pure and critiques essentialist positions of white and not-white. This is not like the Orientalist or nationalistic positions where the subject and object positions are reversed; here one position is mediated by other positions.

> These positions provide for both identification with, and differentiation from, other subject positions in the process of mediating identity positions where "I" is like "you"—is "you"—in some ways, but is different in others. (Kelly 118)

This hyphenated position is not simply about either or both of the dyads; this is a unique spatial condition where everything is positional and situational. This position constitutes, at the same time negates the two essentialist positions, emphasizing evolution rather than stasis. In this condition, "difference is neither one nor the other, but something else besides, in-between [...] (Bhabha 219, *The Location of Culture*). The black and white world of the authors does not close other worlds to them. Their allegiance goes through a process of change and transformation, "not the so-called return to the roots but a coming to-terms-with our 'routes'" (Hall 4). Langford's book is more pragmatic focusing on the shifting subject positions and mediated identities, through the author's marriage to two white men. But Morgan's book is more stereotypical and the attempted cultural recovery is very close to the essentialist position. But she knows that she herself is a product of the dominant discourse, and her mother and grandmother who form the links to the past are not exempt from it. Stuart Hall is right: "Identities are [...] constituted within, not outside representation" (Hall 4).

Earlier, I talked about authenticity and the problem of representation. Radhakrishnan talks about two kinds of representations: axiomatic and the problematic: "In the first instance, representation is reliable, and in the other it is suspect" (Radhakrishnan 203, "Ethnic Identity"). Ruby Langford's book, we can safely say is axiomatic or genuine and the book is a record of her heterogeneous experiences as she is in touch with lived reality. She is obsessed with the questions of survival, and does not polarize experience because it is multiple and heteroglossic. She also focuses on the ambiguity of black position;

> But city blacks couldn't survive there and they couldn't survive in our half black half white world. It was very hard on both sides and for our survival we had to be strong mentally as well as physically (Langford 235).

Langford does not unify the black subjects, nor does she homogenize black experience as she is conscious of her suburban background and her outsiderism in a traditional society. But Sally Morgan's book offers a counter narrative on the surface level: "All our history is about the white man. No one knows what it was like for us [...]. I just want to try to tell a little bit of the other side of the story" (Morgan 208). It appears, as if Morgan is going to reverse the Orientalist position, but on close watch the failure of that position becomes manifest. Her desire to recover the transcendental and pure origin leads her to 'imagine' that primordial uncontaminated period. She goes to Corunna with her mother and imagines the past.

> We were both trying to imagine what it would have been like for the people in the old days [...]. They seemed to us mythical and magical (Morgan 289).

She feels like belonging to that imaginary and mysterious world, the world she can never live practically. Gladys is right; Sally is romantic. She romanticizes the past and feels she belongs, but Nan has lived that life and does not feel like belonging; even Gladys is not very enthusiastic about her roots. So, the anthropological (as told to) autobiographies of Arthur, Gladys, and Daisy are suspect because a pure tribal identity is misrepresented when it is mediated by the language of the dominant culture. The quest does not lead her to anywhere; Daisy keeps her secrets till the end; Gladys' sister remains unknown and Daisy's parentage untraced. Sally's "place" remains Utopian one and the emotional pilgrimage ends with her return to the suburban life.

Morgan appears to focus on the theme of protest, but she herself is a half-blood like her mother. She marries Paul, a school teacher and there is no indication to believe that Paul is an abo. But Langford does not magnify her difference from the gubb culture. She retains the surname of Langford and has five children from two white husbands, Gordon Campbell and Peter Langford. In the beginning of the book, she calls it "an aborigine woman's struggle to raise a family of nine children in a society divided between black and white culture in Australia." This statement is enough to deconstruct a universalizing or fundamentalist identity. In contrast to Morgan's quest for the roots, Langford accepts the 'present' as the belonging place, "That it might give some idea of the difficulty we have surviving between two cultures, that we are here and will always be here" (Langford 269).

Another problem remains for both the authors; they are both black and women, and in a dominant discourse both a black and a woman remain outside representation. But where should they place their allegiance? What are they first of all: writer of colour, woman writer, or woman of colour? Can they represent their womanhood and racial identity at the same time? These questions, I feel, are very difficult to answer because compartmentalising allegiances and loyalties ignores shared and lived experience. Langford faces a lot of problems because she is a black woman; Sam Griffin and Lance Mariot are no better than Gordon Campbell and Peter Langford.

> [...] my generation at this time wandered around as if we were tribal but in fact living worse than the poorest of poor whites, and in the case of women living hard because it seemed like the men loved you for a while and then more kids came along and the men drank and gambled and disappeared [...] my women friends all have similar stories (Langford 96).

So, being a black and a woman suggest a fluid (linguistic, ethnic, cultural) identity where one factor may dominate at a given time, but not a permanent determinant. So, the identity of a postcolonial subject is divided rather than a unified one.

So, both the books, in different degrees, oscillate between two cultures and resist a purist notion of identity. But they have their moments of raw resistance; Langford screams at Mrs. Jenkins, "You don't own the land your house is on, my people were here first, so set off, come on and fight me if you're game you bitch" (Langford 176). But this kind of resistance is used intermittently, the focus being on a common ground where different cultures meet, interact, resist and reconcile. Reconciliation does not ignore resistance; rather it is a prerequisite. We know that both whites and kooris lived in the camping area across the river; Langford's friend Neddy's family was also a mixture of colours; underprivileged black kids stayed with white families. In Morgan's book, the symbol of pure black culture Nan is a half-blood and always wanted to be white. Morgan herself joins a government department like her brother Bill; the white names of her family members indicate that they have not rejected the white ways. Arthur Corunna had arranged a white man for Daisy, that it did not materialize is another story. When Gladys gets a gift from England, she feels ten feet tall, and later when she gets a black doll, she does not quite appreciate it because of its colour. We know how fussy Daisy was about her mixed colour and white ways.

So, the texts are not the symbols of alterity or difference, but what Radhakrishnan calls "common ground," quite unlike the idea of multiculturalism that magnifies difference. Common ground implies sharing, growth and change, not fixity or stasis. The objective of this transethnic collectivism is, according to Radhakrishnan,

> [...] an ever expanding coalition that insists on the need to honor both the irreducible specificity of the ethnic and a connectedness that goes beyond the absolutism of purely local ethnicities (Radhakrishnan 16, "Common Ground").

To remain pure or the attempt at it is to play into the hands of the colonial discourse which insists on difference and alienness; it is to replicate the Western idea of the West and its other. The

Western hegemonic discourse depends on its other to justify its evangelisation and civilizing mission; any attempt to retrieve the pure origin, the prelapsarian, originary time would be an invitation to Orientalism, a self thrust Orientalism. The desire not to change, to remain isolated, distant, and frozen is a corroboration of Orientalist reason. In fact, Orientalist reason wants that the orient remain timeless and alien, its people prehistoric and frozen that will justify its civilizing mission and the mission of disarticulating the native.

The two works of our discussion unsettle the myths of difference in varying degrees. The celebration of a particular culture autonomous from any other culture is an attempt to justify the superiority of that particular culture, yet a desire for equality is implicit. Bhabha says, "The demand for cultural emancipation and recognition on the part of the excluded is based on a prescriptive presumption of equal cultural value" (Bhabha 449, "Minority Maneuvers"). But difference and equality do not go together. Any claim to equality will be a self-defeating enterprise if one demands difference and separate identity at the same time. To be different is to remain outside representation and has disturbing parallels with raw resistance. If the subject remains in an Olympian position, untouched and timeless and is outside discourse and representation, then he will be the first target of assimilationist policies: "fuck them white, train them right."

Postmodernism and multiculturalism are Eurocentric inventions, which, in the name of celebrating difference create unbridgeable gap among the cultures which depend on the master discourse for representation. Gladys is afraid of her vanishing colour, her daughter Sally is also dead against any cultural exchange. Both Morgan and Langford are against assimilation policies of the government. Langford's fear is genuine "My grandchildren are blonde or blue or hazel-eyed, and within two or three hundred years there won't be Aboriginals in suburbia" (Langford 177). But it must be kept in the mind of the reader that the difference between urban black culture and bush black culture is as big as the difference between the urban black culture and white culture, and to homogenize blacks is a grave distortion of reality. Morgan takes a child like delight in the bush life of Corunna aborigines which she calls her root and "place." But nothing is far from the truth; by virtue of their education and suburban life, they are in an unenviable position; both black and white, yet none, "almost the same but not quite" (Bhabha 126, "of Mimicry and Man"). Completely separate existence within the common ground is an illusion; to ask for equal value is asking too much. Laclau makes an insightful observation,

> [...] the right to difference—has to be asserted within a global community—that is, within a space in which that particular group has to coexist with other groups. Now, how could that coexistence be possible without some shared universal values, without a sense of belonging to a community larger than each of the particular groups in question (Laclau 105).

The particular, for its particularism, depends on other particulars as mise-en-scene. Pure particularism has disturbing connotations of biological insiderism leading to an absolute ethnic/tribal identity.

The space of the authors is the liminal space, the space of both resistance and reconciliation. This is the zone where cultures come in contact with each other; they affirm and deny each other and this leads to what I call "bracketed resistance." This is quite unlike the conventional raw resistance (both physical and verbal); this occurs within parenthesis, where one accepts and discards, acknowledges and resists [...] a kind of acceptance through selective rejection. This ambivalent position interiorizes, yet negates the dominant discourse, and it has explicit parallels to Bhabha's concept of mimicry which "represents an ironic compromise" (Bhabha 126, "of Mimicry and Man"). Mimicry is not as innocent as it appears to be, it has connotations of mockery; it is selective appropriation of the master discourse, but not quite assimilation. Daisy's approach to the white culture is more sound than Sally's; she is not a breast beating messiah mourning over the loss of culture like Sally. She tries to follow white ways, entertains white guests; but it is not simply a surrender to the authority. It does not simply substantiate the dominant discourse, but mocks and disturbs it. The difference between Daisy and Sally is that one has lived experience and another is a romantic dreamer. She knows that black colour is fast vanishing,

> Aah, that colour business is a funny thing. Our colour goes away. You mix us with the white man, and pretty soon, you got no black fellas left. Some of these white fellas you see walkin, around, they really black underneath (Morgan 404).

So, she wants to be white: "I wanted to be white, you see. I'd lie in bed at night and think if God could make me white, it'd be the best thing" (Morgan 415). In Langford's book also, we find the dismantling of black/white binary. When the author was staying in the Green valley, there were only three or four aboriginal families and they lived in harmony with the whites. She feels happy when her daughter gets the opportunity to dance with the Prime Minister.

> Pearl had made history being the first aboriginal ever to dance with the Prime Minister [...]. I was so proud I was crying, and then people were gathering around Pearl, looking at her photo and recognising her, so she took my hand and we ran to get away from them laughing (Langford 141).

In all these passages we see the cultural gaps closing in. In the present transnational and diasporic world, nobody can escape acculturation and hybridity. But mimicry is not simply a respect to the authority, it is "at once resemblance and menace" (Bhabha 127, "of Mimicry and Man"). It does not simply resemble, it simply does not create a double; it also ruptures and unsettles. The master discourse feels insecured, because it implies stooping on part of the colonizer and the destruction of master-slave binary. The whiteness of Morgan and Langford, their friends and family members force the white world to reconsider and reconceptualise their difference and superiority.

The texts have their moments of raw nationalism, the story of black fellas as the standardised narrative of Australia as a nation. There is no doubt that they are the first Australians, but given the present situation, nationalism should not be equated with that pure moment. That might lead us to the pitfall of the present as 'loss' or 'lack.' Langford cries, "[...] you don't own the land your house is on, my people were here first, so get off, come on and fight me if you're game you bitch" (Langford 176). Or look at Arthur Corunna's reaction, "They should not get the land, but the white man's had land rights, since this country was invaded, our land rights" (Morgan 266). And at another place,

> Take the white people in Australia, they brought the religion here with them and the commandment, Thou Shalt Not Steal, and yet they stole this country. They took it from the innocent (Morgan 268).

This is not to deny the fact that blacks were the first people of the nation, but race and ethnicity are constructed and reconstructed according to the needs of our time. Nationalism as that uncontaminated moment and pastness means ignorance of the present. Christopher McAll's observation might throw some more light on the matter.

> For nationalism [...] the present is the denial of the natural superiority of the dominated people, the past is the proof of that superiority and the future will provide the opportunity for that superiority to reassert itself (McAll 192).

This notion of nationalism is not only restrictive, but also Utopian. Nationalism is not simply a matter of affiliation and belonging, but also exclusion and rejection. The celebration of a nation's long past and its great knowledge system led Benedict Anderson to wonder, "why do nations celebrate their hoariness, not their astonishing youth?" (Anderson 659). Morgan's search for her place comes to a naught as she could not discover the name of Gladys' sister and Daisy's father. Her attempt was to create an undivided origin for the nation and to celebrate that moment as nationalism. But there is no homogeneous and pure nation, nor any authentic origin, or as Jules Chametzky says, "There is no 'then,' 'then'—that is, no Golden Age, in the past or now, or in future" (Chametzky 13).

Sally Morgan does not simply go on a pilgrimage to find the Holy Grail, but also recreates a pure moment in her mind. Grossman and Cuthbert bring the point home,

> Aboriginality is thus cast as the originary moment in the teleology of Australian civilization which we may now nostalgically revisit precisely because it is a place and time we have left behind [...] (Grossman & Cuthbert 114).

To revive that pure bush life would be a mythologisation of difference. Gyan Prakash, in a thought provoking essay focuses on this point and claims that this nationalism is not a continuous flow or an evolution, but a revival and a return, return of the modern nation in the archaic, which "introduces a sharp break between the past and the present; the past irrupts, it does not evolve, into the present" (Prakash 540). This kind of theoretical and armchair nationalism always celebrates the hoariness, pastness, and loss. Revival of the "before" and "then" and the celebration of the "forgotten" and "dead" is an enterprise in fixity and stagnancy. Langford offers a tenable and practical solution, that past can only be kept alive in ways other than living it; "I have thought that one way we can keep Aboriginal culture alive is through the kids—having Aboriginal studies taught compulsorily in schools" (Langford 177). Unlike Morgan, Langford is vocal about her belongingness to the world she lives in; "That it might give some idea of the difficulty we have surviving between two cultures, that we are here and will always be here" (Langford 269).

So, black culture is not something to dream, not an excursion to a dream vision; it has to accommodate growth and change. In the world of transnational hybridity, culture and identity need to be redefined, focusing on shared experience. Koori identity is not to be judged according to some fixed notions, because it is continuously mediated by other identities, a self in process. This process has to resist all the reductivistic ideas of aboriginality because the formation of identity is an ongoing process; not something given, but formed discursively with culturally and temporally located meanings.

WORKS CITED

Anderson, Benedict. "Narrating the Nation." *Times Literary Supplement*, 13 June 1986.

Bhabha, Homi K. "of Mimicry and Man: The Ambivalence of Colonial Discourse." *October*, Spring, 1984.

——. "Introduction: narrating the nation." *Nation and Narration*. London: Routledge, 1990.

——. *The Location of Culture*. London: Routledge, 1994.

——. "Culture's In-Between." *Questions of Cultural Identity*. Ed. Stuart Hall and Paul du Gay. London: Sage Publications, 1996.

——. "Editor's Introduction: Minority Maneuvers and Unsettled Negotiations." *Critical Inquiry*. 23.3 (1997).

Chametzky, Jules. "Beyond Melting pots, Cultural Pluralism, Ethnicity—or Deja vu All over Again". *MELUS.* 16.4 (Winter, 1989-90).

Grossman, Michele & Cuthbert, Denise. "Resisting Aboriginalities." *Postcolonial Studies.* 1.1 (1998).

Hall, Stuart. "Who Needs Identity." *Questions of Cultural Identity.* Eds. Stuart Hall & Paul du Gay. London: Sage Publications, 1996.

Kelly, Jenniffer. "The Landscape of Grandmother: A Reading of Subjectivit(y)ies in Contemporary North American Native Women's Writing in English." *World Literature Written in English.* 31.2 (Autumn, 1991).

Laclau, Ernesto. "Universalism, Particularism and the Question of Identity." *The Identity in Question.* Ed. John Rajchman. New York: Routledge, 1995.

Langford, Ruby. *Don't Take Your Love to Town.* Victoria: Penguin Books, 1988.

McAll, Christopher. *Class, Ethnicity and Social Inequality.* Montreal: McGill-Queen's UP, 1990.

Morgan, Sally. *My Place.* Fremantle: Fremantle Arts Centre Press, 1987.

Prakash, Gyan. "The Modern Nation's Return in the Archaic." *Critical Inquiry.* 23.3 (Spring, 1997).

Radhakrishnan, R. "Ethnic Identity and Post-structuralism Differance." *Cultural Critique.* No. 6 (Spring, 1987).

____. "Culture as Common Ground: Ethnicity and Beyond." *MELUS,* 14.2 (Summer, 1987).

20

Relocating Minority Space: A Search for Identity in Taslima Nasrin's *Lajja*

C.C. MISHRA

In the postcolonial criticism Multiculturalism as a literary canon has occupied the centre stage for quite a long time. 'Multiculturalism,' has often been considered as a linguistically neutral and politically correct 'term' to effectively deal with ethno-political crisis the world over. However, in the last decade or so, there is a growing awareness that this multicultural policy has by no means solved all the problems surrounding the political representation of ethnic identity. The ethnic or minority feels that it preserves prejudices as well as differences rather than helping to overcome them, while the dominant culture feels that it acts more as a dissolvents. Not only the multicultural policy is being questioned for its ascribed role but also as a canon it is being debated for its role in literary criticism.

In the words of W.M. Verhoeven the taboo surrounding the multiculturalism debate stems from the deep-seated fear of acknowledging that the strained relation between 'ethnic selfhood and 'ethnic otherness' crucially involves:

> a relationship of power of domination of varying degrees of a complex hegemony.[1]

According to Michael Foucault,

> like ethnic selfhood and identity, the notion of equality is an 'indifference' (of no material concern).[2]

Smaro Kamboureli in her essay "The Technology of Ethnicity" reminds us:

> The ideological margins separating the literary and the political problematised the discursive site where contestation occurs and where alternate lines of action can be pursued.[3]

It is not surprising that the Postcolonial Third world literature both from the native and immigrant writers should have become a major discursive site in the present-day ethnicity debate. What concerns us here is not the position of the racist writer or critic rather how they privilege the ethnic self over the ethnic other whenever faced with a contestation of power.

On examining the present-day literature it may be felt that ethnic anxieties are increasingly being reflected not only mostly by the writers from minority communities but also by those from many segments of the larger community. There is no dearth of such writing from the Jewish, African, Caribbean or Asian origin either. But such anxieties especially in India and its neighbouring countries like Pakistan, Sri Lanka and Bangladesh were being felt after the partition. Though these have been extant for long in Bangladesh, they are being felt more after events like demolition of Babri Masjid at Ayodhya in India. The scope and visibility of writers of South Asian origin like Taslima Nasrin have made these anxieties and apprehensions so tangible that it would be worthwhile having these examined for a better understanding of her minority characters.

In this paper I shall attempt to trace the paradigm of ethnicity which Taslima uses to re-locate the minority Hindu community against the backdrop of national history of Bangladesh in order to project their desperate search for an identity in the face of a hostile race and alien culture.

In the preface of the book the author comes out quite boldly and authoritatively with her clarion call against fundamentalism and communalism.

> The disease of religious fundamentalism is not restricted to Bangladesh alone and it must be fought at every turn. I am convinced that the only way the fundamentalism forces can be stopped is if all of us who are secular and humanistic join together and fight its malignant influence.[4]

Quite surprisingly the novel has been forwarded to the people of Indian subcontinent. The back ground of the novel is the aftermath of demolition of Babri Masjid on 6th December 1992 in Ayodhya, India. It took her only seven days to complete this controversial novel. However, a deeper analysis of the various historical events and facts in the novel since 1947 shows that it traces the minority Hindu characters not just as mere victim of a fanatic religious extremism, on the other hand, there is a serious attempt on the part of the author to portray the characters with their idealism, idiosyncratic cultural behaviour, and their desperate attempts to achieve self-identity.

The ethnic anxiety of the repressed Hindu Community as reflected in "Lajja" centres around four members of the family father Sudhamoy, mother Kironmoyee, son Suranjan and daughter Maya. The family lived in Myemensingh in their rich ancestral home. To the sincere injunctions of his uncles, friends and neighbours who were leaving Bangladesh in 1947, afraid of religious persecution, Sudhamoy, like his father Sukumar had learnt to say:

> Why should I leave my homeland and go somewhere else? If I live, it will be in this soil, and if I die it will be in the very same place.[5]

The inexorable migration of Hindus to India continued but Sudhamoy stayed on. In time he earned a medical degree and started his practice as a doctor. Authentically enough the Bangladeshi Census since 1901 shows the gradual decline of Hindu population. It had been 33.1 per cent of the national population but after partition of India on communal line in 1947 had reduced to 22 per cent. Furthermore, in 1981, it was a mere 12.1 per cent and it was expected to decline still further. It was in 1992 that Sudhamoy is confronted with this question himself.

> Were the Hindus now expected to leave the country?[6]

In 1952 Sudhamoy, as an energetic youngman of twenty-four had participated and often headed the processions demanding the use of Bengali as national language. The city road were awash with blood of the protesters shed by Jinnah's brutal police force. Before his very eyes his friend Rafiq Salaam Barqat Jabbar was shot. There was every likelihood that he too would be shot and declared a martyr but he survived. For Sudhamoy the nationalist brimming with patriotism and leftist idealism, there was no national movement in which he had not participated eagerly. The United Front Elections of 1954, The Education Movement of 1962, the six clause movement of 1966, the movement protesting against Agartala Conspiracy case 1968, the General Elections of 1970 and Freedom Movement of 1971—these were all rallying points for the nationalist minded Bengalis and each one of these had underlined the fact of Sudhamoy's sacrifice for his nation.

The Freedom Movement of 1971 was a still more critical time when the 1947 exodus was being repeated. Sudhamoy was furious and cursed all those running away Hindus as cowards. The Pakistani army was out on the street and hounding out Hindus and killing them. When his friend Nemai reported this and urged him to run away. Sudhamoy assumed the same stance as before:

> You go if you want to [...]. I am not running away from my home. We'll kill those Pakistani's dogs and get and our freedom. Come back if you can at that time.[7]

Eventually Sudhamoy stayed on only to see the strong mountain of idealism that he had built over years crumbling to pieces. Sensing threat to his family, he had gone out to buy a lock when he was caught by the Pakistani Army and questioned in Urdu about his name. He realised that his Hindu name would not go well with his tormentor. In order to doze them off he uttered the name 'Sirajuddin Hussain' but it was an exercise in futility. They yanked open his Lungi and took him to the internment camp. At this moment of blindling clarity he saw just why all his friends had run away from the country. He received from his captors a broken leg, three broken bones in his rib cage and a brutally mutilated penis for resisting conversion to Islam. These scars on his heart would always remain.

Sudhamoy had never really recovered from his incarceration during the country's war of independence. He had returned alive from the internment camp but ever since he had never felt truly alive. The life of deception and fear he had to live with the following seven years in a small bamboo hut in the guise of Abdus Salaam in a remote village Arjunkhila in Phulpur away from his ancestral home had its toll on his mental state. When he recalled that time, he would feel that the broken rib that had almost pierced his heart had hurt him less than the shame of calling his beloved wife 'Fatema.' In December when the freedom fighters had come down to Phulpur with reverberating cries of 'Jai Bangla' he had finally been able to repeat the name 'Kironmoyee' which he so dearly loved. The flaming pain that had been burning in his heart subsided now. That he can call his dearest wife by her own name and his restoration to his own ancestral home was Sudhamoy's own idea of having achieved independence.

But the anxiety and fear bred in the heathen fire of communalism wouldn't let him have that freedom either. His six year old daughter Maya was kidnapped on her way back from school. Despite all their attempt she could not be traced and two days later she returned all by herself. For months afterwards she behaved strangely, sleeping fitfully and waking up abruptly in the middle of the night. She refused to meet people altogether. Anxiety and tension further escalated in the family when they received anonymous letter threatening to kidnap her again unless a ransom was paid. Sudhamoy complained to the police but they took no further action except registering it. His family life was further aggravated when local boys started invading his orchard, plucking away the fruits, trampling the vegetable garden and stripping flowers from the bushes. They were all helpless. Realizing the futility of protesting to officialdom, he complained to his neighbours who replied with authoritarial indifference:

> What can we do? This is how it has always been. There won't be any improvement.[8]

Tension goaded him still further in the form of his neighbour Shaukat Ali who tried to fake documents and occupy a sizable part of his property. Sudhamoy was too tired to battle him in court. Circumstances had pushed him to such a brink that he decided to leave his ancestral home and property for a little security in the capital city of Dhaka. When he had first come to Dhaka, Asit Ranjan, one of his friend who had hired a house for him had reported how he had to send away his grownup daughter Utapa to Calcutta afraid of eve-teasing and abduction in the local colleges. Ironically, it is the very same place to which Sudhamoy shifts for his family peace and security.

In Dhaka Sudhamoy had applied for a senior government job, a promotion on his present official position. Often he went to the ministry to enquire about the fate of his application. Almost always he was responded in monosyllables and asked for free medical favour instead. At his retirement when he should have been an Associate Professor, he finally retires as an Assistant Professor. On the day of his retirement, one of his Hindu colleague had put a garland of marigolds around his neck and voiced the sentiment of his community:

> It is not right to expect too many benefits in a Muslim country, what we are getting is more than enough for us.[9]

Sudhamoy had realized that while the country did not blatantly discriminate against the Hindus and though there was no constitutional prohibition against Hindus for employment and upgradation there was none holding the post of Secretary or Additional Secretary in the administration. No Hindu ever hold post of Superintendent of Police or the higher ranks in the Army either.

His wife Kironmoyee had her own series of traumatic experiences and feelings in search of her identity. She had indeed suffered a lot because of her husband's idealistic life. She had always wanted to perform her prayers in the traditional Hindu way, but he had warned that such prayers were not allowed in his house. She had been an excellent singer in her youth. But when she began singing in public, people of the other community had abused her as a shameless Hindu woman: So offended she had been by these accusations that she had given up singing completely. At this moment of crisis her idealistic husband had neither stood by her nor supported her. For twenty-one years he had literally slept with her as if perversely guarding her chastity. She had to chock up all her physical cravings and become used to deprivation as her husband had been emasculated in the internment camp by the Pakistani Army because of his resistance to conversion.

Her husband had somehow managed to carry his frail body with broken ribs and legs and fallen at her feet. Though she shuddered at the sight of his bleeding body, she had summoned immense courage to take her husband and two children to safer place. Althrough the months of their disguised living she had shown the same strength as her husband and resisted all attempts for conversion to Islaam. With the cheering slogan of 'Jai Bangla' that finally she had let loose her pent up feelings and cried bitterly in her husband's arms. Yet joy of regaining self-identity and freedom had been as fleeting as her husband's with the kidnapping of her daughter Maya and loss of their ancestral home.

Their son Suranjan too had learnt to love and work for Bangladesh inspired by his father's leftist idealism. Despite the traumatic experience of seven years long hybernated life and loss of their sweet home on the bank of Brahmaputra in his early years he had overcome his racial inferiority. He had excelled both as a good student and a student leader. Even he hold a membership in the governing body of college union and had eagerly participated in the Freedom Movement of 1971. In Dhaka too he had proved himself sharper than his Muslim counterparts and earned a master degree in Physics.

But the ugly hand of racial discrimination did not spare him either. Though he was much better than his fellow students it was they who scored better marks than him. When he went in search of a job too the same story was repeated. It was those who had scored less marks than him and those who grieved with disappointment for not having fared well in the interview received the appointment letters. His failure was due to his resistance to say 'Asalaam Aleikum' or 'Namaskar' indiscriminately. To him this was not the only way to show respect. It may be for this or because he was a Hindu, there were no jobs forthcoming with the government. At last, he did land a job in a private firm but resigned it after three months.

Suranjan's sister Maya, too had to undergo the same racial anxiety and tension since her childhood. A darkly beautiful girl who threw her tantrums for new cloths and visit puja mandaps was often scolded by her brother not to behave like a Hindu to which she would ask innocently:

Why? Aren't Hindus human?[10]

A year after their disguised living Suranjan would often call her by her pseudonym to which she would protest and scowl angrily at him.

Yet her childhood innocence and joyfulness was short-lived. At the age of six she had to face her first trauma of being kidnapped by some Muslim hooligans. She was completely shocked and dazed. For days together she behaved like a neurotic. Her suffering and insecurity compelled his idealist father to leave their ancestral home at Myemensingh altogether. In Dhaka, she seems to bear an assimilating and liberal attitude like her father. There were instances when she was ready to let go off such minor harassment considering it as a weakness of her community.

Sudhamoy an atheist, still believed with a naive mix of optimism and idealism that his motherland would not let him down. But the demolition of Babri Masjid in Ayodhya in December 1992 triggered a spurt of communal violence in Bangladesh. The Hindus there who had never ever dreamt of having anything to do with India, those like the Duttas became victim of a fanatic religious persecution. There were massacre, vandalism, plundering and brutal torture unleashed on them. Thousands of temples and Hindu houses were destroyed and their religious shrines desecrated. Woman irrespective of their age were kidnapped and raped, sometimes before the very eyes of their family members. Sudhamoy's family which is the focal point in the novel depicts the pangs of sorrow and anxiety of their community through the personal suffering of each member of his family.

Sudhamoy's fate is the fate of all such members of a minority race who had shed their life blood for their nation and who lived throughout their life with patriotic idealism. His house was completely ravaged and Maya, his grown up daughter was forcefully kidnapped before his very eyes. Helpless Sudhamoy suffered a severe attack of paralysis and his voice became slurred. Kironmoyee, who ran after the kidnappers was hurt in the head and she fell down unconscious on the road. Suranjan, the son brought up with his father's idealism was now at the verge of a helpless desperation and complete frustration. He seeks the help of his friend Haider to trace Maya but realises that he was of no help at all. All attempts to find his sister were fruitless.

Suranjan realises that he had been victim of racial discrimination at every step of his life. He recalls how his brief stint with Parveen came to an end because he was a Hindu. Even his last hope to make up for his wasted life by settling down with Ratna, a girl of his community too was thwarted when she accepts a Muslim husband for herself. Blinded by a fury of frustration, he intends to rape a Muslim girl on victory day the independence day of Bangladesh. But he only ends up bruising, scratching and raping a poor prostitute Shamima who had to trade her body for a little food. His question to her betrays his concern for his own identity:

> You people are in the habit of changing names. Have you gone and changed yours too?[11]

However, during all these moments of crisis Kironmoyee remains poised and nurses her husband as she had done earlier. The mass exodus of 1947 was being repeated once again. Yet she is undaunted and courageous enough to reply to Aleya Begum's suggestion to migrate to India that she wouldn't do so because this was her own country. Aleya was surprised at her reply but Sudhamoy lying on the bed realises that the two women can never be equal citizen in this country.

Still further, to his utter dismay, Sudhamoy finds his youthful son burning all the books of Lenin, Marx, Dostoevsky, Nehru and Azad and many more. One more realisation descends on him that his idealist secular minded son has already been forced to the brink of racism. He was wounded and full of pain. He had been hurt by his family, society and above all his country and today he was burning himself in the surging flames of an inferiority complex which is typical of every ethnic community striving to survive.

Suranjan was determined now not to cling to his father's empty idealism anymore. The inhuman cruelty and violence that had been heaped on his community at the wake of every national disturbance must bring sense to his father. He implores him to leave such a nation that has betrayed them again and again.

> However much we call ourselves atheists, however much we call ourselves humanists, these people out there will call us Hindus. They'll call us bastards. The more we love this country, the more we think of it as our own, the more we'll be forced into a corner. The more we love the people of this country, the more they will isolate us.[12]

Sudhamoy replies with concern:

> It will be a rootless existence [...].[13]

To which his son's question is emotionally charged:

> What will you do with your roots, Baba? If your roots are so powerful then why are you hiding behind locked doors and windows? Will you stay this way all your life?[14]

Sudhamoy's reply was a firm 'No' at the moment:

> Is India your father's home or your grandfather's? From your family, who the hell stays in India? Do you want to run away from your own homeland [...] doesn't it make you feel ashamed?[15]

Later in the darkness of the night awakening of a sinister kind rises inside him and his heart quacks with fear and apprehension. Before his very eyes the ivory tower of his life long idealism and sacrifice had crumbled to pieces. The nation of his blood and hope has let him down. Now he must leave with his wife and son for a life free from worries and anxieties, insecurity, torture and death. He must deliver his battered and bruised family from the clutch of this ever-hunting nightmare. Sudhamoy's decision to migrate to India, a foreign land with his family might seem as a defeat of his race at the moment yet it also suggests a renewed attempt to re-assert their identity.

In addition to the central characters there are many other minor characters through whom the author has successfully expressed the anxiety of the Hindu Community. None can be as large hearted and liberal as Sudhamoy even in a sacrilegious act like beef eating. He not only teaches his son to rise above such petty religious prohibition but also he goes to the extent of cooking it in his own hearth and share it with his family in order to dispel the gloom of a separate entity and inferiority complex bred through racial discrimination. In order nor to breed communal and religious complex in his children he forbids his wife from performing traditional religious rites. However, despite all his idealism and liberal attitude he and his family remains an alien till the end.

Taslima Nasrin's success as a novelist lies in her faithful portrayal of the characters of a minority community undergoing an ethnic crisis. It must be understood clearly that the demolition of Babri Masjid was not the prologue to this crisis. Such crisis have been extant earlier too. By re-locating the minority characters in the construction of the nations history and attributing them thcir due space the author has very successfully projected the identity crisis confronting them.

REFERENCES

1. Verhoeven, W.M. "How Hyphenated can you get?: A Critic of Pure Ethnicity" in Mosaic vol. 29, No. 3, September 1996.
2. Focault, Michael. "What is an Author?" Language, Counter-Memory, Practice: Selected Essays and Interviews. Trans. Donald F. Bouchard and Sherry Simon. Ed. and Intro. Donald F. Bouchard 1977. Ithaca: Cornell UP, 1992.
3. The Alphabet of the self: Generic and other Slippages in Michael Ondaatje's Running in the Family." Reflection: Autobiography & Canadian Literature Ed. K.P. Stich Ottawa: University of Ottawa P., 1988, 79-91.
4. Nasrin Taslima 'LAJJA' Translated from Bengali to English by Tutul Gupta. New Delhi: Penguin Books (P) Ltd., 1994.
5. Lajja 7.
6. Lajja 11.
7. Lajja 9.
8. Lajja 15.
9. Lajja 21.
10. Lajja 51.
11. Lajja 212.
12. Lajja 213.
13. Lajja 214.
14. Lajja 214.
15. Lajja 213.

21

Major Themes in Commonwealth Poetry

KH. KUNJO SINGH

By "Commonwealth Poetry" we mean poetry written in the commonwealth countries. It is of recent origin as the commonwealth countries have emerged after the dissolution of the British Empire. As the term "Commonwealth" connotes a common social, political and economic bond for all these countries, it is quite natural that the literatures of these countries, specially the poetry, have a common phenomenon. This phenomenon is landscape and national identity.

To begin with Africa, the theme of landscape and national identity predominates its poetry. The African poets like Bernard Dadie, Okot P'Bitek, Dennis Brutus, Wole Soyinka, J.P. Clark, Christopher Okigbo, David Rubadiri, Noemia De Sousa and Flavien Ranavio are conscious of African landscape and national identity and the image of "Africa" lives vividly in their poetry. They have a sense of "belonging" as expressed thus:

> I thank you God for creating me black
> For making of me
> porter of all sorrows,
> setting on my head
> The World. ("I thank you God")

> The negro labourer in Liverpool
> That from his motherland
> A heart heavy
> With the load of a century's oppression
> Gloriously sought for an identity
> Grappled to clutch the fire of manhood

In the land of the free
But here are only the free dead
For they too groping for a light
("A negro labourer in Liverpool")

African consciousness is poignantly revealed in Noemia De Sousa's poem "If You What to Know Me":

Africa from head to foot
This is what I am.
If you want to understand me
Come, bend over this soul of Africa
In the black dock worker's groans
The chope's frenzied dances
The changanas' rebellion
In the strange sadness which flows
From an African song through the night.

There is a sense of liberty and freedom in the African poetry. The image of "Africa" dominates the thought process of the African poets and they seek an enduring and lovable identity. A poet's desire to celebrate his motherland is clearly expressed in David Diop's poem "Africa":

Africa my Africa
Africa of proud warriors in ancestral savannahs
Africa of whom my grandmother sings.
On the banks of the distant river
I have never known you
But your blood flows in my veins. ("Africa")

In African society the voice of the poet is the voice of vision in his own time. In this sense Wole Soyinka remarks: "The artist has always functioned in African Society as the recorder of mores and experiences of his society and as the voice of vision in his own time."[1] African poets are generally realists and the famous African poet Dennis Brutus remarks: "A writer must write about what he sees around him and he must write truthfully about it, or he must come to terms with what is ugly in it and pretend that it is not there or that is not bad."[2]

One important technique of African poets is the employment of native tradition in their creative writings. Instead of blindly following the British poets they write poetry in their own way. Thus African poetry shares the popular phenomenon of the commonwealth poetry. Poets like Wole Soyinka and Christopher Okigbo have tried to infuse their sense of belonging and belief into the texture of their poetry and so Soyinka writes:

And no one speaks of secrets in this land
only, that the skin be bared to welcome rain
And earth prepare, that seeds may swell
And roots take flesh within her, and men
Wake naked into harvest tide.

Okigbo writes on traditional religion and belief in his poem, "Heavens-gate":

Before you, mother Idoto
naked I stand;
before your watery presence
a prodigal
leaning on an oilbean
lost in your legend.
Under your power wait I
on barefoot,
Watchman for the watchword
at Heavens gate;
Out of the depths my cry:
give ear and hearken
DARK WATERS of the beginning.

African poets also deal with contemporary problems like—corruption, oppression and exploitation. Expressing contemporary politics Osundare writes:

Let me be
a grass in the meadow
matching heads with others
to repel oppressive storms
with stalks steeled by shared resolve.

Stressing this aspect of Nigerian poetry Adermi Bamikunle has rightly remarked: "An important new note in Nigerian poetry which is best exemplified in Osundare's poetry is the confidence of the peasantry to put right a system which they built but which has gone wrong in the hands of those who make a profession out of distributing economic products they do not produce."[3]

One important theme in African poetry is love. J.P. Clark, Gabriel Okara and Dennis Brutus have written beautiful love poems. J.P. Clark has depicted love in a subtle way in the poem "Olokun":

I love to pass my fingers
(As tide thro' weeds of the sea
And wind the tall fern—fonds)
Thro' the strands of your hair
Dark as night that screens the naked moon:

I am jealous and passionate
like Jehovah, God of the Jews
And I would that you realize
No greater love had woman
From man than the one I have for you:
(Olokun)

Passion and intimacy are conveyed through the action of passing finger through the beloved's hair that is as dark as night which hides the moon. The allusion to mythical figures like Jehovah to explain the lover's jealousy and passion involves the acclimatization of traditional belief to the commonwealth language (English).

The difference between the two states of a woman—before consummation and after consummation; and the desire and fulfilment in love are depicted artistically in Gabriel Okara's "The Mystic Drum":

The mystic drum beat in my inside
and fishes dance in the rivers
and men and women danced on land
to the rhythm of my drum

But standing behind a tree
with leaves around her waist
She only smiled with a shake of her head.

("My Mystic Drum")

Thus African poetry has freshness, originality and the potentiality to endear itself to the readers with its process of indigenization and modernization.

In Australian poetry the image of the native land has become the central theme since 1823 when William Wentworth wrote his poem "Australisia" at the Cambridge University for the Chancellor's Gold Medal Poetry Competition. This image has been finely portrayed by poets like A.D. Hope, Judith Wright,

Mary Gilmore, Douglan Stewart and James Mc Auley. Mc Auley writes:

And I am fitted to that land as the soul is to the body
I know its contractions, waste and sprawling indolence
They are in me and its triumphs are my own
Hard won in the thin and bitter years without patience.

The ageless antiquity of Australia, the young country, is expressed in Judith Wright's poem "The Cycads":

Their smooth dark flames flicker at time's own root [...]
Only the antique cycads sullenly
Keep the old bargain life has long since broken;
and cursed by age, through each chill century
they watch the shrunken moon, but never die,
for time forgets the promise he once made,
and change forgets that they are left alone [...]

The image of Australia is best expressed in A.D. Hope's poem "Australia":

A nation of trees, drab green and desolate gray
In the field uniform of modern wars
Darkens her hills: those endless outstretched paws
of Sphinx demolished or stone lion worn away.

("Australia")

The Australian poetry is original because it successfully extricated itself from the British influence. Acclimatization of indigenous tradition, ritual, culture to English language has been done successfully.

In the same vein Judith Wright has used "kite" as her theme and turns it into a symbol that touches the chord of Australian heart as in the following lines:

"Carved out of strength, the furious kite
shoulders off the winds hate
the black mark that bars his white
is the pride and hunger of cain
perfect, precise, the angry calm of
his closed body that snow storm
of his still eye that threatens harm
Hunger and force his beauty made
and turned a bird to a knife blade.

("Black-Shouldered Kite")

Important poets like Judith Wright, A.D. Hope, James Mc Auley and Kenneth Slessor have metamorphosed landscape and the life of the land into poetry. They have also grasped nationalism and universal myths to broaden the basis of their poetry. Judith Wright has adapted Christian myth to the modern situation and context.

As a component of Commonwealth Poetry, Canadian poetry also adapts the theme of landscape and geography. Canadian poets like A.J.M. Smith, P.K. Page, Margaret Avison, Margaret Atwood, Anne Wilkinson, Charles Mair, Robert Finch, Dorothy Livesey and A.M. Klein have shared the predicament of the commonwealth poet of our time. And Margaret Atwood depicts this predicament:

In this country you can say what you like
because no one will listen to you any way,
it's safe enough, in this country you can try to write
the poem that can never be written
the poem that invents
nothing and excuses nothing,
because you invent and excuse yourself each day.

Again Margaret Atwood has used landscape as an integral part of her poetry and she writes:

That the hills
Which the eyes make flat as a wall, welded
together, open as I move
to let me through [...]
whatever I do I must
keep my head. I know
It is easier for me to lose my way
forever here, than in other landscapes

("Journey to the Interior")

Canadian poets take up "love and self" too as the major themes, Dorothy Livesey writes on this aspect as:

Sun, stun me, sustain me
turn me to stone:
stone, goad me and goll me
Urge me to run..........
....
The fire in the farthest hills

Is where I'd burn myself to bone:
Clad in the armour of sun stand anew alone.
Take off this flesh, this hasty dress
Prepare my half-self for myself;
One unit, as a tree and stone
Women in men, and Man in womb,

("On Looking into Hennry Moor")

Indian English poetry forms a major chunk of Commonwealth poetry and is known for its originality and authenticity. The place and status of the pre-independence and post-independence Indian English poetry are open to debate. P. Lal and Adil Jassawalla join hands with R. Parthasarathy in denouncing the poetry of Sri Aurobindo and his contemporaries. But critics likc V.K. Gokak and C.D. Narasimhaiah and a few others have lauded the poetry of Sri Aurobindo and his contemporaries like Sarojini Naidu. Gokak classifies the Indian poets in English before Independence into two groups: "neo-symbolists" and "neo-modernists." The neo-symbolists dive deep into mysticism and the neo-modernist's vision rests on humanism. Famous critics and scholars like K.R.S. Iyengar, Sisir Kumar Ghose and M.K. Naik also appreciate Sri Aurobindo and Sarojini Naidu as poets of importance. But sceptics denounce post-independence Indian English poets beginning with Nissim Ezekiel. The real Indian English poetry came to be written only in the sixties and after.

The Indian English poetry has acquired a distinct character and discovered its own voice. Post-Independence Indian English poetry is both a break with the past and a continuation with it too. It tries hard to set its roots and develop its own artistic credo. It is acquiring new dimensions in the hands of brilliant poets like Nissim Ezekiel, A.K. Ramanujan and R. Parthasarathy by rising above "decadent romanticism." Poets like Jayanta Mahapatra, A.K. Ramanujan, R. Parthasarathy, Arun Kolatkar and Kamala Das turn inward to get into their roots. Jayanta Mahapatra's "Relationship" is set in Orissa—a land of "forbidding myth." Kamala Das also expresses her emotional and sexual traumas in poems of unexceptionable frankness reminiscent of the medieval Shaja poets who espoused free love as means of realizing oneself. A.K. Ramanujan dives deep into the areas of strength and weakness of his Hindu heritage.

The superstition and folk belief existing in Indian society have become a favourite theme of recent poetry. In the "Night of the Scorpion" Nissim Ezekiel handles such a theme with superb irony and subdued mockery. The mother is stung, the nationalist and sceptical father tries, "every curse and blessing/ power, mixture, herb and hybrid, "as the peasants swarm in to console her offering advice of a strongly ritualistic and faith healing kind. The mother's reaction to her own suffering, "Thank God, the scorpion picked on me/ and spared my children," ironically rejects both the responses. Ramanujan in his poem "River" records the details about the twins, which the woman would have born, bringing the experience to its simple and painful humanity. O.P. Bhatnagar examines the implication of the exodus of the Indian intellectuals to foreign lands and makes a fervent appeal to them to return home. In his poem "Look Homeward Angel," Bhatnagar ironically calls them angels. Likewise, Shiv K. Kumar portrays the unprincipled and time-serving politicians in "Epitaph on an Indian Politician."

Vasectomized of all genital urges
For love and beauty
he often crossed floors
as his wife leaped across beds.

Some Indian poets have tried to evoke the sense of "Indianness" in content and language in their poetry. Ezekiel's "Very Indian poem in Indian English," "Good-bye party for Miss Pushpa T.S.," Keki N. Daruwalla's "The Professor Condoles" and R. Parthasarathy's "Incident at Ahmedpore Station" are bright examples of this effort. Ezekiel, Daruwalla, Margaret Chatterjee and Lila Ray take a different attitude, a historical, amoral, neutral, stoic and ironic. O.P. Bhatnagar joins them in making pointed, objective and thought provoking observations on the reality around us. Thus Post-Independence Indian English poets have attempted and succeeded to a limited extent in evolving a new Indo-English idiom.

In New Zealand poets like Allen Curnow; A.R.D. Fairburn, Edward Tregear, James Baxter, Gordon Chellis have become popular with their treatment of landscape and "self" in their poetry. Giving a new dimension to the theme of identification Allen Curnow writes:

I, Time, am all these yet these exist
Among my mountainous fabrics like a mist,
So do they the measurable world resists.
....
....
Am island, am sea, am father, farm and friend
Though I am here all thins my coming attend,
I am, you have heard it, the Beginning and the End.

"The green myth" in Curnow's poem "Sailing or drowning," connects the past and the present making the evening and the morning one. Some of the New Zealand poets the theme of love and metaphysical problems. A.R.D. Fairburn in his love poem "Epithalamium" compares might with lover's robe and writes:

Now at the brink of being, in our pride of blood
let us remember lost lovers,
....
O love, how many of our faith have fallen
Endless the torrent of time, endless and swollen
with tributaries from the broken veins of lovers.

To the modern man living in an irreligious milieu faith is religion. Gordon Challis describes a scene where a post is given a letter to deliver to God in his poem "The Postman":

She startled me as well the other day
gave me a glass of lemonade and slipped
me a letter to deliver—"Don't you say
a word to anyone, it's no concern
of theirs, or your's. Nor no more it was except
here was this letter plainly marked "To God"
and therefore insufficiently addressed.
I cannot stamp it now "Return to sender"
for addressee and sender may be one.

("The Postman")

Coming to the West Indies poetry, it can be said that the poets are largely dispossessed of their past. The poet critic John Figueroa mentions Derek Walcott, Evan Jones, Edward Brathwaite and Mervym Morris to have used the West Indian language continuum creatively and dreams have been forged into visions. Derek Walcott's poetry shows how a poet is conscious of resolving the conflict of native dialect and the syntactical power of English. Walcott and Brathwaite are aware of the colonial problem and they make an effort to "transcend it and heal it." John Figueroa, the Editor of *Caribbean Voices*, discerns the vision of a "Brave New World" as he writes in his exultation:

> Where else have Africans, Asians, Americans, Europeans and every possible mixture of these, come together to form a new people? Which makes the "melting pot" look like an innocent cup of tea.[4]

Derek Walcott celebrates the island and islanders in "A sea-chantey" as he writes:

A sea faring Christian,
And intrepid people
Now an apprentice washes his chicks
With sea water and sun light.

The following lines express the dilemma of choosing between the native dialect and the English language:

I who am poisoned with the blood of both
Where shall I turn, divided to the vein?
I who have cursed
The drunken officer of British rule, how choose
Between this Africa and the English tongue I love?
Betray them both, or give back what they give?
How can I face such slaughter and be cool?
How can I turn from Africa and life?

("A Far Cry from Africa")

Again the West Indies poets share with the commonwealth poets in acclimatizing an indigenous tradition to English language and so E. McG Keane writes:

Africa is not lost,
My fathers sing the sun in one remembered syllable,
And freedom is preserved in private whispers.

("The Age of Chains")

Commonwealth poetry is found in Singapore, Malaysia and Sri Lanka also. Shirley Lim and Kripal Singh have emerged as poets of significance. Sri Lankan poetry is divorced from the oral tradition of the country. Shirley Lim reminds us of A.K. Ramanujan in his nostalgia. Kripal Singh complains against the attitude of visitors to Singapore in the following lines:

You come to my country loaded with your riches
we offer you a convenient stop
allow you to tempt us, lure our pretty girls
corrupt our innocence
because we need money to survive.

("To a Visitor to Singapore")

I conclude with the answer to the question "What is common in Commonwealth Poetry?" The answer is "to use a common language *i.e.*, English and a shared experience like the colonial rule which made the commonwealth poets to seek their roots and establish a national identity."

REFERENCES

1. Wole Soyinka. "The Writer in a Modern African State," *The Writer in Modern Africa* ed. per ASTBER (Uppsalle, 1986) 15-16.
2. Dennis Brutus. "Protest Against Apartheid," *Protest and Conflict, African Literature* (1986) 93.
3. Aderemi Bamikunle. "New Trends in Nigerian Poetry: The Poetry of Niyi Osundare and Chinweizu," *The Literary Criterion*, Vol. xxiii, No. 1 and 2 (1988) 84.
4. Bijay Kumar Das. "Trends in Commonwealth Poetry," *Aspects of Commonwealth Literature* (New Delhi: Creative Books, 1995) 25.

22

FROM IMPERIALISM TO NATIVISM

ALKA GOPAL

Indian writing in English was an outcome of the interaction between the imperial British culture and the native Indian culture. It was an offshoot of the mainstream English literature and was an assertion of independence from the imperial authority. However, this offshoot of British literature soon developed qualities and characteristics markedly its own. It came to be firmly rooted to the Indian soil and culture. Being born out of the marriage of an imperial language and a native culture, Indian writings in English, very naturally, became a hot subject for critics and writers alike. The first question for debate is quite understandably—Why write in English when one has the choice of one's mother tongue?

Being a multi-lingual and mufti-cultural society India has a long and continuous tradition of rich and varied regional literatures, which continued to be at its height even in the colonial rule. The difference with Indian English is mainly that the advent of colonialism played a direct role in its evolution. Depending on the diversity of its native formative cultures it came to assume a complex multiculturality and sought to discover new myths, new modes of expression which embodied the diverse traditions in its complex fabric. This multi traditional basis of Indian writings in English gave rise to a host of questions like—the 'Indianness' of Indian writing in English, the adequacy of the borrowed imperial language to capture and portray the native Indian culture and sensibility and the competence and ability of its practitioners to use it creatively *et cetera.*

Such questions are a natural consequence of a desire to achieve literary de-colonization, a desire to recreate a pre-colonial past. This desire comes logically to a society, which has suffered the consequences of colonization. But ours was a hybrid post-colonial society and not only in our writings in English but in all other regional literatures the marks and traces of colonization have left an indelible mark. In fact some critics think that this hybrid nature of our society is a source of strength rather than weakness. Commenting on the hybrid nature of post-colonial writings, TaherBen Jalloun, a Moroccan writer says: "We have two cultures; it is as if we had two mothers and two fathers. Perhaps we don't have total control like writers in the west, but we have two possible inner worlds, I think we are doubly clever; firstly to use the narrative techniques of the west and secondly, to exploit the narrative tradition of the folklore, the stories from our respective countries. And we've come up with a third type of literature that is unlike western writing, which is essentially provincial, egocentric and inward looking. We have created literature, which is open to other cultures and situations."

The circumstances that brought English language and English education in India are well-known. The Britishers propagated the English language in India to preach their own values and culture and transcend their hegemony down to the grass-roots of native India. Rajeshwari Sunder Rajan comments:

> Though the overt purpose of English education was to create an amenable native elite population that would be impressed by, conform to, and propagate the values of the secular English book—was undoubtedly served, the English text was also, in complex and mediated ways, appropriated within native arguments for political representation, for articulating demands and for questioning the rulers.

People who acquired English education, however, defeated the very motive for this education by questioning England's very presence in India. P.K. Rajan has very aptly remarked, "The English language, the powerful instrument of British colonialism had to play the paradoxical role of being both perpetuator of colonialism and the promoter of nationalism, modernity and freedom. The tool of colonialism also became a tool for its destruction; the language of oppression became a medium for liberation and modernity."

The irony of the situation was that the Indian writers of English adopted the western literary forms and techniques and used them creatively in the native cultural background. They exploded the myth of universality by the west and established a unique style of their own. Almost all the writers of this literature while being deeply indebted to the western literary forms and concerns, use the medium to probe their native roots in terms of empirical experiences and for invoking their native myth, legends, narrative forms, folk traditions *et cetera.* They also use the medium to explore the concerns of a society in the throes of modernity but under colonial subjugation and the preoccupation and dilemmas of a post-colonial situation.

But resistance and subversion of the foreign language is only half the story the other half is reconstruction. The challenge that Indian writers faced was that of creating a distinct voice of their own. Raja Rao has put it very aptly in the preface to *Kanthapura* "One has to convey in a language that is not one's own, the spirit that is one's own [...]. After language, the next problem is that of style. The tempo of Indian life must be infused into our English expression." The history of Indian writing in English is a story of how these writers have overcome these challenges and have established a unique voice and style of their own. Inspired by the classical Indian tradition, they use this medium to search for the metaphysical and transcendental realms of experience and attempt a rediscovery of the quintessential India. The representative Indian English writers from Tagore, Aurobindo, Mulk Raj Anand, Raja Rao, R.K. Narayan, Kamala Markandaya, A.K. Ramanujan, Amitav Ghosh, to Salman Rushdie, practice in differing degrees this cultural identity. This is where the Indian English literature stands distinguished from other literatures thereby demanding its own parameters of critical evaluation. They have succeeded in forging a separate identity by invoking their history and tradition and by emphasizing on cultural diversity as a positive value.

The 1980s needs a special mention as it brought about a sudden boom in Indian fiction. It was a distinctly productive period which emerged out of a fairly long intellectual and literary gestation that had begun in the 1930s and was given a new impetus, strength and whiff of fresh air, free from any sort of inhibition and residual hangover of the pre-independence era. The 1980s heralded a new era in Indian English fiction with a change in tone, tenor and contents. In wake of Salman Rushdie's writings in the 1980s, there emerged an impressive array of young novelists. These included Amitav Ghosh, Allan Sealy, Shashi Tharoor, Vikram Seth, Upmanyu Chatterjee and Vijay Singh. The new crop of these novelists unfettered Indian fiction in English from pre-independence complexes and strove successfully to forge a new idiom by handling English language more freely, creatively and unself-consciously.

REFERENCES

1. Bill Ashcroft Gareth Griffiths & Halen Tiffin. *The Empire Writes Back: Theory and Practice in Post Colonial Literatures* (London: Routledge, 1989).
2. TaherBen Jalloun in an interview with Vaiju Naravane. (*The Sunday Times of India*—28-1-1996).
3. Rajeswari Sunder Rajan. *The Lie of The Land: English Literary Studies in India* (Delhi: Oxford UP, 1992).
4. Raja Rao, *Kanthapura* (New York: New Directions).
5. M.K. Naik. "The Achievement of Indian English Poetry," *Dimensions of Indian English Literature* (New Delhi: Sterling, 1984).
6. R. Parthasarathy. "Introduction," *Ten Twentieth Century Poets* (Madras: OUP, 1976).
7. Man Mohan Bhatnagar. *Indian Writings in English* Vol. 1 (New Delhi: Atlantic Publishers).
8. Avadesh K. Singh. *Contemporary Indian Fiction in English* (New Delhi: Creative Books, 1993).

23

I Heard the Owl Call My Name: The Twentieth Century in Retrospect

MOHIT K. RAY

Standing at the threshold of the new millennium when we look back at the twentieth century as a historical phenomenon we feel like saying—what Dickens said about the year 1775:

> "It was the best of times, it was the worst of times, it was the age of wisdom, it was the age of foolishness, [...] it was the season of Light, it was the season of Darkness [...]."

The twentieth century has been a time of quick changes: The merciless onslaught of the new upon the old; the fierce struggle for possession and survival between aggressors and victims; the upsurge and assertion of ethnic identities. Caught up in this turmoil one may tend to forget the other, less obvious aspect of the scenario. It is that area of history where, if rarely, assimilation took the place of confrontation, love and harmony ruled over forces of hostility and dissension. Margaret Craven, in her novel, *I Heard the Owl Call My Name* (1967) explores this layer of the twentieth century experience with reference to a remote island in Canada, where wisdom, kindness and love had brought disparate people together. It is a reassuring vision of the possibility of exchange and interaction through love in spite of all the countervailing forces operating against it.

F.J. Niven, while underscoring the comparatively better situation of the Canadian Indians, *vis-a-vis* the Indians of America or Mexico, had also admitted: "As far as it is possible for a race that sees its lands in the keeping of newcomers, the

Canadian Indian is happy" (1148). The question is how far is it possible? Perhaps not too far, as becomes evident from the pervasive feeling of grievance that has provided an impetus for the so-called Native Canadian Renaissance since the late 1960s. Lots of writing in recent times appear to have focused on the white's abrogation of the non-white, the colonizer's usurpation of the colonized in Canada.

However, Margaret Craven's *I Heard the Owl Call My Name* (1967) is a refreshing if rare example of departure from the above trend. It is about an outsider's response to native Canadian life in an island in British Columbia; but here the outsider does not superimpose himself on the native rather he slowly gets merged with them as one of their own. The author is aware of the binary oppositionalities of a Canadian society, but nevertheless tries to stress the possibility of a unique harmonious solution. It is not the relationship of the colonizer and the colonized, but between man and man on equal footing, that achieves the solution.

In a remote island under British Columbia a priest had come to devote the last two years of his life in the service of the local church. All the objective attributes of the ethnic group that lived in the region through ages were unique and distinctly differentiating; language, territory, colour, diet, dress, even religion separated them from others; Christianity had entered the place, but only feebly, and old rites, rituals along with the belief behind them still continued more or less undisturbed. Similarly distinctive were the subjective feelings of the group as well as their behaviour pattern regarding the outsider.[1] They were conscious and proud of their ethnicity and were ashamed of those who betrayed the island to the outside world by their un-Kwacutal action or ways.

Craven recaptures here, with meticulous thoroughness and remarkable artistic effect, a special demography, including its unique terra ferma, flora fauna, its beachline, the unpredictable rivers, the 'noisy Rocks', jungles, its special idiom, its own community memory embedded in the traditional myths and legends, and above all its special people with their unique way of life, pursuing age-old vocations and practices. They belonged to an even more ancient way of life than Thomas Hardy's "slow, silent man" harrowing clods through millenniums; they retained the practices of a time when men were hunters and food-gatherers totally depending on the bounty of nature. However, signs of an impending and inevitable change were already appearing at the time of this story, which the author carefully indicates; the totems were falling from old house-tops, the kids no more knew all the stories of the island, and some of the young ones were leaving their own people for a nook in the cities. The big sophisticated life beyond the river and the straits had already been reaching out its tentacles into these islands; tremors of change were being felt, for better/for worse.

A doomed man came among these doomed people; he was "from the great outside world" (22) of those "white intruders" (23). But he came here quietly and tried to embrace and understand a people and a place, both unfamiliar and mysterious to him as the wilderness of the region. The story (the little of it that there is) evolves out of the interaction between the indigenous and the newcomer who slowly outgrows the status of an outsider and gets merged into this life. In this novel the writer explores the possibility of a development (very rare though) by which distance between strangers might be removed through a reversion of the conventional procedure of acculturation, where transfusion between two cultures implies the domination of the culture of the powerful that overpowers the culture of the dominated. Here Gordon, an island boy, opts for this acculturation, and, after initial conflict, gets alienated from his fellow-islanders. But Mark, the white man from the city, goes over to the other side and humbly reaches out to the countrymen with respect and love. As result there is no confrontation of values, and Mark's alienation is overcome. Of course he had to pay a price in order to achieve this identification; it was two years' dedicated service prompted by sincere feeling for a people. Coming from the outside he showed no trace of the snobbery/high-handedness that attended the assumption of superior culture; rather he came to learn and respect the culture of the indigenous, their rich heritage of the past, while recognizing their helpless bafflement in face of imminent changes, and to help them a bit through their daily troubles. Naturally he generated no hostility, mistrust or helpless anger. Ultimately a stage came when the tribe would provide him a means of becoming rooted in the land.

The doctor had told the bishop that Mark Brian, the young vicar, had only two more years to live; so the bishop sent him to his remotest, most inaccessible and difficult diocese that he could utilise this last brief spell in a meaningful way. Thus, at twenty-seven Mark Brian came to the bishop's "hardest parish" on patrol of the Indian villages at Kingcome. At the beginning everything was new and alien to him in this remote island of quiet people who were still hunters and fishers "born with a paddle and fish-hook in your hand" (90): "They lived where they had always lived. They fished as they had always fished, known for their intelligence and a culture that was perhaps the most highly developed of any native band of the continent" (3). Mark had to go the hard way, like a patient explorer set for a new archipelago, and he learnt bit by bit about the tribe. Pride and arrogance marked the 'chiefs' of the olden days. Pride was still there in the sad eyes of the young Indian though no arrogance. And "Behind the pride was a sadness so deep it seemed to stretch back into ancient mysteries Mark could not even imagine" (7). Later in the day he would recognize the same expression in the picture of Christ inside the church: "His face was the Indian's face, His eyes the Indian eyes and in them the depth of sadness" (16). He also learnt about the Indian's feeling for his village which meant for him not only the ancient strip of land, but also the myths, the winds, the rains, the river, the killer whales, the salmon and the seal who followed the salmon, the village talking bird, the owl who called the name of the man who was going to die, the mountain goat, the fifty-foot totem by the church and the cedar-man at the bottom holding up the eagle, the wolf and the raven (12-13). Later the vicar would also come to share this feeling. But when he arrived first the broad outlines as well as the minute details of this world were strange wonders to which he had just awakened; the potlatch paintings on the rocks, the hand of the welcome totem above the trees, the death-rites in strange language for a child who had gone to "the land of the owl," (17) the ceremonial house with its battered eagle and totem pole, the two carved killer whales, inches above the high tide-mark, topped by a full moon. The journey and the arrival are thus, for Mark, an introduction to the unknown. Even a piece of rock had its own story and associations and Mark learnt them bit by bit ("My people call it 'Whale Pass,'" Jim tells the priest, "because long ago the gods turned a whale into that rock.") (10).

In a way this life was counterpoised and threatened by the outside world from which the vicar had come. Naturally interactions was not always easy or uninterrupted. The suspicion and pain caused on occasions by the "white intruder" (23) is evident in Mrs Hudson, the matriarch's anguished accusation: "What have you done to us? What has the white man done to our young?" (62). Her granddaughter had been ruined by a white man, and this question was addressed to Mark; the latter's response was marked only by genuine sorrow, remorse and sympathy, which ultimately won back the aggrieved.

It is not that Mark's response was typical. Rather his difference from the norm is underscored by placing him alongside other outsiders. The only other resident white man in the village was the school teacher. And "he did not like the Indians and they did not like him" (25). The callous and impolite man gets no love or respect. His contrast to Mark is brought out by his failure "to join the others" which meant "to care, and to care was to live and to suffer" (137). This was what Mark did and this was what made him different from others like the American tourists who could not "tell the Indians apart" (86), or the English woman anthropologist who combined rude contemptuous snobbery with unfeeling curiosity (87-88), or the youth who had cheated Keetah's sister and her family for personal gain, or the liquor boat agents who came to squeeze the hard-earned money of these simple people. None of these intruders could make any inroad into the heart of the tribe. Rather, each of these encounters only helps to bring into sharp focus, by contrast, Mark's innate fineness, dignity and love which made him appreciate the fineness, dignity, and trust of the tribe.

Before Mark had set out for Kingcome, his well-informed friend Caleb had warned him: "He (the Indian) will watch you [...] and in his own time he will accept or reject you" (4). And in the beginning, for months "it was always the same. The sad eyes [...]. The cautious waiting" (29). There were understandably moments of alienation, hopelessness, and consequent depression; because whereas the "Indians belonged here as the birds and fish belonged [...] he was a guest in their house, and he knew, also, that this might never change" (29). But he waited. Then one day he had his first visitors—two children "watching him from their soft, dark, sad eyes, as their ancestors must have watched the first white man in the days of innocence" (31); these "first friends" were followed by a steady flow of friends. He also began to pick up his first words in the local dialect (Kwakwala, "Bakbakwalanuksiwae," "Weeksas-weeksas," etc.). The first time the look of "watchful waiting" left Jim's eyes was occasioned by the priest's address to the run of salmon entering the river; it was a prayer—"Come swimmer [...]" (34). Jim recalls his grandfather addressing the salmon the same way. For Mark it had been a very difficult and painstaking process of self-knowledge attained through identification with the collective as the bishop had predicted: "The village is you" (13). The knowledge had come through long days and nights of waiting; at last "Both knew there was friendship between them now, forged without words and needing none" (41). "It was loneliness that Indians had lived through all the centuries, and it was in loneliness Mark came to know them best" (103). So Kingcome could become so much of a home for him that when he looked up some college friends on a brief visit to the city, "he realized with a shock that he no longer talked the same language" (92), and he eagerly looked forward to the simple warm reception awaiting him in his island vicarage. At the end when he gets the signal for departure "the thought filled him with a twinge of sudden anguish and fear [...]. How would he live again in the old world he had almost forgotten [...]?" (125). And as Keetah implores him on behalf of the village not to leave—"because this is your village and we are your family. You are the swimmer who came to us from the great sea"—Mark does not have words to thank for this recognition and acceptance, "for the sudden, unexpected gift of peace which they had offered him in their quiet, perceptive way" (131).

After his death in the river Mark's body is received back by the village in accordance with the ancient rites and in the night that follows Marta, the old woman, softly bids him adieu to "the land of the owl," while at the end of the village Peter the carver sits up in the faint hope that the departed might come back in the form of some bird whom he would address softly, "It is only old Peter, the Carver, who waits here, friend" (138). Thus the last homecoming in death shows how complete the assimilation had been. Mark's sad simple self-realization on the eve of approaching death may serve as an appropriate epitaph:

> He had learnt a little of the truth of one tribe in one village. He had seen the sadness, the richness, the tragic poignancy of a way of life that each year, bit by bit, slipped beyond memory and was gone. For a time he had been part of it, one of the small unknown men who take their stand in some remote place, and fight out their battle in a quiet way (126).

Mark's simple quiet 'experiment with Truth' in the faraway island seems to ring a note of conviction which is, indeed, rare in our times. On the one hand, the twentieth century has been an era of huge knowledge explosion far surpassing the accumulated knowledge of previous centuries. But unfortunately what is conspicuously absent is wisdom. Ours has been an age of technological and communication revolution; but we have nothing to communicate; the technological advancement has led to world wars and we are yet to get over the holocaust of that traumatic experience. Yet all is not lost. There are definite silver-linings, and occasional lone voices that hold out the promises of hope and redemption and reaffirm a faith in the essential goodness of man. Margaret Craven's novel precisely re-affirms this faith.

We can conclude with the words of Faulkner:

> I decline to accept the en of man. It is easy enough to say that man is immortal simply because he will endure; that when the last ding-dong of doom has clanged and faded from the last worthless rock hanging tideless in the last red and dying evening, that even then there will be one more sound: that of his puny inexhaustible voice, still talking. I refuse to accept this. I believe that man will not only endure: he will prevail. He is immortal, not because be alone among creatures has an inexhaustible voice, but because he has a soul, a spirit capable of compassion and sacrifice and endurance.

(William Faulkner's address accepting the 1949 Nobel Prize for Literature. December 19, 1950.)

NOTE

1. Paul R. Brass uses subjective, objective, and behavioural definitions to identify ethnic groups in *Ethnicity and Nationalism : Theory and Comparison.* New Delhi: Sage Publications, 1991, 18.

WORKS CITED

Craven, M. *I Heard the Owl Call My Name.* Toronto: Clarke, Irwin and Co. Ltd., 1967.

Niven, F.J. 'Canada' *People of All Nations* II (Ed. J.A. Hammerton). London: Educational Book Co. Ltd., N.D.

Burland, C., Nicholson, I., Osborne, H. *Mythology of the Americas.* (London; N.Y.: Hamlyn Publishing Group, 1970), 22-47.

Contributors

Alka Gopal, Assistant Professor of English, Saifia College, Bhopal, Madhya Pradesh.

B. Indira, Department of Humanities and Social Sciences, University College of Engineering, Andhra University, Vishakhapatnam, Andhra Pradesh.

Basavaraj Naikar, Professor and Chairman, Department of Studies in English, Karnataka University, Dharwad, Karnataka.

C.C. Mishra, Assistant Professor of English, K.G. Arts and Science College, Raigarh, Chhatisgarh.

Dipankar Chakrabarti, Department of English, Tripura University, Tripura.

Elsa Linguanti, Via Dei MILLe 26, 56100 Pisa, Italy.

Gajendra Kumar, Department of English, Agra College, Agra, Uttar Pradesh.

Jyotirmay Tripathy, Department of English, Christ College, Cuttack, Orissa.

K.M. Pandey, Department of English and Modern European Languages, Mahatma Gandhi Kashi Vidyapeeth, Varanasi, Uttar Pradesh.

Kalpana Purohit, Department of English, JNV University, Jodhpur, Rajasthan.

Kh. Kunjo Singh, Associate Professor, Department of English, Manipur University, Manipur.

Kuldeep Kumar, Department of English, N.P.G. College, Shikohabad, Uttar Pradesh.

Mallikarjun Patil, Lecturer, Department of English, Gulbarga University, Gulbarga, Karnataka.